# CONTEN



---

**IMPORTANT**

The information in this guide has been published in good faith on the basis of information submitted to the English Tourist Board and Pastime Publications by the proprietors of the premises listed. The English Tourist Board and Pastime Publications cannot guarantee the accuracy of the information in this guide and accept no responsibility for any error or misrepresentation. All liability for loss, disappointment, negligence or other damage caused by reliance on the information contained in this guide, or in the event of the bankruptcy, or liquidation of any company, individual or firm mentioned, or in the event of any company, individual or firm ceasing to trade, is hereby excluded.


The publishers thank all tourism officers and regional tourist board staff who have helped in the preparation of this guide and all the English hoteliers who provide such an excellent service to the public.

*Consultant Editor:* James Grassie
*Editor:* Drew Jamieson
*Cartography/Illustrations:* Kate Isles
*Lay-out:* Hugh Smith


---


Published by Pastime Publications, 15 Dublin Street Lane South, Edinburgh, EH1 3PX, in association with the English Tourist Board, Thames Tower, Black's Road, Hammersmith, London, W6 9EL. Distributed by W.H.S. Distributors.
Typeset by Opus, The Old Toffee Factory, 120a Marlborough Road, Oxford, OX1 4LS. Printed in the U.K.

# INTRODUCTION

This is the first edition of **England for Fishing.** It brings together a taste of the best that is readily available to the visiting angler, whether his interest is game, coarse or sea fishing.

The pleasures of angling are many and varied. For some these can be the continuity and contentment of fishing the same pond each week and watching the changes brought by each season. For others they are the challenge of exploring new rivers, lakes or beaches close to home; and for yet others they are found at the end of journeys to previously untried waters at home and abroad. It is for them, whether they come from other parts of the UK, Europe or North America, that this guide is designed.

Within its covers the angler will find enough information, in readily accessible form, to choose a location for fishing or to identify the possibilities of a particular area, and be able to check when fishing is permitted, which rod licence is needed, the type of fish available and where to obtain permits.

Such is the scope that every water has not been included in every detail. The editor has selected waters where visitors are particularly welcome; some, of course, are bound to have been omitted in this first edition and he will be pleased to have details of them sent to him at the publishers.

He has also had to choose what information to provide about each fishery. This he has limited to identifying a locality, a fishery and the contact where permits — and more detailed local knowledge — can be acquired.

**England for Fishing** is not the "Complete Guide" for the "Compleat Angler". It tries, nevertheless, to point the visiting angler towards some interesting fisheries — and once there, he will find many more.

# WELCOME TO ENGLAND

It should come as no surprise that Izaac Walton — "Father of the Angle" — should have lived and fished and written his classic book, "The Compleat Angler", in England. There are few countries in the world where an angler can be "complete" within such a small radius. Other lands may boast larger specimens, greater numbers or more exotic species of fish, but none offer the variety of angling challenges in river, lake, pond or sea as can be found in most regions of England.

But angling may be only part of the charm of a holiday in England. Packing a rod offers an excuse to fish the Stratford Avon while the rest of the family enjoy the delights of Shakespeare, or to cast a line in the Ouse beneath York Minster, or in the Thames under Oxford's "dreaming spires". The National Parks and the seaside need no excuses, of course, and the delights of fishing among incomparable scenery fit in well with the other family activities in the Lake District, Yorkshire Dales, Exmoor and England's long and varied coastline.

So, welcome to England! May your stay be memorable. Catch a fish for the record book — and come back again.

# HOW TO USE THIS GUIDE

England for Fishing is divided into nine areas which correspond to those of the regional water authorities. These are identified on the key map on page 14. Each section begins with a map showing fishing locations and major towns and resorts. This is followed by information on the appropriate water authority, regional tourist board, local angling clubs, types of fish and fishing seasons. Individual waters are then listed with types of fish and permit sources; a section on sea angling names the resorts and coastal towns where it is available.

Hotels and guest houses are given alphabetically by county under the town in which they are situated. All establishments listed are registered with the English Tourist Board, have paid for their entries and have supplied their own descriptions. They have all undertaken to meet Tourist Board Standards and to abide by the "Fair Deal" Code of Conduct. As a condition of entry to this guide, each hotel or guest house must:

- be registered with the English Tourist Board
- be situated within 15 miles of at least one good fishing ground for at least one of the following types of fishing: coarse; game; sea
- allow guests upon reasonable request, 24 hour access to and from the establishment
- make available to guests, upon reasonable request, packed lunches
- make available, upon reasonable request from fishing guests, the use of a fridge or freezer for bait or catch, either within the hotel or through a local fishmonger/butcher/trader
- provide guests, upon reasonable request, with an area to dry wet clothes

Some of the establishments also offer discounts for children. Details of the Crown Classification scheme and the symbols used in each hotel or guest house entry are given overleaf. Prices given are per person, sharing a double room, per night, including VAT (at the current rate of 15%).

*Colin Housego and 34lb cod caught off the Needles*

## THE NEW NATIONAL CROWN CLASSIFICATION SCHEME FOR SERVICED ACCOMODATION

The national Crown Classification Scheme for all types of serviced accommodation has been introduced throughout Britain by the National Tourist Boards for England, Scotland and Wales. The scheme is operated in England by the 12 Regional Tourist Boards.

One of the main objectives of the scheme is to make it easier for you, the customer, to identify accommodation you can use with confidence and which provides the facilities and services you seek.

All establishments classified under the national scheme are inspected regularly to ensure that high standards of cleanliness, courtesy and service are maintained.

There are six classifications which indicate the level of facilities and services provided: the higher the classification, the more facilities and services offered. A low classification does not necessarily mean, however, that the quality of what is provided is lower than that available in an establishment with a higher classification.

Listed

*Relatively simple accommodation with a limited range of facilities and services.*

*Accommodation with a wider range of facilities.*

*Accommodation offering a more extensive range of facilities and services.*

*Well appointed accommodation with one-third or more of the bedrooms having bath or shower and WC ensuite.*

*Particularly well appointed accommodation with a wide range of facilities and services and with three-quarters or more of the bedrooms having bath or shower and WC ensuite.*

*Exceptionally well appointed accommodation with an extensive range of facilities and services and with all bedrooms having bath and shower and WC ensuite.*

Some establishments in this guide have applied for classification but, since it was impossible to complete all the inspections between the introduction of the scheme and the publishing deadline for the guide, they are marked 'Classification not yet known'.

## SYMBOLS

To help you choose your possible holiday accommodation quickly and easily, symbols are used to show:

- Restaurant
- Swimming Pool – Indoor
- Swimming Pool – Outdoor
- Bar
- Facilities for Disabled People
- Baby Minding Facilities
- Dogs Admitted
- M Member of a Regional Tourist Board
- T May be Booked through Travel Agent/Commission Paid
- LF Lock up facilities for fishing
- LP Local permits
- AL Water Authority licences
- HT Hiring of tackle etc.
- i Tourist Information Centre

# HOW TO BOOK

At the back of this guide you will find enquiry forms to help you make a booking. All you have to do is choose your hotel and fill in the enquiry form, giving the dates when you wish to go on holiday and any alternative dates in case the hotel is full at the time you want to go. Please try to give as much information as possible as this will help proprietors decide whether they can offer exactly what you want, and so avoid disappointment.

You then send the completed form straight to the hotel or guest house. The proprietors will write back to you saying whether they have vacancies for the dates you have indicated, confirming the price quoted and sending any further information and brochures that you may request. They will probably ask for a deposit to secure your booking.

If the hotel or guest house of your choice has indicated that it accepts travel agency bookings (shown by the [T] symbol) you may instead go to a travel agent who will make your booking for you.

You should always make your reservation well in advance if you can, to be sure of getting in to the hotel of your choice. Since it is easy for misunderstandings to occur over the telephone, we recommend that, time permitting, all bookings should be made in writing.

Please note that the English Tourist Board does not make reservations. You should address your enquiry direct to the establishment or to the central reservations office, if applicable.

**When making a booking**

- mention 'England for Fishing'
- book in advance to be certain of receiving all the facilities promised by the establishment as a condition of entry in this guide.
- check prices and other details listed.
- give your arrival and departure dates.
- indicate acceptable alternative dates, if any.
- state your expected time of arrival particularly if you may arrive late.
- specify what accommodation is needed and any particular requirements – twin beds, private bath, private shower, child's cot, special diet, lock-up garage, and so on.
- check what facilities will be available – golf, tennis, disco, swimming pool, etc.
- check which credit cards are acceptable if you wish to pay by this method.

**CANCELLATIONS**

When you accept offered accommodation, on the telephone or in writing you will be entering into a legally binding contract with the proprietor of the establishment. This means that if you cancel a reservation, fail to take up the accommodation or leave prematurely, the proprietor may be entitled to compensation if the accommodation cannot be relet for all, or a good part of the booked period. If a deposit has been paid, it is likely to be forfeited and an additional payment demanded.

However, no such claim can be made by the proprietor until the end of the booked period, before which time he should make every effort to relet the accommodation. The circumstances which lead to cancellation or curtailment of a booking may, of course, be taken into account.

# USEFUL INFORMATION

**INSURANCE**
Travel and holiday insurance protection policies are available quite cheaply and will safeguard you in the event of your having to cancel or curtail your holiday. Your insurance company or travel agent can advise you further on this. Some hotels offer insurance schemes.

**PROBLEMS AND COMPLAINTS**
We naturally hope that you will not have any cause for complaint but problems do inevitably occur from time to time. If you are dissatisfied make your complaint to the management at the time of the incident. This gives an opportunity for action to be taken at once and to put things right without delay.

**SUGGESTIONS FOR SINGLE PARENTS**
If a hotel indicates that it does not charge a single room supplement and offers a reduction for children, it may also offer a reduction for children sharing a single room with a parent. Please ask about this when booking, even if the hotel of your choice does not specifically advertise any reductions.

# HOW TO GET FURTHER INFORMATION

England has a widespread tourist information network to help holidaymakers find out about holiday destinations, attractions, sports and evens.

**Regional Tourist Boards**
In each section of the gazetteer are the addresses of the appropriate Regional Tourist Boards which provide comprehensive information on the holiday facilities in the area covered by that section.

**Tourist Information Centres**
Most resorts and major towns have Tourist Information Centres which are the best source of information about the area where you are staying. The friendly staff will be delighted to help. Just go in and ask any question you like about the area – where to go, what to see and how to get there. Ask about anything from boat trips to tickets for summer shows.

Plenty of brochures and pamphlets are always available; some are free, others are for sale. By browsing around, you can get a good idea of all there is on offer in the area.

You can easily spot a Tourist Information Centre; they are all identified by the English Rose and the words 'Tourist Information Centre'. Some are open all the year round while others are open during the holiday season only. The former are marked with ℹ on the map at the beginning of each section of the gazetteer.

# FISHING'S MY PLEASURE

JACK CHARLTON, OBE

My love affair with fishing goes back a long way. A full day on any of the rivers in the North of England trying for salmon is close to my idea of paradise.

Just lately I have had a slight diversion. I bought a boat at Filey in North Yorkshire to go fishing with my old pal Matt Haxby, a retired coble fisherman. I have known Matt for 30 years and have spent many days with him crabbing and long-lining just for pleasure. Now that he is retired we have arguments about our status — who is captain and who is chief engineer? I lose all the time because I have to bow to his superior knowledge of the tides, location of the fish and so on. We do quite well taking mainly cod, but also mackerel, whiting and the occasional haddock. Sometimes, but not very often, we go deep-sea wreckfishing, but jigging in deep water is a bit too much for Matt. He likes bait and handline. We have some wonderful days.

Like most fishing folk we seem to have as much fun talking about the sport as we do when taking part. He loves to hear me tell of my experiences catching salmon and I am fascinated when he re-lives his days of fishing for tunny in the North Sea and how they could watch them chasing the herring or mackerel under the boat. Matt is a real old professional.

Another friend, Mac, is a real amateur. I took him for a few days on the Border Esk last year. It was his first experience of fishing of any kind. I gave him a quick lesson on how to cast using my 10'6" Hardy carbon rod, put on a weight-forward floating line for him and then took him to a narrow part of the river which was easy to fish. I left him there. I visited him regularly during the rest of the day to monitor his progress. He had not moved. I suggested to him that he might move up and down the stretch of water because he had worn a channel where he had moved in and out. He wouldn't listen. He said he was quite happy and argued that the fish would have to pass him anyway. After changing his fly and putting on a new leader for him I left him to it. Towards the end of the second day I had had enough and wandered, fishless, back to see him. He was slumped on the river bank, soaking wet, holding a shattered rod with a beautiful 14 pound salmon at his feet!

"What do you think of that son?" he said with a huge grin breaking all over his face. "Sorry about your rod but I chased that fish up and down the river on my knees and when the rod went, the only way I could get it out was to drag it with the rod over my shoulder".

That fish cost me £150 but it was worth every penny. Mac was an instant convert. He is now hooked and memories of that first fish will stay with him forever no matter how many fish he catches in the future.

I like people who like fishing whether it's for trout, sea trout or salmon, or casting for dabs off the shore. I get as many telephone calls from fishing friends as I get from football folk and the conversation is invariably more interesting. It is my pleasure, where football is business.

I fish various rivers in Northern England — Eden, Tyne, Wear, Esk, Coquet, Tweed. It would be impossible to single out a favourite. I love them all when I am there. My local rivers are the Tyne, Coquet and Tweed. The former has good spring fishing at the lower end and is fine all over during the autumn. The Coquet offers nice brown trout fishing, a few salmon and plenty of sea trout, but damned hard to catch. The Tweed is a big river. I have a day a week on one beat and have taken some nice salmon. A 28 pound specimen at the end of last year was the best fish I have ever had, caught on a Thunder and Lightning tube fly. I don't do much reservoir fishing for trout now since I moved from Yorkshire to Northumberland to live, but I used to have some lovely days at places like Rutland Water, Draycote and Ladybower Reservoir with my friend Dennis Woodhead, another ex-player who loves his fishing. I miss his humour in the boat and his grumbling when I catch fish and he doesn't. I had a 5 pound rainbow at Rutland, hooked while I was asleep in the bottom of the boat with my line dangling over the side on one of those hot summer days when nothing is happening. "You don't deserve that", he said, smacking the side of his head in frustration. He moaned all the way to the pub — and laughed about it all the way home. My favourite fishing is unquestionably in the dark for sea trout. There is something special about fishing all night — the smells and the sounds and playing a fish when you cannot see it. I have never had a whopper — 4–5 pounds is the biggest — but they seem twice as big in the dark.

Throughout the years footballers have constantly asked me what I see in fishing. I suggest they come and try it. Usually they say they have no time. I make sure I find time. It is a rewarding sport you can do on your own or with friends. Dawn to dusk, the day flies by, no matter what the weather. There are times when my wife, Pat, thinks I am crackers. After a night match at Birmingham or Manchester I will drive home in the early hours of the morning, snatch a little sleep and be off at 6 or 7 the following morning for a day's fishing. That night I will arrive home shattered but hopefully with a big fish, which I show off to a wife who has seen it all before. Even without a fish I will have enjoyed the day and wonder if there will be time to go again tomorrow.

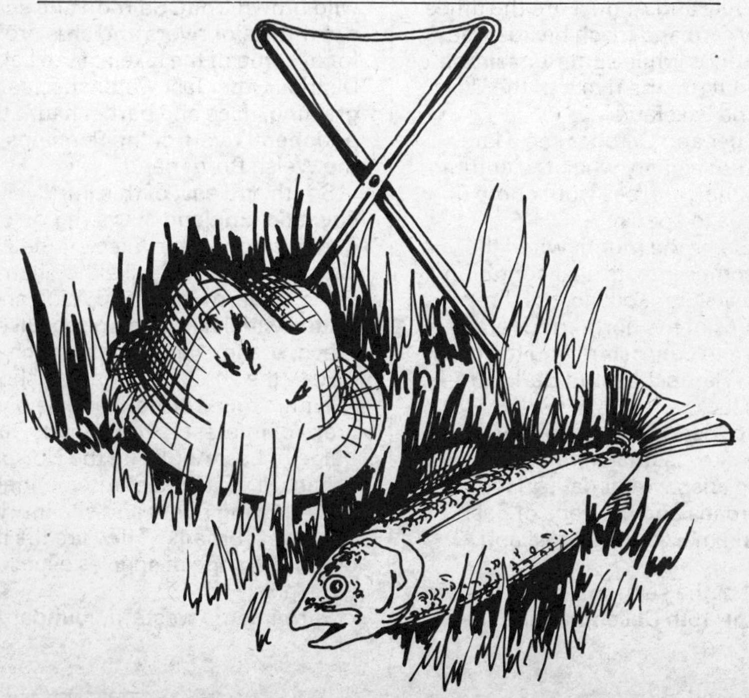

# "OH! TO BE IN ENGLAND — NOW THAT APRIL'S HERE"

DREW JAMIESON

Although there is no guarantee that the original poet who penned these lines was a trout angler, the emotion is one which, each season, swells in the breasts of this vast clan of trout fishing enthusiasts as the sap rises in the spring. However, anglers' thoughts can turn to England at all seasons of the year.

April, May and June may be prime times for trout on the chalk streams of the south, the wild rivers of the north and the west or the big reservoirs of the Midlands and Wessex, but June 16th is the great start of the coarse fishing season when lowland rivers, canals, meres and ponds have the pilgrimage of individual, club and match fishermen to "sit on cowslipped bank" and watch float or swing-tip indicate the attention of roach, bream, tench or perch.

Balmy summer evenings and misty dawns of July and August are the times for mighty carp and tench beside tree-lined lily ponds while summer salmon and sea trout run the rivers of the West Country and Lakeland.

September and October see a late flurry of trout activity while the autumn runs of salmon and sea trout come up from the sea to spawn.

November is the month when the grayling comes into its best condition and enthusiasts set out across the rippling runs of the northern rivers of Yorkshire and Lancashire and the chalk streams of Hampshire and Berkshire — if they are lucky.

The first frosts of November or December are a signal to the hardy pike angler and crisp winter days in the Norfolk Broads and the Fens of East Anglia yield memories of pike and zander.

The last of the salmon fishing ends in Cornwall on 15th December and the keen rod can be back in action again on the Eden in Cumbria on 15th January.

The first of the brown trout fishing starts on the 15th of March but there are now rainbow trout fisheries in many areas which stay open all winter, when the fish are often at peak condition.

In terms of its geography, and to a large extent, its fishing, England divides itself into a 'highland' half and a 'lowland' half roughly along a line drawn from the mouth of the River Exe in Devon to the mouth of the River Tees in Northumbria. To the north and to the west of this line lie the main upland areas of old, hard rocks and fast-running rivers — areas such as Dartmoor, Exmoor, the Lake District, Pennines and North York Moors. These are the traditional 'game fishing' grounds. Fast, clear rivers and upland lakes and tarns hold good population of wild brown trout. Salmon and sea trout run the major rivers and char are fished for in some of the lakes of the Lake District. Other fast water species like grayling, dace and barbel haunt the peripheral rivers of the Pennines and the Welsh Borderland.

South and east of this line lies 'lowland' England. It is a region of gentle slopes, clay vales drained by slower major rivers like the Thames, Trent, Severn, Ouse and Avon and dotted with lakes and ponds full of roach, bream, tench, carp, perch and pike — the so-called 'coarse fish'.

Within this wide lowland lie particular areas of interest to the angler. Out in the bulge of East Anglia lie the Norfolk Broads, a vast area of interconnected slow-flowing rivers and shallow lakes known as 'broads'. They are the haunt of a wide range of species especially large pike.

Forming the western boundary of

Norfolk and occupying that part of Cambridgeshire and Lincolnshire surrounding the Wash, lies the area known as The Fens. Formerly an arm of the sea, this area is now reclaimed and criss-crossed with a multitude of drains, dykes and ditches full of roach, bream, pike and zander. This is England's "Little Holland".

On the west side of the country, intruding into 'highland' England, lies the Cheshire Plain, a low-lying area undermined with salt workings and studded with shallow reed-fringed meres which harbour shoals of bream.

Game fishing is not forgotten in lowland England. The most famous trout fisheries of all — the chalk streams like Test, Itchen and Kennet, are to be found rising on the chalk and limestone uplands of the Cotswolds and Chilterns and the downs of Hampshire and Berkshire. These classic fisheries of clear water, rich feeding and large trout are well preserved and access for the casual visitor is difficult.

However, spread across the face of lowland England is a great number of Water Authority reservoirs — from Blagdon and Chew in Wessex to Rutland in Northamptonshire — where public access to brown and rainbow trout fishing is excellent. Added to the big waters is a large number of smaller, more intimate rainbow trout fisheries operated on a 'put and take' basis. These are widely distributed from Kent to the Scottish Border.

So come to England in April — or November — or any month of the year, if you are a 'Compleat Freshwater Angler'. The sea angler's year is different — but just as full of opportunities — but that is another story.

# ENGLISH 'BIG-GAME'

TREVOR HOUSBY

"Big-Game" fishing in English waters is primarily for various species of shark. In this respect the English angler is well catered for. Initially, shark fishing was confined to the waters off south Cornwall. Then as more and more anglers began to take an interest in this branch of the sport it became obvious that shark — and big ones at that, could be caught in many places beyond the Cornish peninsula. In all, four species of sporting shark exist in English water — the Blue, the Mako, the Porbeagle and the Thresher shark. The blue shark has always been the mainstay of the south Cornish shark charter industry. Ports like Looe (home of the Shark Club of Great Britain), Fowey, Mevagissey and Falmouth are the main traditional sharking ports. Blue shark up to — and just over — 100 pounds are the target species with the ever-present chance of a huge mako shark thrown in to add spice to the fishing.

Most mako caught have been accidental fish, although one Falmouth skipper — Robin Vinnicombe — made a name for himself and his boat "Huntress" by specialising in the catching of large mako shark. Strangely enough, mako are now something of a rarity, the record for this species having stood firm for over twenty years. Although always few and far between in home waters, mako have captured the hearts of all shark anglers. Unlike the comparatively sluggish blue shark, the mako is a fighting species – a jumping shark which specialises in a display of fiery acrobatics that few other species can match. The record 500-pounder was a big fish but paled into insignificance against some of the monster sharks that were hooked off Falmouth. Both of the Vinnicombe brothers hooked and lost mako sharks over 700 pounds in weight. Mako seem to be confined to the mouth of the Channel. I have never heard of one being hooked east of Start Point in Devon.

Probably the most popular shark is the porbeagle. In English waters it can grow to weights in excess of 450 pounds and although it doesn't jump when hooked, it is strong enough to put up a good fight on all but the strongest of tackle. At present, there are two major porbeagle strongholds in English waters, the Isle of Wight and the north coast of Devon and Cornwall. The Isle of Wight grounds are normally fished by boats operating from Portsmouth, Emsworth, Langstone and Lymington, while off north Devon and Cornwall, the boats operate from Appledore and Bude. Originally, the Isle of Wight grounds were the most productive. These days, however, it is the north coast of Cornwall and Devon that seems to produce the larger fish. There may be a number of other areas that could easily produce porbeagle in quantity. Packs of these fish certainly appear off Weymouth and Poole and, I believe, off Scarborough in North Yorkshire.

Most English sharks are rather limited in distribution — the exception being the thresher shark which can occur just about anywhere. In English waters thresher sharks can easily attain weights in excess of 500 pounds and possibly as much as 800 pounds. The thresher is, in its way, a spectacular species. Its huge scythe-like tail makes it impossible to mistake. Once hooked, most thresher will jump "mako-style". Fast and visually exciting, a good-sized thresher is one of the three big game fish – a monster that many dedicated anglers dream about catching. Many of the largest shark have been caught off the Isle of Wight. Far larger fish have been sighted and occasionally caught

*Portbeagle Shark*

by commercial fishermen in many other areas. Thresher shark can often be caught from inshore areas in depths of less than 60 feet.

A near-relative of the larger sharks already described is the tope. Widespread in distribution, tope are caught off many sections of the English coastline. In most areas a 50 pound tope can be classed as a very good catch.

Recently, however, the Essex coast has started to produce tope in excess of 70 pounds. These fish, including a magnificent 80 pound specimen, have been taken in comparatively shallow water. Tope are pack fish. Find one and you should find others. This is particularly true of the male fish. Off St. Catherine's Point on the Isle of Wight no less than 84 tope were taken from one boat in a single day. The best was a magnificent 62 pounder. Most of the fish weighed between 20 and 35 pounds — big enough to provide some hot fishing. Tope are essentially a light-tackle species. For maximum sport a 30 pound class outfit should be used. A good-sized tope hooked on this sort of tackle can be guaranteed to give even the most experienced angler some exciting fishing.

Big skate, which were at one time a common species, now seem to have disappeared completely from the English scene, probably due to over-fishing by sporting anglers. Any big-game fish takes a long time to grow and develop. Fortunately, conservation is now practised by anglers and charter boat skippers. The practice must continue, otherwise big fish of all types will be totally exterminated – at one time we had blue-fin tuna. Possibly these fish are slowly beginning to return; as yet however they are not common enough to warrant a serious fishing session. We may not have the more exotic species of big-game fish in English waters but we have enough large sporting fish to provide most English anglers with good sport.

# FISHING REGIONS USED IN GAZETTEER

## BASED UPON WATER AUTHORITY BOUNDARIES

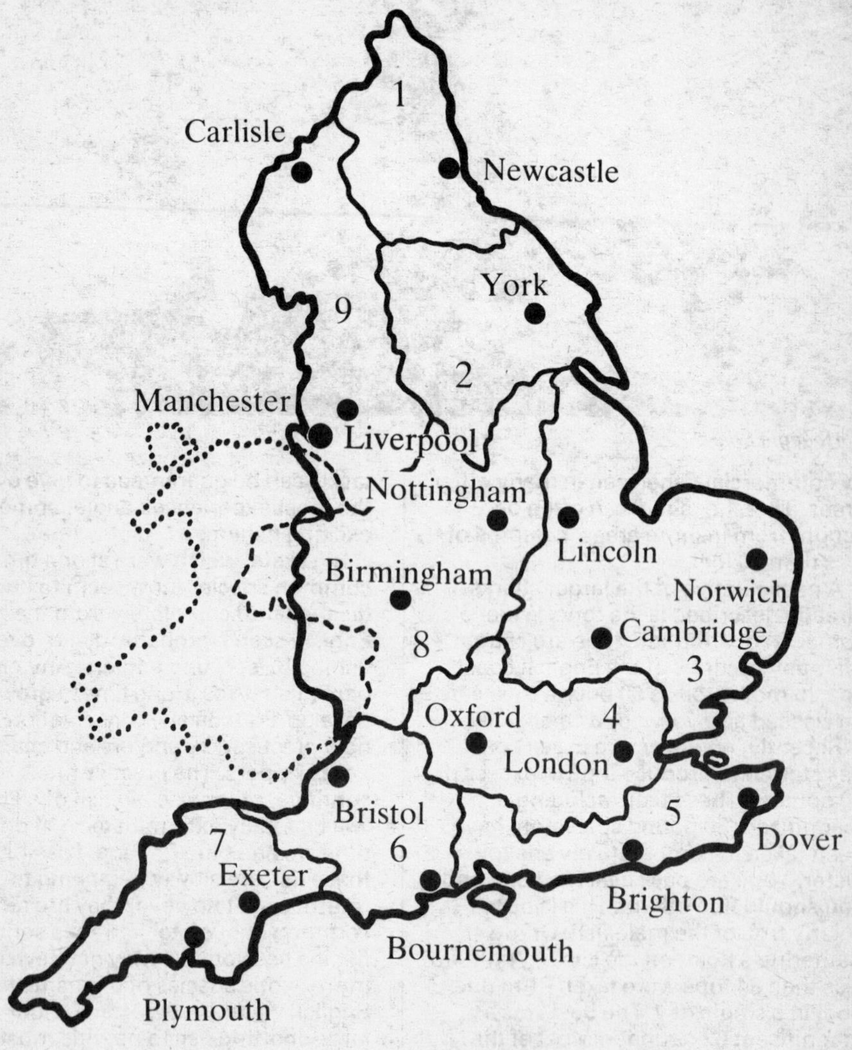


1. NORTHUMBRIA
2. YORKSHIRE
3. ANGLIA
4. THAMES
5. SOUTHERN
6. WESSEX
7. SOUTH-WEST
8. SEVERN-TRENT
9. NORTH-WEST

# USING THE GAZETTEER

The following gazetteer is divided into geographical regions which correspond to those of regional water authorities. For ease of reference it begins with Northumbria in the north east and then moves clockwise round England to end in the North West.

The water authorities have a statutory responsibility for the protection of the fisheries within the areas in which they operate and for the issuing of rod licences. The address of the relevant authority is given at the beginning of each regional section.

Within each regional section, **Rivers and Canals** are listed alphabetically; **Lakes and Reservoirs** follow and these include ponds, gravel pits and other stillwaters. Each fishery is related to the nearest town. A third category is provided by **Sea Angling**, the facilities for which are listed by coastal resorts and towns and expert comment is given by Trevor Housby. (Two regions, Severn Trent and Thames have no sea angling of significance.) Hotels and guest houses which give anglers a particular welcome are then listed alphabetically by county under the town in which they are situated.

The names and addresses of the appropriate regional tourist boards are given at the beginning of each section.

All freshwater anglers must have a rod licence. This can be obtained from water authority offices or authorised outlets such as tackle shops. Licences are normally issued for salmon and migratory trout and for trout and coarse fish but each water authority follows its own practice. No licence is needed for sea angling.

Byelaws determine the fishing seasons which are listed at the beginning of each section. Within the limits set by the byelaws, some individual fisheries fix their own dates and these are available on inquiry at permit agencies.

In addition to the rod licence, a "permit to fish" is also required from the owner of the stretch of river, canal or lake. This can be obtained from a variety of sources, such as a local hotel, club secretary, tackle shop or, in some cases, from a bailiff patrolling the banks. But each fishery is different so that the most important information in this guide is where "permits to fish" are obtainable. Permits themselves provide all the further information that is necessary — details of times of fishing, type of bait allowed, use of keepnets and other advice, all of which can vary from fishery to fishery.

Costs of permits vary enormously. Salmon fishing is expected to be expensive though some of the small west coast rivers are very reasonable. Trout fishing can range from £1 or £2 a day in rough streams in the north to £30 for a boat for two on a big reservoir. Coarse fishing is generally much cheaper, the exception being specialist carp fisheries.

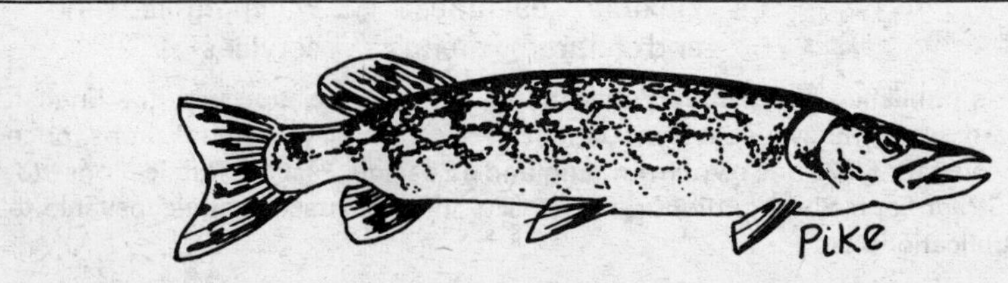

## USEFUL ADDRESSES

**The Angling Foundation**, Prudential House, 10th Floor (East Wing), Wellesley Road, Croydon CR0 9XY

**British Waterways Board**, Melbury House, Melbury Terrace, London NW1 6JU Tel: 01-262 6711

**Carp Anglers Association**, Peter Mohan, Heywood House, Pill, Bristol BS20 0AE Tel: (027581) 2129

**English Tourist Board**, Thames Tower, Black's Road, London W6 9EL Tel: 01-846 9000

**The Grayling Society**, Secretary, Derek Frome, 3 Broom Road, Hale, Altrincham, Cheshire

**National Anglers Council**, Executive Director, P.H. Tombleson, OBE, FZS, 11 Cowgate, Peterborough PE1 1LZ Tel: (0733) 54084

**National Federation of Anglers**, Halliday House, 2 Wilson Street, Derby DE1 1PG

**National Federation of Charter Skippers**, (Littlehampton Representative), Brian Parkin, 13 Linden Road, Littlehampton, West Sussex

**National Federation of Sea Anglers**, Secretary, R. Page, 26 Downsview Crescent, Uckfield, East Sussex TN22 1UB

**National Trust**, 36 Queen Anne's Gate, London SW1H 9AS Tel: 01-222 9251

**Nature Conservancy Council**, North Minster House, North Minster, Peterborough PE1 1UA Tel: (0733) 40345

**The Pike Angler's Club of Great Britain**, Secretary, Malcolm Bannister, 7 Sunny Road, Southport, Lancashire PR9 7LU

**Salmon and Trout Association**, Fishmongers Hall, London Bridge, London EC4R 9EL Tel: 01-283 5838

**The Sports Council**, 16 Upper Woburn Place, London WC1H 0QP Tel: 01-388 1277

**Water Authorities Association**, 1 Queen Anne's Gate, London SW1H 9BT Tel: 01-222 8111

*Phil Williams with a good catch of mullet*

# NORTHUMBRIA

# NORTHUMBRIA

Northumbria is a region of contrasts between the high moorlands of the Northumbrian National Park and the industrialized lowland plain along the North Sea coast. Major rivers like Tyne, Tees and Wear run as crystal trout streams through upland valleys before becoming home to grayling, dace, roach and chub as they slow down upon the plain. A heritage of industrial pollution is being rectified and salmon and sea trout now run all the major rivers. To feed the water to industry many reservoirs — from Derwent to the new Kielder — have been created and are developed as major trout fisheries.

**Water Authority**
Northumbrian Water, Northumbria House, Regent Centre, Gosforth, Newcastle-upon-Tyne NE3 3PX
Tel: (091) 284 3151

**Northumberland and Tyne Division**
Northumbria House, Town Centre, Cramlington NE23 6UP
Tel: Cramlington 713322

**Wear Division**
Wear House, Abbey Road, Pity Me, Durham DH1 5EZ
Tel: Durham 44222

**Tees Division**
Trenchard Avenue, Thornaby, Stockton, Cleveland
Tel: Stockton 760216

**Fishing Seasons**
Salmon — 1 Feb–31 Oct (inclusive)
Sea Trout — 3 Apr–31 Oct
Trout — 22 Mar–30 Sept and 1 May–31 Oct*
 * Derwent Reservoir
 * Hallington Reservoirs
 * Broomlee, Crag and Greenlee Loughs
 * Bakethin Reservoir
 1 June – 31 Oct
 ** Kielder Reservoir

Coarse Fish — 15 Jun–14 Mar (rivers and streams)
Coarse Fish — No close season (lake, reservoir, pond)

**Northumbrian Water Licence Required**
Full lists of outlets available from Northumbrian Water, which also publishes an Angling Guide containing much useful information.

**Regional Tourist Board**
Northumbria Tourist Board, Aykley Heads, Durham City, County Durham DH1 5UX
Tel: 0385 46905

## NORTHUMBRIA ANGLING CLUBS

**Aln Angling Association**
John Gibson, 45 Chapel Lands, Alnwick, Northumberland
**Alston & District Angling Association**
Gerry Hagon, Secretary, The Firs, Alston, Cumbria
**Bishop Auckland Angling Club**
John Winter, Secretary, 7 Royal Grove, Crook, Co. Durham
**Chester-le-Street & District Angling Club**
T. Wright, Secretary, 156 Sedgeletch Road, Houghton-le-Spring, Tyne & Wear DH4 5JY
**Felling Fry Fishing Club**
J Irving, 25 Sherwood Close, Washington, Tyne & Wear NE38 7RJ
**Hartlepool & District Angling Club**
J.J. Hartland, Hon. Secretary, 7 Chillingham Court, Billingham, Cleveland TS23 3UT
**Redcar Angling Club**
Mrs Bell, Secretary, Foxrush Farm, Kirleatham Lane, Redcar, Cleveland
**Saltburn and District Sea Anglers' Association**
Mr Brewer, Secretary, 2 Falcon Way, Guisborough, Cleveland
**Teesbay Angling Club**
Mr Goupillot, Secretary, 10 Griffin Road, Middlesbrough, Cleveland
**Westwater Angling Club**
Secretary, 6 Rectory Green, West Boldon, Tyne & Wear NE36 0QD
**Willington & Dist Angling Club**
Mr R Lumb, 18 Shipley Tce, West View Est, Crook, Co. Durham

Details of other angling clubs can be found in the NWA Angling Guide.

# RIVERS

| Water | Location | Species | Permits |
|---|---|---|---|
| **Aln** | Alnwick | Salmon<br>Sea Trout<br>Trout | Aln Angling Association<br>R.L. Jobson, Tower Showroom, Alnwick |
| **Coquet** | Rothbury | Salmon<br>Sea Trout<br>Trout | Rothbury and Thropton Angling Club<br>Phillips Newsagents, Towntoot, Rothbury |
| | Weldon Bridge<br>(Nr Rothbury) | Salmon<br>Sea Trout<br>Trout | Anglers Arms Hotel<br>Weldon Bridge, Morpeth<br>Tel: 066 570 655 |
| **East Allen** | Allendale | Brown Trout | Allendale Angling Association<br>Allendale Post Office<br>Tel: 043 483 201 |
| **North Tyne** | Falstone | Salmon<br>Trout | Black Cock Inn, or<br>Mr JG Sanderson, 9 The Croft, Falstone<br>Tel: 0660 40313 |
| | Hexham | Salmon<br>Trout | George Hotel<br>Chollerford, Hexham, Northumberland<br>Tel: 043 481 611 |
| **Rede** | Otterburn | Salmon<br>Sea Trout<br>Trout | Percy Arms Hotel<br>Otterburn, Northumberland |
| | Otterburn | Salmon<br>Sea Trout<br>Trout | Otterburn Tower Hotel<br>Otterburn, Northumberland |
| **South Tyne** | Alston | Salmon<br>Sea Trout<br>Trout | Alston and District Angling Association<br>A. and P. Struthers, Newsagents, Front St, Alston<br>Kirkstile Inn, Knarsdale, Eals<br>Lowbyer Manor Hotel<br>Hexham Road, Alston, Cumbria<br>Tel: 0498 81230 |
| | Bardon Mill | Salmon<br>Sea Trout<br>Brown Trout | Greggs Sports Shop,<br>Main Street,<br>Haltwhistle |
| **Tees** | Middleton-in-Teesdale | Salmon<br>Sea Trout<br>Trout | Teesdale Hotel<br>Middleton-in-Teesdale, County Durham |
| | Darlington | Salmon<br>Trout<br>Coarse Fish | Croft Spa Hotel<br>Croft on Tees, Nr Darlington, North Yorkshire |
| **Till** | Chatton | Salmon<br>Sea Trout<br>Grayling | Percy Arms Hotel, Chatton, Nr Alnwick<br>Northumberland NE66 5PS<br>Tel: 066 85 244 |
| | Cornhill<br>on Tweed | Salmon<br>Sea Trout<br>Grayling | Tillmouth Park Hotel<br>Cornhill-on-Tweed, Northumberland<br>TD12 4UU Tel: 0890 2255 |
| **Tweed** | Cornhill<br>on Tweed | Salmon<br>Sea Trout<br>Grilse | Tillmouth Park Hotel<br>Cornhill-on-Tweed, Northumberland<br>TD12 4UU Tel: 0890 2255 |

| Water | Location | Species | Permits |
|---|---|---|---|
| **Tyne** | Hexham | Salmon<br>Sea Trout<br>Brown Trout | Tourist Information Centre,<br>Hexham<br>Tel: 0434 605225 |
| | Ovingham<br>(Nr. Wylam) | Salmon<br>Sea Trout<br>Brown Trout | Mr P A Hall,<br>Northumbrian Anglers Association<br>3 Ridley Place, Newcastle NE1 8JQ |
| **Wear** | Chester-Le-Street | Trout<br>Eels<br>Dace<br>Roach<br>Occasional<br>Migratory Fish | Chester-Le-Street and District Angling Club<br>Photo and Sports, Front Street, Chester-Le-Street<br>F. Armstrong, North Burns, Chester-Le-Street |
| | Eastgate | Salmon<br>Sea Trout<br>Trout | Northumbrian Water<br>Mr R.W. Bell, West End Filling Station,<br>Stanhope |
| | Bishop Auckland | Salmon<br>Sea Trout<br>Brown Trout<br>Grayling | Bishop Auckland Angling Club<br>Windrow Sports, Fore Bondgate, Bishop<br>Auckland, County Durham<br>Tel: 0388 603759 |

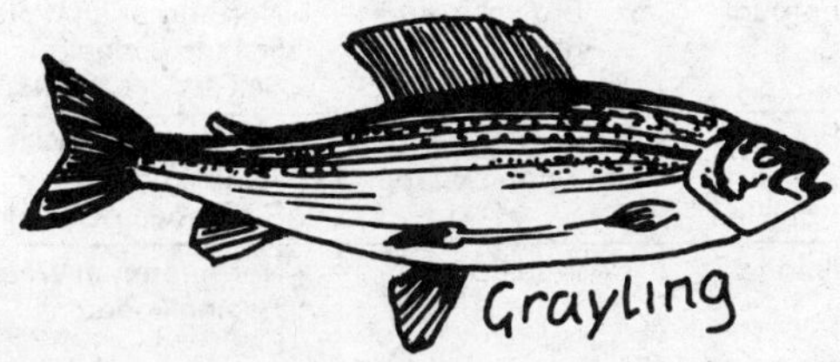


## LAKES AND RESERVOIRS

| | | | |
|---|---|---|---|
| **Bakethin** | Kielder | Brown Trout | Northumbrian Water<br>Self service system at fishing lodge<br>Advance Bookings — Bellingham 40398<br>Boat Hire |
| **Balderhead** | Cotherstone | Wild Brown Trout | Northumbrian Water<br>Willington & District Angling Club<br>To be announced |
| **Blackton** | Cotherstone | Brown Trout | Northumbrian Water<br>Felling Fly Fishing Club<br>To be announced |
| **Bolam Lake** | Belsay,<br>Nr Morpeth | Pike<br>Perch | Bolam Lake, Country Park, Northumberland<br>National Parks<br>Wardens Office on Site |
| **Burnhope** | Wearhead | Brown Trout<br>Rainbow Trout | Moorland Fisheries<br>Mr M. Graham Tel: Alston 81263<br>Self service system at Fishing Lodge |
| **Cow Green** | Teesdale | Wild Brown Trout | North Country Anglers<br>Self service system at Fishing Lodge |
| **Derwent** | Consett | Brown Trout<br>Rainbow Trout | Sunderland and South Shields<br>Water Company<br>Utilities Building at Reservoir |

| Water | Location | Species | Permits |
|---|---|---|---|
| **Fellgate Fishery** | Gateshead | Rainbow Trout<br>Carp<br>Tench<br>Bream<br>Chub<br>Roach<br>Dace | Reception Desk, Fellgate Fishery |
| **Fontburn** | Rothbury | Wild Brown Trout | Northumbrian Water<br>Fishing Lodge<br>Self service |
| **Grassholme** | Middleton | Brown Trout<br>Rainbow Trout | Northumbrian Water<br>Fishing Lodge<br>Self service |
| **Hury** | Cotherstone | Brown Trout<br>Rainbow Trout | Northumbrian Water<br>Fishing Lodge<br>Self service, disabled facilities |
| **Kielder** | Kielder | Brown Trout | Northumbrian Water<br>Fishing Lodge<br>Self service<br>Advanced booking phone Bellingham 40398 |
| **Lockwood Beck** | Guisborough | Brown Trout<br>Rainbow Trout | Northumbrian Water<br>Fishing Lodge<br>Self service, Boat hire |
| **Scaling Dam** | Guisborough | Brown Trout<br>Rainbow Trout | Northumbrian Water<br>Fishing Lodge<br>Self service, Disabled facilities |
| **Selset** | Middleton | Wild Brown Trout | Northumbrian Water<br>Fishing Lodge<br>Self service |
| **Sweethope Lough** | Kirkwelpington | Brown Trout<br>Rainbow Trout | Percy Arms Hotel<br>Otterburn, Northumberland |
| **Tunstall** | Wolsingham | Brown Trout<br>Rainbow Trout | Northumbrian Water<br>Fishing Lodge<br>Self service, boat hire |
| **Waskerley** | Consett | Brown Trout<br>Rainbow Trout | Northumbrian Water,<br>NW Durham Anglers<br>Fishing Lodge<br>Self service |
| **Whittledene Reservoirs** | Heddon on the Wall | Rainbow Trout | Westwater Angling Club<br>Self service dispensary at Fishing Hut |

## SEA ANGLING

**Whitley Bay**
Whitley fishes best in the winter months when the winter codling move inshore to feed in the kelp-lined rock gullies that abound throughout the bay. Some anglers firmly believe that winter is the only time that Whitley Bay is worth fishing. This is far from true, for a few codling can always be found in the area around the kelp beds. Coalfish are present at all times of the year and localised sandy areas within the bay fish fairly well for plaice and dabs.
Mackerel can turn up during the summer months. Local specialists invariably fish the Whitley Bay marks on the first half of the ebb tide up to the first half of the flood tide. At these times conditions are right to drop a bait into the most productive gullies. The varying nature of the shoreline means that even in bad weather there is always some section of the shoreline that can be fished. All sections are likely to produce good codling. Although

low water conditions are the most favoured, one or two places also fish well at high tide, so it is possible to fish somewhere within the area, irrespective of prevailing tidal conditions. Rocky Island at Seaton Sluice is a good place to head for where rock scarps or ledges provide good comfortable fishing stations. A high ledge known as the Sump is a good all – round mark. This ledge produces reasonable year-round fishing at all states of the tide and is therefore popular with visiting anglers and locals alike.

South of Seaton Sluice, at Collywell Bay, vast beds of heavy kelp weed attract the visiting cod shoals. The cod caught here often run into double figures. Local anglers fishing this area usually head for Middle Scaur or Round Rocks. At the southern extremity of Collywell Bay, Crag Point provides a good high-water cliff mark that fishes well in rough weather, but it is not a place for the nervous angler. On a north or north-easterly blow, Hartley Scaur can produce good bags of codling on an ebb tide but basically fishing at this point is patchy.

St Mary's Island is another kelp-filled area which is extremely popular with local anglers. Apart from the usual codling this rough, weed-covered mark occasionally produces wrasse and the odd pouting or two. St Mary's Island is connected to the mainland by a short causeway, access to the island being possible approximately two hours either side of the top of the tide. Another cod hot-spot noted for the high proportion of double-figured fish it produces is situated in a 200-yard stretch north of the boat station. Again this area fishes best when a north-easterly sea is running. Whitley Bay Beach, roughly one and a half miles in length is a sandy beach interspersed with outcrops of rock. Casting out to these rock patches can be most productive with good-sized codling and coalfish providing most of the action. Little Bay, a narrow gully at the extreme end of the North Promenade, is a good place to take flounders on an ebb tide. Watts Slope, Big Bay, North Wilkinsons, The Panama, and Whitley Pipe are well known fishing spots. Any local angler will tell you the exact locality of these marks. Whitley Pipe is a comfortable flat rock stance which allow anglers to cast into fairly deep water. Most of the local specialists seem to congregate at the end of the pipe but good catches can be taken at the bend. This particular mark can generally be relied upon to fish well at any time of the year. Great caution should be used when fishing the end of the Pipe.

Whitley Bay is something of a shore fisherman's paradise. Practically any section of the bay can fish well and noted marks are numerous. The south Promenade and a rock mark known as the Chair are both good high-water venues which allow for comfortable fishing positions at all times. Crawleys, a noted rock point situated beside the disused Table Rock Swimming Pool is very popular locally, yielding coalfish and fair codling. Brown's Bay and Marconi Point also fish well on high water, whereas North Crab Hill to the south of the Brown's Bay Lagoon is essentially a low water station. Great care should be taken here for it is easy to become too engrossed in the fishing and not notice the incoming tide.

One of the main advantages of the Whitley Bay marks is that they can be fished comfortably by anglers with only average casting ability. For general fishing, lug and ragworm make the best baits. During the winter months mussel is an effective cod bait and peeler or soft-backed crab, when obtainable, is the best bait of all. Lugworm can be dug at the north end of Whitley Bay Beach or obtained from local bait diggers or tackle dealers. Crabs and mussels have to be gathered from rocks. Small boats can be launched by the private boat compound. Cod, small whiting, coalfish, haddock and mackerel are the main quarry of the boat fishermen in this area. A leash of three baited feathers is the best terminal rig to use.

**Tynemouth**

South of Whitley Bay, Tynemouth produces good fishing to anglers who know where to fish. Cod, flounder, dab, plaice, pouting, whiting and dogfish can all be caught in the Tynemouth area. Tynemouth has many shore marks to choose from. The long sands to the south of Cullercoats, Stony Bottom, Barge Bottom, King Edward's Bay, Tynemouth Haven, Sharpness Point and Cullercoats Harbour are all good shore fishing points

giving access to a wide variety of fish.
For anglers who enjoy pier fishing, the estuary, the fish quay wall and Howden Staithes make good casting platforms. Boat fishing in the area is reasonably good, particularly for cod and coal-fish. Ragworm, lugworm and the locally favoured white worm can be dug in the Tyne estuary. Bait digging here is hard work.

**South Shields**
Directly across from Tynemouth, South Shields offers similar opportunities for sport. Local anglers are inclined to fish the one and a half mile long pier regularly and when fish are on the move, this pier can produce excellent catches. Shore fishing marks like South Beach, Herd Beach, Black Rock, White Rock, Blow Hole and Cammis Island wall are also worth trying.
Frenchman's Point, although a fairly good spot, can be a very dangerous place to fish.

**Sunderland**
Very little boat fishing is done in the Sunderland area although the offshore marks can fish fairly well. Shore fishing is fairly good.
Ryhope Beach, the estuary of the River Wear and Lizard Point all fish well enough at times. Bass occasionally occur in this area, although most catches are made up of codling and small flatfish. Seaburn Promenade, and Roker Pier are good places to head for during the winter months, with codling being the main catch.

**Seaham**
The farther south one comes, the more varied the fish become. At Seaham, for example, boat anglers get skate and conger as well as codling, dogfish, mackerel, pouting and the usual flatfish. Shore fishing is the most popular form of angling here and marks such as Hail Beach to the north of Seaham and Blast Beach to the south are favoured venues. The North Pier is also very popular, particularly during the winter months, when shoals of codling and whiting put in a regular appearance. Like most places in the north-east, charter boat trips are difficult to arrange, although anglers launching their own boats can find good sport all along this section of coastline. Catches of twenty or more good-sized codling are commonly made by inshore boat fishermen.
Baited feathers on a two hook paternoster rig baited with mussels, worms or fish cuttings should be used.

**Redcar**
Shore fishing in the Redcar area is good but often dangerous. The Coatham and Redcar Rocks are favourite venues but the surrounding shallow water troughs tend to fill rapidly on an incoming tide. Unless great care is taken it is easy to become cut off from safety in a remarkably short time. A sandy patch near the Coatham Hotel provides a safe beach-fishing stance, although fishing at this point is rather patchy. The South Gare Breakwater and Saltburn Pier are worth trying. Charter boats are virtually non-existent in Redcar and Middlesbrough, but inshore fishing is good.

# ACCOMMODATION

## NORTHUMBERLAND
## Alnwick

**PERCY ARMS HOTEL**
Chatton, Nr Alnwick,
Northumberland, NE66 5PS
Tel: 06685 244
6 Bedrooms
M LF LP AL HT
An attractive, small country hotel situated in beautiful countryside near the banks of the River Till (private fishing for residents). A family-run hotel renowned for good food and friendly hospitality. We can arrange facilities for sea fishing, loch fishing and expert tuition and gillie (by pre arrangement). Washing and drying facilities. Freezer. Solarium for extra relaxation.

| | B & B £ |
|---|---|
| High Season | 12.50 |

Children's discounts available

## Chollerford

**GEORGE HOTEL**
Chollerford, Nr. Hexham,
Northumberland, NE46 4EW
Tel: 043481 611
54 Bedrooms (All with private bathroom/shower).
M T LF LP AL
Set in beautiful Northumbria, this attractive hotel enjoys a unique and tranquil riverside setting, providing a peaceful and friendly venue for that well deserved relaxing weekend. The George has comfortable bedrooms, most with a view of the gardens. A fine restaurant, and a leisure centre with an indoor swimming pool, sauna, solarium and spa bath.



See page 4 for details of symbols

| | B & B | Half Board |
|---|---|---|
| | £ | £ |
| High Season | 27.50 | 35.00 |

Children's discounts available

## Cornhill-on-Tweed

**TILLMOUTH PARK HOTEL**
Cornhill-on-Tweed,
Northumberland, TD12 4UU
Tel: 0890 2255

13 Bedrooms (All with private bathroom/shower).

M T LG LP HT

A Victorian Mansion, situated in over 1000 acres of Northumberland countryside, banking on the famous salmon river — the River Tweed — offering salmon, sea trout and grilse fishing from February to November with boat and ghillie provided. Only 9 miles from Berwick on Tweed where sea-fishing can be arranged or loch fishing at nearby Coldingham Loch. An angling paradise renowned for food, wines and whiskies!

| | B & B | Half Board |
|---|---|---|
| | £ | £ |
| High Season | 25.00 | 36.50 |

Children's discounts available

## Morpeth

**ANGLERS ARMS INN**
Weldon Bridge, Morpeth,
Northumberland, NE65 8AX
Tel: 066 570 655

5 Bedrooms

M LG

The Anglers Arms is a veritable haven for fisherman. Lying on the beautiful River Coquet and situated 20 miles north of Newcastle-upon-Tyne, just a few miles off the A1 (M) it is well placed for visiting all historic landmarks and beauty spots of Northumberland. We have an established first class reputation for the excellence of our cuisine. A wide range of traditional and continental dishes is offered, prepared and served to perfection by our chef.

| | Bed Only | B & B |
|---|---|---|
| | £ | £ |
| High Season | 20.00 | 24.00 |

Children's discounts available

*Mullet on spinner*

# YORKSHIRE

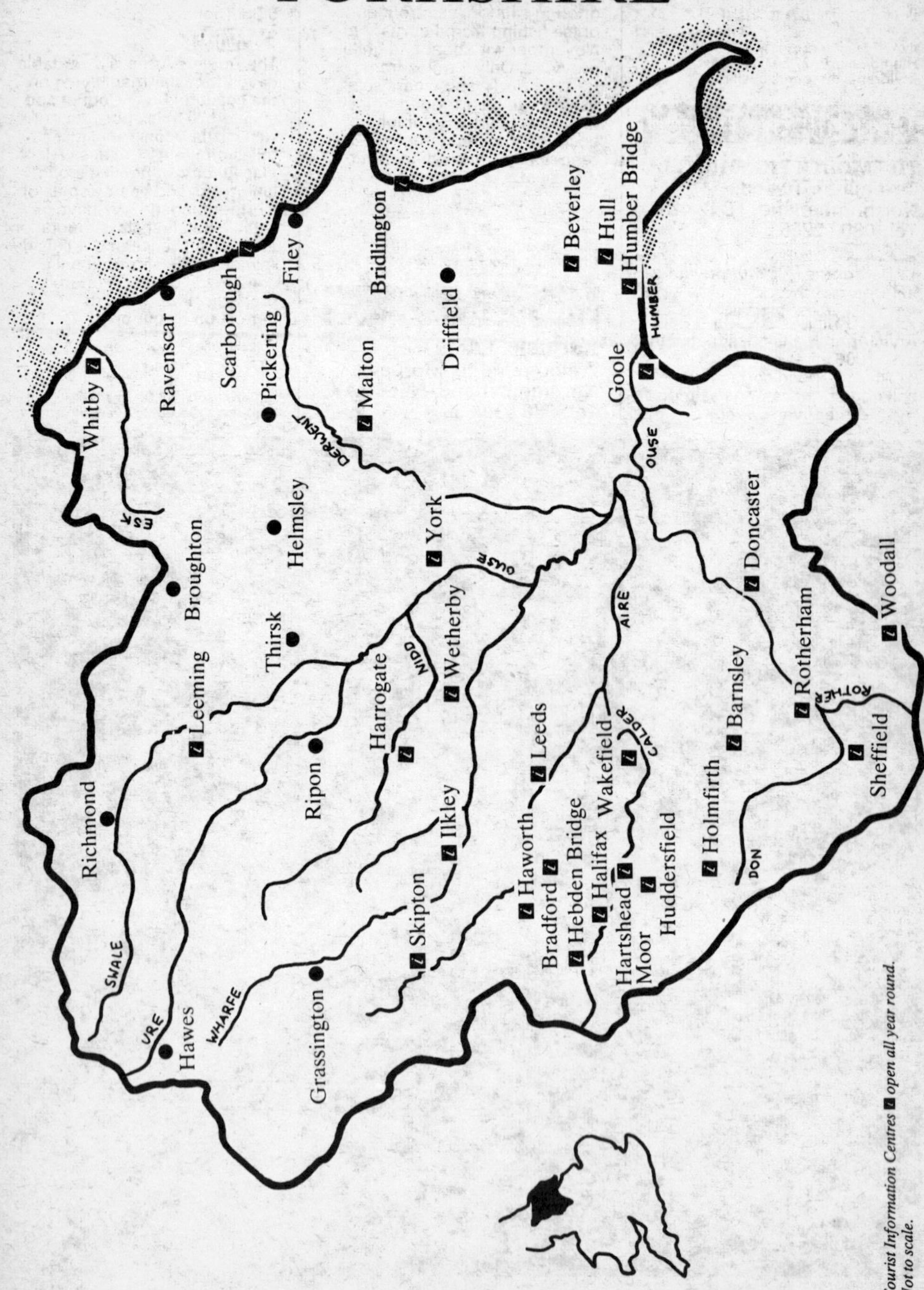


*Tourist Information Centres* [i] *open all year round. Not to scale.*

# YORKSHIRE

"If you can't catch it in Yorkshire — it's extinct". This area is the epitome of English fishing with a wide range of species available for capture. The great plain of York gathers the many exciting tributaries of the River Ouse and channels it down to the Humber estuary. The Swale, Ure, Aire, Wharfe and Nidd rise in the high Pennine Moors of the Yorkshire Dales National Park and provide fishing for trout, grayling, barbel, dace and chub amid spectacular scenery. On the east bank the rains falling on the North York Moors National Park bring salmon and sea trout up the Yorkshire Esk and feed the delightful trout and coarse fisheries of Rye and Derwent.

**Water Authority**
Yorkshire Water, Amenity and Recreation Officer,
21 Park Square South, Leeds LS1 2QG
Tel: Leeds (0532) 440191

**Fishing Seasons**
Salmon — 6 Apr–31 Oct

Sea Trout — 6 Apr–31 Oct

Trout — 25 Mar–30 Sept

Coarse Fish — 1 Jun–27 Feb

**Regional Tourist Board**
Yorkshire and Humberside Tourist Board,
312 Tadcaster Road,
York YO2 2HF
Tel: (0904) 707961

---

## YORKSHIRE ANGLING CLUBS

**Bingley Angling Club**
Secretary, P. Exley, 5 Highfield Road, Frizinghall, Bradford
**Bradford City Angling Association**
M. Briggs, 4 Brown Hill Close, Birkenshaw, Bradford BD11 2AS
**Bradford No. 1 Angling Association**
C.W. Smith, Secretary, 44 Fleet Lane, Queensbury, Bradford BD13 2JQ
**Chapeltown & District Angling Association**
J.W. Rowlinson, Secretary, 8 Brook Road, High Green, Sheffield S30 4GG
**Hull & District Anglers Association**
J. Haldenby, Secretary, 1 Grebe Road, Newport, Brough, North Humberside
**Marsden Star Angling Society**
D. Brown, Secretary, 36 Western Avenue, Riddlesden, Keighley, W. Yorks
**Preston Park Angling Club**
N.G. Wickman, Secretary, 7 Skelwith Road, Berwick Hills, Middlesbrough, Cleveland TS3 7PT
**Ryburn Angling Society**
W. Rust, Secretary, 55 Westcliffe Drive, High Road Well, Halifax, W. Yorks
**Selby & District Angling Association**
3 Ferndale Road, Selby, N. Yorks YO8 9DQ
**Sheffield & District Angling Association Ltd**
F.E. Turner, Secretary, 30 Mather Walk, Sheffield S9 4GL
**South Hunsby Fly Fishing Club**
Elm Cottage, 13 Mill Street, Hutton Cranswick, N. Humberside
**Tadcaster Angling & Preservation Association**
S. Barker, Secretary, 4 Westfield Square, Tadcaster, N. Yorks LS24 9JJ
**Todmorden Angling Club**
R. Barber, 12 Grisedale Drive, Manor Park Farm, Burnley BB12 8AR
**Unity Angling Club**
E.K. Mann, 19 Busfield Street, Bradford BD4 7QX
**Wensleydale Angling Association**
Mrs Penny Thorpe, Secretary, Rose & Crown Hotel, Bainbridge, Leyburn, N. Yorks
**York & District Amalgamation of Anglers**
J.M. Lane, Secretary, 39 Lowfields Drive, Acomb, York YO2 3DQ

# RIVERS AND CANALS

| Water | Location | Species | Permits |
|---|---|---|---|
| **Aire** | Parts | Trout<br>Grayling<br>Coarse Fish | Bradford No. 1 Angling Association<br>Local Tackle Shops |
| | Parts | Trout<br>Grayling<br>Coarse Fish | Bradford City Angling Association<br>Secretary, M. Briggs, 4 Brown Hill Close,<br>Birkenshaw, Bradford<br>Tel: 0274 684906<br>Local Tackle Shops |
| | Bingley<br>Cottingley | Trout<br>Grayling<br>Coarse Fish | Bingley Angling Club<br>Secretary, P. Exley, 5 Highfield Road,<br>Frizinghall, Bradford Tel: 0274 493409 |
| **Bain** | Bainbridge | Brown Trout<br>Grayling | Wensleydale Angling Association<br>Rose and Crown Hotel, Bainbridge, Leyburn,<br>North Yorkshire<br>Victoria Hotel, Worton<br>Crown Hotel, Askrigg |
| **Calder** | Bradford | Trout<br>Coarse Fish | Unity Angling Club<br>Secretary, E.K. Mann, 19 Busfield St,<br>Bradford BD4 7QX |
| | Sowerby Bridge | Trout<br>Coarse Fish | Ryburn Angling Society<br>Jewson Gun Shop, 1 Westgate, Halifax<br>Calder Anglers Supplies, 38 Gooder Lane,<br>Brighouse |
| | Parts | Trout<br>Coarse Fish | Bradford No. 1 Angling Association<br>Local Tackle Shops |
| **Derwent** | Parts | Mixed | Bradford No. 1 Angling Association<br>York and District Amalgamation of Anglers<br>Goole and District Angling Association<br>Local Tackle Shops |
| **Esk** | Danby | Salmon<br>Sea Trout<br>Brown Trout | Preston Park Angling Club<br>Secretary, Mr N.G. Wickman,<br>7 Skelwith Road, Berwick Hills,<br>Middlesbrough Tel: 0642 211139 |
| **Leeds and Liverpool Canal** | Longings<br>Barnoldswick to<br>Bank Newton Top<br>Lock | Carp<br>Tench<br>Trout<br>Roach<br>Bream<br>Pike | Marsden Star Angling Society<br>Tackle Shops in Keighley |
| | Parts | | Bradford No. 1 Angling Association<br>Local Tackle Shops |
| **Leven Canal** | Waterloo<br>Sandholme<br>Leven | Mixed Coarse<br>Fish | Hull and District Anglers Association<br>Everetts, Minster Tackle Shop, Beverley<br>11 The Meadows, Leven<br>Caravan Site, Sandholme Lane, Leven |
| **Nidd** | Parts | Mixed Coarse<br>Fish | York and District Amalgamation of Anglers<br>Bradford No. 1 Angling Association<br>Local Tackle Shops and Post Offices |
| **Ouse** | Parts | Most<br>Freshwater<br>Species —<br>including Barbel | York and District Amalgamation of Anglers<br>Local Tackle Shops and Post Offices |

| Water | Location | Species | Permits |
|---|---|---|---|
| **Rye** | Hawnby | Trout<br>Grayling | Hawnby Estate<br>Hawnby Hotel, Hawnby Tel: (043 96) 202 |
| | Parts | Mixed | York and District Amalgamation of Anglers<br>Local Tackle Shops and Post Offices |
| | Nunnington | Trout<br>Grayling | Ryedale Lodge and Restaurant<br>Station Road, Nunnington, Nr Helmsley, North Yorkshire Tel: 04395 246 |
| **Selby Canal** | Brayton Bridge to Burn Bridge | Roach<br>Tench<br>Bream<br>Chub | Selby and District Angling Association<br>Tackle Shop in Selby<br>On Canal Bank |
| | Part | | Goole and District Angling Association |
| **Seph** | Hawnby | Trout<br>Grayling | Hawnby Estate<br>Hawnby Hotel, Hawnby, North Yorkshire<br>Tel: (043 96) 202 |
| **Swale** | Gatenby | Barbel<br>Dace<br>Chub<br>Roach<br>Grayling | Preston Park Angling Club<br>Secretary, N.G. Wickman, 7 Skelwith Road, Berwick Hills, Middlesbrough<br>Tel: 0642 211139 |
| | Richmond | Trout<br>Grayling<br>Barbel<br>Dace<br>Chub | Richmond and District Angling Society<br>Metcalfe's Sports Shop, Richmond<br>Sports and Tackle Shop, Richmond |
| **Swale (and Codbeck)** | Topcliffe | Trout<br>Grayling<br>Barbel<br>Coarse Fish | Bradford City Angling Association<br>Secretary, M. Briggs, 4 Brown Hill Close, Birkenshaw, Bradford |
| | Parts | | Bradford No. 1 Angling Association<br>Local Tackle Shops |
| **Ure (Yore)** | Leyburn<br>Hawes | Trout<br>Grayling | Wensleydale Angling Association<br>Rose and Crown Hotel, Bainbridge<br>Victoria Hotel, Worton<br>Crown Hotel, Askrigg |
| | Boroughbridge | Trout<br>Coarse Fish | Unity Angling Club<br>Secretary, E.K. Mann, 19 Busfield Street, Bradford BD4 7QX |
| | Parts | Mixed Coarse Fish | Bradford No. 1 Angling Association<br>Local Tackle Shops |
| | Parts | Trout<br>Grayling<br>Coarse Fish | Bradford City Angling Association<br>Per Secretary |
| | Parts | Mixed Coarse Fish | York and District Amalgamation of Anglers<br>Local Tackle Shops and Post Offices |
| **Wharfe** | Parts | Mixed Trout and Coarse Fish | Bradford No. 1 Angling Association<br>Local Tackle Shops |
| | Tadcaster (Grimston Park East Side) | Chub<br>Dace<br>Barbel<br>Roach<br>Bream<br>Pike | Tadcaster Angling and Preservation Association<br>"Bay Horse", Commercial Street, Tadcaster<br>Westmoreland's, Newsagent<br>Chris's Tackle Shop |

| Water | Location | Species | Permits |
|---|---|---|---|
| **Wharfe** contd. | Buckden | Trout | Bradford City Angling Association<br>Hartrigg Hotel, Buckden |
| | Burnsall | Trout<br>Grayling | Red Lion Hotel, Burnsall, Nr Skipton,<br>North Yorkshire Tel: 075 672 204 |
| | Burnsall | Trout<br>Grayling | Manor House Hotel, Burnsall, Nr Skipton,<br>North Yorkshire BD23 6BW Tel: 075 672 231 |
| | Bolton Abbey | Trout | Devonshire Arms, Bolton Abbey, Skipton,<br>North Yorkshire BD23 6AJ Tel: 075 671 441 |

# LAKES AND RESERVOIRS

| Water | Location | Species | Permits |
|---|---|---|---|
| **Calderbrook Bottom Dam** | Littleborough | Trout<br>Carp<br>Tench<br>Bream<br>Roach<br>Rudd | Todmorden Angling Society<br>Summit Stores, Todmorden Road, Summit |
| **Farmire** | Knaresborough | Brown Trout<br>Rainbow Trout | Farmire, Farmire House, Farnham,<br>Knaresborough, North Yorkshire<br>Tel: 0423 866417 |
| **Leeming Reservoir** | Oxenhope | Trout | Bradford City Angling Association<br>Per Secretary |
| **Leighton Reservoir** | Masham | Brown Trout<br>Rainbow Trout | Swinton Estate<br>Masham, Ripon, North Yorkshire<br>Fishing hut by reservoir |
| **Malham Tarn** | Settle | Brown Trout<br>Perch | Malham Tarn Field Centre, Settle<br>Available on site |
| **Moorland Trout Lake** | Pickering | Rainbow Trout | Moorland Trout Farm<br>Newbridge Road, Pickering, North Yorkshire<br>Tel: (0751) 73101<br>Tackle Shop at Fishery |
| **Newbegin Pond** | Sheffield | Carp<br>Tench<br>Bream<br>Roach | Chapeltown and District Angling Association<br>Max Dolby's, Tackle Shop, Station Road,<br>Chapeltown, Sheffield<br>Bailiffs on Water |
| **Thrybergh Reservoir** | Rotherham | Rainbow Trout<br>Brown Trout | Rotherham Metropolitan Borough Council,<br>Thrybergh Country Park<br>Permits at Visitor Centre |
| **Ulley Reservoir** | Rotherham | Bronze Bream<br>Perch<br>Pike<br>Roach | Rotherham Metropolitan Borough Council<br>Ulley Country Park<br>Permits available on site |
| **Waterwood Trout Fishery** | Leeds | Rainbow Trout<br>Brown Trout | Waterwood Trout Fishery<br>Manor Farm, Thorner Lane, Scarcroft<br>LS14 3AN Tel: Leeds (0532) 892288 |

## SEA ANGLING

The rugged coastline of Yorkshire with its vast cliffs, jutting rock ledges and weed-encrusted rocks, can usually be relied upon to produce some good sport for the keen sea angler. Shore fishing here is a long established recreation and over the years local anglers have developed a highly characteristic style of angling that consistently catches fish from areas which would appear at first sight to be totally unfishable. The coastline is a challenge to the skill and endurance of any angler. The fish are there in plenty. All it takes to catch them is know-how, perseverance and a total disregard for weather and sea conditions.

In terms of geographical layout and fish population the Yorkshire coastline is divided into two sections. North of Flamborough Head is rough, tough rock fishing where cod are the main fish caught. South of Bridlington the shoreline changes considerably. Rocks give way to sandy, easily accessible beaches. Cod are still caught in this area but they are not so common. Instead thornback ray, dabs and even tope can be taken. This softer section of coastline can produce good shore fishing but it is better known as a boat fishing area.

**Whitby**

In the north of the county, this resort caters for sea angling in a big way. Boats are readily available in the Whitby area, mostly for cod fishing. Cod are the mainstay of sport all along the Yorkshire coastline. Despite the fact that cod are the most commonly-caught species on the Yorkshire coast, the average size of fish is well below the average for cod caught in more southern waters. A 20 lb Yorkshire cod is a veritable monster by local standards, whereas a fish of this size caught off the Kent coast, for example, would be regarded as a reasonable, but by no means exceptional, specimen.

Codling (small cod in the 3 lb to 7 lb range), are extremely prolific and boat anglers fishing known Yorkshire cod grounds can reasonably expect to catch boxes of fish of this size.

Cod over 10 lb are, however, a much scarcer breed and it is here that the shore, or rather rock, fisherman often scores. The larger cod seem to come close inshore to take full advantage of the rich feeding grounds round the rock ledges on which anglers normally stand. A favourite spot in the Whitby area is Saltwick Nab just south of the town.

**Ravenscar and Scarborough**

This is another area well worth visiting. Good boat fishing can be found all along this section of coastline and boat trips can be arranged from all the main resorts. The Scarborough area is extremely rich for the shore angler: Scalby Ness, Jackson's Bay and Cloughton are firm favourites with local anglers and visitors alike.

Yorkshire anglers are as hardy a breed as you will find anywhere in the British Isles. Any section of coastline which has any form of access, no matter how dangerous the descent may be, will be hard-fished solidly throughout the entire year. Local anglers also occasionally fish directly from the tops of the towering cliffs. This is not to be recommended, particularly where visiting anglers are concerned, for unless you know the terrain extremely well, this spectacular cliff-hanging style of angling can be extremely dangerous.

Huge tunny were once common off the Yorkshire coast and big game fishermen from all over the world made a habit of visiting Scarborough, which at one time held the world record for the blue fin tunny, to take full advantage of the migrating tunny packs.

During the period between the wars, tunny fishing here reached its peak, catches were high and fish of between 500 to 700 lb were commonplace. An attempt was made after the Second World War to re-establish tunny fishing as a sport, but by this time commercial harvesting of the herring shoals had taken its toll of the tunny's main food supply. A few fish were caught, but nothing was seen of the vast packs of big tunny that once frequented the area, and local sportsmen reluctantly gave up the idea of tunny hunting as a productive pastime. Tunny apart, the Yorkshire coastline holds some wonderful fishing, with a wide choice of venues to try, and fish to catch.

**Filey Brigg**

A huge natural breakwater on the extremity of Filey Bay, this is a vast natural pier giving rock fishermen every opportunity to scramble out along its rugged length to cast into particularly productive waters.

**Bridlington**
Fishing trips on local boats are easy to arrange here and extremely popular, for catches are often exceptionally good, although big fish are far from common. Beach anglers find the occasional medium-sized bass, boat anglers may encounter that ugly cold monster, the catfish, with its slippery body, ungainly head and lethal looking jaws.
Porbeagle shark are also known to visit this coastline.

# ACCOMMODATION

## HUMBERSIDE Driffield

**THE TRITON INN**
Sledmere, Nr. Driffield,
N. Humberside, YO25 0XQ
Tel: 0377 86644
Classification not yet known
6 Bedrooms (2 with private bathroom/shower).

M T LF LP AL HT

Situated in the shadow of the famous Sledmere House, the Inn is a favourite stopping off point for travellers along the scenic route between Bridlington and York. Sledmere is 8 miles from Driffield on the B1252, 17 miles Bridlington/Scarborough. The guests are guaranteed a warm and friendly welcome. Family-run, old inn, offering a selection of excellent home cooking and hand pulled traditional ales. Central heating. Colour TV. Tea/coffee-making facilities.

| | Bed Only £ | B & B £ | Half Board £ |
|---|---|---|---|
| High Season | 6.00 | 10.60 | 15.00 |

Children's discounts available

## NORTH YORKSHIRE Hawes

**WHITE HART INN**
Main Street, Hawes,
N. Yorkshire, DL8 3QL
Tel: 09697 259
7 Bedrooms

M LF LP AL

The White Hart is a small, friendly inn situated in the lovely market town of Hawes. Closely located (100 yds) to some of the best trout and grayling fishing in North Yorkshire. There is extensive fishing within a 4-mile radius of Hawes. The Inn has a residents' TV lounge made for relaxing, restaurant serving home cooked meals and a friendly, local bar serving good beers.

| | B & B £ |
|---|---|
| High Season | 11.00 |

Children's discounts available
Closed Dec, Jan

## Pickering

**MILBURN ARMS HOTEL**
Rosedale Abbey,
Nr. Pickering, N. Yorkshire,
YO18 8RA
Tel: 07515 312
7 Bedrooms (5 with private bathroom/shower).

M LP

Beautifully situated traditional country inn with comfortable well-appointed accommodation for fishermen with outstanding food and wines. Our friendly atmosphere makes for easy relaxation, and being the village pub we can ensure a convivial evening in the low-beamed bar with log-fires and handpulled real ales, plus a vast array of malt whiskies and cognacs. Scenic drives to many game, sea and coarse waters.

| | B & B £ | Half Board £ |
|---|---|---|
| High Season | 19.50 | 26.50 |
| Mid Season | 18.00 | 25.00 |
| Low Season | 17.00 | 24.00 |

Children's discounts available
**HS** Easter, 20 May–30 Sep
**MS** 1 Apr–19 May, Oct
**LS** 1 Nov–31 Mar
Supplements: Single room £7. Dogs £3.50 per stay

## Scarborough

**THE VICTORIA HOTEL**
79 Westborough,
Scarborough, N. Yorkshire,
YO11 1TP
Tel: 0723 360376
Classification not yet known
32 Bedrooms (8 with private bathroom/shower)

M LF LP AL HT

The Victoria Hotel, a central, licensed and friendly hotel is close to all Scarborough's amenities. 5 minutes from the sea and close to the Mere, an idyllic setting for a day's coarse fishing. Sea wreck fishing trips can be organised on the Valhalla (38 ft) or the Wand'rin Star (34 ft), eight rods per boat. Small and large parties catered for. Phone for further details.

| | B & B £ | Half Board £ |
|---|---|---|
| High Season | 21.90 | 33.80 |

Children's discounts available
Closed 1 week at Christmas

## Skipton

**DEVONSHIRE ARMS**
Bolton Abbey, Skipton,
N. Yorkshire, BD23 6AJ
Tel: 075 671 441
38 Bedrooms (All with private bathroom/shower).

M T LF LP AL HT

The Devonshire Arms at Bolton Abbey is a comfortable hotel in the Yorkshire Dales National Park. It is adjacent to the River Wharfe. The fisheries manager continually checks the River to ensure an appropriate supply of trout. Traditions of hospitality reach back to the 12th century. The hotel lies on the A59 Skipton to Harrogate road in the lovely Dales.

| | B & B £ | Half Board £ |
|---|---|---|
| High Season | 60.50 | 84.00 |
| Mid Season | 60.50 | 84.00 |
| Low Season | 60.50 | 80.00 |

Children's discounts available
**HS** 22 May–31 Oct
**MS** 27 Mar–21 May
**LS** 1 Nov–26 Mar

**MANOR HOUSE HOTEL**
Burnsall, Nr. Skipton, North Yorkshire, BD23 6BW
Tel: 075672 231
7 Bedrooms
M T LP AL HT
Yorkshire Dales National Park. Situated in some of the most beautiful scenery in the Dales. Food and hospitality recommended. Open December until end of October. Manor House is licensed and there are also two public houses in the village. Free trout and grayling fishing available to all residents all the year round. Brochure: Manor House Hotel, Burnsall, Nr. Skipton, N. Yorks Tel. 075672 231.

| | B & B £ | Half Board £ |
|---|---|---|
| High Season | 10.00 | 14.00 |

Children's discounts available
Closed last 3 weeks in November

**RED LION HOTEL**
Burnsall, Nr. Skipton, N. Yorkshire, BD23 6BU
Tel: 075672 204
12 Bedrooms (4 with private bathroom/shower).
M LP
Day and weekly tickets available. 7 miles keepered club waters. Trout June/September, grayling November/January. Fly only. Beautiful stretch Wharfe. Hotel offers comfortable accommodation with en-suite facilities, good food with bar meals and restaurant. Two-star AA and RAC. Also Michelin guide, Routiers and Ashley Courtenay recommended.

| | B & B £ | Half Board £ |
|---|---|---|
| High Season | 14.00 | 21.00 |
| Low Season | 14.00 | 18.00 |

Children's discounts available
**LS** Nov–Mar
Supplements: Room with bath/shower & WC £5. Single room £5

## Thirsk

**SHIRES COURT HOTEL**
Knayton, Nr. Thirsk, North Yorkshire, YO7 4BS
Tel: 0845 537210
15 Bedrooms (All with private bathroom/shower).
M LF LP AL HT
Excellent facilities for coarse and game fishing. Most rooms on the ground floor with own entrance. Detailed list of more than 15 fishing sites within 30 mile radius available on request. Situated in Herriot country, excellent centre for golf, gliding, pony trekking, walking, zoos, pleasure parks, ancient abbeys, stately homes, in fact something for everyone. Excellent meals in our restaurant on your return! Send or ring for brochure and full details.

| | B & B £ |
|---|---|
| High Season | 36.00 |
| Mid Season | 32.00 |
| Low Season | 22.00 |

Children's discounts available
**HS** 9 May–26 Sep
**MS** 28 Mar–8 May, 27 Sep–31 Oct
**LS** 28 Feb–27 Mar
Closed 1 Nov–27 Feb
Supplements: Single room £3

## York

**HEWORTH COURT HOTEL**
76–78 Heworth Green, York, North Yorkshire, YO3 7TQ
Tel: 0904 425156
16 Bedrooms (All with private bathroom/shower).
M T LF LP AL
A three-acre private coarse fishing pond in pleasant surroundings owned by the hotel proprietors, Mr. Smith being a keen angler. A Yorkshire River Board licence is all that is required to fish. Other day ticket waters are available in the area. Smith's pond, situated seven minutes walk from the hotel, includes roach, rudd, perch, tench, carp, bream, pike and trout. No fishing allowed after dusk.

| | Bed Only £ | B & B £ | Half Board £ |
|---|---|---|---|
| High Season | 27.50 | 27.50 | 38.00 |
| Low Season | 25.00 | 25.00 | 35.50 |

Children's discounts available
**HS** 1 Jun–30 Sep
**MS** Break terms available
**LS** 1 Oct–31 May
Supplements: Single room £6

**RYEDALE LODGE & RESTAURANT**
Station Road, Nunnington, Nr Helmsley, York, North Yorkshire, YO6 5XB
Tel: 04395 246
Classification not yet known
7 Bedrooms (All with private bathroom/shower).
M T LF
Ryedale Lodge is a small secluded country house hotel situated by the River Rye with 1000 yards of private fishing. Access to a further 2½ miles brown trout and grayling. The Lodge is renowned for fine food and relaxing atmosphere. All bedrooms beautifully appointed, with private bathroom, colour TV, direct-dial telephone, trouser press, hairdryer, tea-making facilities and a welcome bowl of goodies. Personally managed by chef proprietors Jon and Janet Laird.

| | B & B £ | Half Board £ |
|---|---|---|
| High Season | 27.00 | 43.75 |
| Low Season | 24.50 | 40.25 |

Children's discounts available
**HS** Jun–Sept
**LS** Oct–May

## SOUTH YORKSHIRE Sheffield

**THE LINDUM HOTEL**
91 Montgomery Road, Nether Edge, Sheffield, S. Yorks, S7 1LP
Tel: 0742 552356
10 Bedrooms
M LF HT
The Lindum Hotel is conveniently situated in a quiet residential area between the city centre (and its night life) and the Derbyshire countryside. Trout 20 minutes away, coarse at Dam Flask and Under Bank. Trout at Moorhall and Ladybower Reservoir, all day ticket waters. The hotel offers colour TV, radio alarm and tea/coffee-making facilities in all rooms. A la carte menu and packed lunches on request. AA, RAC listed.

| | B & B £ | Half Board £ |
|---|---|---|
| High Season | 11.75 | 16.50 |

*Prices in England for Fishing are per person, sharing a double room, per night, including VAT (at the current rate of 15 per cent).*

See page 4 for details of symbols

# ANGLIA

*Tourist Information Centres open all year round.*
*Not to scale.*

# ANGLIA

This is 'big sky' country of gentle slopes and far horizons occupying the major part of 'lowland' England, Lincolnshire and East Anglia. Large slow rivers meander at a leisurely pace past meadows and willows to the North Sea. This is predominantly coarse fishing country with rivers, drains, ponds and lakes stocked with bream, roach, carp, perch and pike. The Fens are a land on their own — England's "Little Holland" – of dykes and drains full of bream, roach, pike and the recently-introduced zander, or pike-perch. The Norfolk Broads is a world of reed-lined meres and inter-connected rivers important for nature conservation and boating, famed for bream and specimen pike. Anglia is also a centre for reservoir trout fishing with waters like Rutland and Grafham setting international standards for stillwater trouting.

**Water Authority**
Anglian Water, Ambury Road, Huntingdon, Cambs PE18 6NZ

**Cambridge Division**
Great Ouse House, Clarendon Road, Cambridge, CB2 2BL
Tel: Cambridge (0223) 61561

**Colchester Division**
33 Sheepen Road, Colchester, Essex CO3 3LB
Tel: Colchester (0206) 69171

**Lincoln Division**
Waterside House, Waterside North, Lincoln LN2 5HP
Tel: Lincoln (0522) 25231

**Norwich Division**
Yare House, 62/64 Thorpe Road, Norwich NR1 1SA
Tel: Norwich (0603) 615161

**Oundle Division**
North Street, Oundle, Peterborough PE8 4AS
Tel: Oundle (0832) 73701

**Fishing Seasons**
Salmon, Sea Trout, Brown Trout, Rainbow Trout — not in enclosed waters — 1 Mar–28 Sept

Brown Trout — 1 Apr–29 Oct (enclosed waters)

Rainbow Trout — No closed season (enclosed waters)

Coarse Fish — 16 Jun–14 Mar

**Water Authority Rod Licences Required**
Widely available throughout the region. Full List from Water Authority

**Regional Tourist Boards**
East Midlands Tourist Board, Exchequergate, Lincoln LN2 1PZ
Tel: (0522) 31521

East Anglia Tourist Board, Toppesfield Hall, Hadleigh, Suffolk IP7 5DN
Tel: (0473) 822922

Thames & Chilterns Tourist Board
8 The Market Place, Abingdon, Oxfordshire, OX14 3UD
Tel: (0235) 22711

# ANGLIA ANGLING CLUBS

**Beccles Angling Club**
R.J. Pigney, Secretary, 25 Pleasant Place, Beccles, Suffolk
**Boston & District Angling Association**
Secretary, 6 Churchill Drive, Boston, Lincs PE21 0NH
**Colnes Angling Society**
P. Emson, Secretary, 16 Station Road, Colne Engaine, Colchester, Essex
**Earls Barton Angling Club**
B.F. Hager, Secretary, 113 Station Road, Earls Barton, Northampton NN6 0NX
**East Dereham & District Angling Club**
S.R. Allison, Secretary, "Seuqitna", Cemetery Road, East Dereham, Norfolk
**Gipping Angling Preservation Society**
George Alderson, Manager, 19 Clover Close, Ipswich IP2 0PW
**Hitchin & District Angling Association**
L. Day, Secretary, 14 Thatchers End, Hitchin, Herts SG4 0PD
**Kettering & District Fly Fishers Association**
River Secretary, 17 West Furlong, Kettering, Northants NN15 7LF
**King's Lynn Angling Association**
G.T. Bear, Secretary, 1 Cock Drove, Downham Market, King's Lynn, Norfolk
**Leighton Buzzard Angling Club**
M.B. Holmes, Secretary, 8 The Stile, Heath & Reach, Leighton Buzzard, Beds
**Linear Fisheries Club**
Secretary, 23 Cemetery Road, Houghton Regis, Dunstable, Beds
**Louth C.A.W.A.C.**
G. Allison, Secretary, 15 Florence Wright Avenue, Louth, Lincs LN11 8EJ
**Milton Keynes Angling Association**
T. Jeans, 6 Bolton Close, Bletchley, Milton Keynes MK3 6LJ
**Peterborough & District Angling Association**
W. Yates, Secretary, 75 Lawn Avenue, Peterborough PE1 3RA
**Wellingborough Nene & District Angling Club**
G.W. Barker, Secretary, 139 Knox Road, Wellingborough, Northants NN8 1HX

# RIVERS AND CANALS

| Water | Location | Species | Permits |
|---|---|---|---|
| **Ant** | Stalham Dyke | Pike<br>Perch<br>Roach<br>Bream | Free Fishing from Public Staithe<br>Other permits from Richardsons Boatyard |
| | Ludham Bridge | | Anglian Water |
| **Bure** | Woodbastwick | Pike<br>Tench<br>Bream | Anglian Water |
| | St Benet's Abbey | Bream | Norwich and District Angling Association<br>Ludham Post Office |
| | Upton | Bream<br>Roach | Anglian Water |
| **Cam** | Grantchester Meadows | Roach<br>Dace<br>Chub | Free Fishing |

| Water | Location | Species | Permits |
|---|---|---|---|
| **Cam** contd. | Cambridge | | Cambridge Fish Preservation and Angling Society<br>Cambridge Albion Angling Society |
| | Waterbeach | | Waterbeach Angling Club |
| **Chelmer and Blackwater Canal (Parts)** | Chelmsford | Mixed Coarse Fish | Public Fishing |
| | Chelmsford | Coarse Fish | Chelmsford Angling Association<br>Bailiffs on site |
| **Colne** | Aldham and Fordham | Coarse Fish | Colnes Angling Society<br>P. Emson & Son, Tackle Shop, 86 High Street, Earl's Colne<br>Tel: 078 75 3413 |
| **Cut Off Channel** | Denver | Bream<br>Roach<br>Pike<br>Zander | Anglian Water |
| **Fenland Drains** | March<br>Wisbech<br>Chatteris<br>Downham Market | Bream<br>Roach<br>Perch<br>Pike | March Working Men's Club<br>Ramsey Angling Society<br>Chatteris Angling Club<br>Permits available locally |
| **Gipping** | Ipswich | Mixed Coarse Fish | Gipping Angling Preservation Society<br>Local Tackle Shops |
| **Glen (and Northdrove Southdrove Counterdrain Venattsdrain)** | Spalding | All Coarse Fish | Spalding Angling Club<br>D. Ball, Hawthorn Bank, Spalding<br>Tel: (0775) 4001<br>Red Lion Hotel, Spalding<br>Tel: (0775) 2869<br>Bulstrode Guest House, 11 Holland Road, Spalding<br>Tel: (0775) 69465 |
| **Great Ouse** | Milton Keynes | Barbel and Other Coarse Fish | Linear Fisheries Club<br>Site Office, Linford Lakes<br>Local Tackle Shops |
| | Milton Keynes | Mixed Coarse Fish | Milton Keynes Angling Association<br>Local Tackle Dealers |
| | Buckingham | Roach<br>Dace<br>Chub | Buckingham and District Angling Association<br>Local Tackle Shops |
| | Bedford | Mixed Coarse Fish | Leighton Buzzard Angling Club<br>Bedford Angling Club<br>Local Tackle Shops |
| | St Neots | Mixed Coarse Fish | St Neots and District Angling and Fish Preservation Society<br>Permits on bank |
| | Offord | Bream<br>Chub<br>Carp<br>Tench | Offord and Buckden Angling Club |
| | Godmanchester | Bream<br>Chub<br>Carp<br>Tench | Godmanchester Angling Society |

| Water | Location | Species | Permits |
|---|---|---|---|
| **Great Ouse** contd. | Huntingdon | Bream<br>Chub<br>Carp<br>Tench | Huntingdon Angling and Fish Preservation Society |
| | St Ives | Bream<br>Chub<br>Carp<br>Tench | St Ives Angling and Fish Preservation Society<br>Local Tackle Shops |
| | Earith | Bream<br>Chub<br>Carp<br>Tench | Earith and District Angling Club |
| | Southerby to Denver Sluice | | Kings Lynn Angling Association |
| | Chatteris | Coarse Fish | Cross Keys Hotel and Restaurant, 16 Market Hill, Chatteris, Cambs Tel: 03543 3036 |
| | Emberton Olney | Coarse Fish | Leighton Buzzard Angling Club<br>D. Ayres, 52 Montmore Road, Leighton Buzzard, Beds |
| **Nar** | King's Lynn | Mixed Coarse Fish | King's Lynn Angling Association<br>Local Tackle Shops |
| **Nene** | Northampton | Mixed Coarse Fish | Northampton Nene Angling Club<br>Castle Angling Club<br>Long Buckby Angling Club<br>Local Tackle Shops |
| | Wellingborough | Mixed Coarse Fish | Wellingborough Nene and District Angling Club<br>Irthlingborough Angling Club<br>Local Tackle Shops |
| | Thrapston | | Rushden Angling Club<br>Kettering and T.D.A.A. |
| | Peterborough | | Sibson Fisheries Office, New Lane, Stibbington Tel: 0780 782621<br>Bailiff, D. Moisey, 47 Church Lane, Stibbington |
| | Oundle | | Oundle Angling Club<br>Coventry and District A.A. |
| | Earl's Barton | Roach<br>Bream<br>Tench | Earl's Barton Angling Club<br>M. Perkins, Tackle Shop, The Square, Earl's Barton |
| | Peterborough (15 miles) | Most Coarse Fish Species | Peterborough and District Angling Assn.<br>Local Tackle Shops<br>Bailiff on the bank |
| **Relief Channel** | Denver Sluice to King's Lynn | Bream<br>Roach<br>Pike<br>Zander | Anglian Water |
| **South Forty Foot Drain (Bargate and Sibsey Trader Drains)** | Boston | Carp<br>Pike<br>Tench<br>Bream<br>Ruffe<br>Roach | Boston and District Angling Association<br>Local Tackle Shops<br>Bailiff on bank |

| Water | Location | Species | Permits |
|---|---|---|---|
| **Stour** | Sudbury | Roach<br>Bream | Sudbury and District Angling Association |
| | Sudbury | Coarse Fish | "The Henny Swan", Great Henny, Sudbury<br>Mill Hotel, Walnut Tree Lane, Sudbury<br>Suffolk Tel: 0787 75544 |
| | Flatford | Pike<br>Dace | Elm Park, Hornchurch & District Angling Soc.<br>King Catchers Angling Club |
| | Colchester | | Colnes Angling Society<br>Emson & Son, Tackle Shop, 86 High Street, Earl's Colne |
| **Thurne** | Martham Ferry | Bream<br>Roach<br>Pike<br>Tench | Anglian Water<br>Permits from Bailiff<br>Waterside Holidays |
| | Potter Heigham | | Anglian Water<br>Free Fishing |
| | Cold Harbour | | Norwich and District Angling Association<br>Ludham Post Office |
| **Waveney** | Beccles Quay | Roach<br>Bream<br>Pike | Anglian Water<br>Free of charge |
| **Welland** | Market Harborough to Stamford | Dace<br>Chub<br>Roach | Market Harborough Angling Club<br>Uppingham and District Angling Club<br>Oakham Angling Club<br>Stamford Welland Angling Association |
| | Stamford to Spalding (9 miles) | | Peterborough and District Angling Association<br>Deeping St James Angling Club<br>Permits available locally |
| | Spalding | | Anglian Water<br>Free Fishing |
| **Wensum** | Lenwade | Trout<br>Roach<br>Dace<br>Pike | Lenwade House Hotel<br>Rose Cottage, Common Lane, Lenwade |
| | Norwich | | Norwich City Council<br>Free Fishing |
| **Wissey** | Stoke Ferry<br>Mildenhall | Mixed Coarse Fish<br>Trout | King's Lynn Angling Association<br>Local Tackle Shops<br>Smoke House Inn<br>Beck Row, Mildenhall, Suffolk<br>Tel: 0638 713223 |
| **Witham** | Grantham | Roach<br>Chub<br>Dace<br>Bream<br>Pike | Grantham Angling Association<br>Permits available locally |

| Water | Location | Species | Permits |
|---|---|---|---|
| **Witham** contd. | Lincoln | | Lincoln and District Angling Association<br>Permits available locally |
| | Lincoln to Boston | | Witham and District Joint Anglers Federation<br>Permits available locally<br>New England Hotel, Wide Bargate, Boston<br>J. Morely Sports, 5 Wide Bargate, Boston |
| **Yare** | Trowse | Bream<br>Roach<br>Perch | Norwich and District Angling Association<br>Available locally |
| | Whitlingham | | Free Fishing |
| | Rockland Broad Dyke | | Anglian Water<br>Free Fishing |
| | Buckenham | | Anglian Water<br>Free Fishing |

# LAKES AND RESERVOIRS

| | | | |
|---|---|---|---|
| **Alton Reservoir** | Ipswich | Most Coarse Fish | Gipping Angling Preservation Society<br>Local Tackle Shops 30 miles radius Ipswich |
| **Ardleigh Reservoir** | Colchester | Brown Trout<br>Rainbow Trout | Fishery and Estates Officer<br>Ardleigh Reservoir, Colchester<br>Tel: Colchester 230642<br>(Open all year for Rainbow Trout) |
| **Aveley Lakes** | Aveley | Rainbow Trout<br>Brown Trout<br>Brook Trout | Aveley Lakes, Romford Road,<br>Aveley, Essex Tel: 0926 613344 |
| **Barton Broads** | Smallburgh | Pike<br>Bream<br>Roach<br>Tench | Boat Fishing Only<br>Boat Hire: Cox Bros, Barton Turf Staithe |
| | Barton-on-Humber | Carp<br>Bream<br>Tench<br>Roach | Barton Broads<br>Chemical Lane, Barton-on-Humber,<br>South Humberside<br>Permits at Shop/Cafe |
| **Blickling Hall Lake** | Aylsham | Bream<br>Tench<br>Roach<br>Rudd<br>Pike | The National Trust<br>Park Warden, Blickling, Norwich<br>Tel: Aylsham 734181<br>Permits on site from Park Warden |
| **Bure Valley Lakes** | Aylsham | Brown Trout<br>Rainbow Trout | Bure Valley Lakes Trout Fishery<br>Oulton, Nr Aylsham, Norfolk<br>Tel: (026 387) 666<br>Permits on site |
| **Castle Ashby Lakes** | Northampton | Carp<br>Tench<br>Bream<br>Roach<br>Perch<br>Pike | Estate Office, Castle Ashby, Northants<br>Bailiff, Brickyard Lodge, Castle Ashby |

| Water | Location | Species | Permits |
|---|---|---|---|
| **Castle Leisure Park** | Tattershall | Trout<br>Pike<br>Roach<br>Bream<br>Tench<br>Rudd<br>(Numerous Lakes) | Castle Leisure Park<br>Sleaford Road, Tattershall, Lincolnshire<br>Recreation Office (Open all year) |
| **Chigborough** | Maldon, Essex | Eels<br>Perch<br>Crucian Carp<br>Tench<br>Roach<br>Rudd | Leisure Sport Angling<br>Scraley Road, Maldon, Essex<br>Bailiffs on bank |
| **Chigboro' Fisheries** | Maldon, Essex | Brown Trout<br>Rainbow Trout<br>Carp<br>Tench<br>Bream<br>Roach | Chigboro' Fisheries<br>Chigborough Road, Maldon, Essex<br>Tel: Maldon (0621) 57368<br>Permits on site |
| **Daventry Reservoir** | Daventry | Carp<br>Bream<br>Roach<br>Rudd<br>Pike | Daventry District Council<br>Daventry Country Park<br>Warden at Park |
| **Earith Complex of Gravel Pits** | Earith | Coarse Fish | Amey Anglers Association<br>Arc Linch Hill Fishery, Stanton Harcourt, Oxford |
| **Elinor Trout Fishery** | Oundle | Brown Trout<br>Rainbow Trout | Elinor Trout Fishery, Aldwincle, Northants<br>Tel: (0832) 73671 (Eves), Permits on site<br>(Open all year) |
| **Eyebrook Reservoir** | Corby | Brown Trout<br>Rainbow Trout | Eyebrook Reservoir<br>Caldecott, Leicestershire<br>Tel: Rockingham 770 264 |
| **Fen Drayton Complex of Gravel Pits** | Fen Drayton | Coarse Fish | Amey Anglers Association<br>Arc Linch Hill Fishery, Stanton Harcourt, Oxford |
| **Ferry Meadows** | Peterborough | Mixed Coarse Fish | Peterborough and District Angling Association<br>Local Tackle Shops |
| **Fritton Lake** | Fritton | Carp<br>Tench<br>Bream<br>Pike | Fritton Country Park Lake<br>Permits and Boat Hire<br>Mr W. Mussett, Lake Cafe |
| **Grafham Water** | Huntingdon | Brown Trout<br>Rainbow Trout | Anglian Water<br>Fishing Lodge at Reservoir<br>Bookings (0480) 810247 |
| **Hanningfield Reservoir** | Chelmsford | Brown Trout<br>Rainbow Trout | Essex Water Company<br>Fishery Office on site<br>Tel: Chelmsford 400381 |
| **Hatchery House Trout Lakes** | Bury St Edmunds | Rainbow Trout | McRae Farms Limited<br>Hatchery House, Barrow, Bury St Edmunds<br>Tel: (0284) 810300<br>Permits book in advance |

| Water | Location | Species | Permits |
|---|---|---|---|
| **Hatton Trout Lake** | Horncastle (Lincs) | Brown Trout<br>Rainbow Trout<br>Brook Trout | Hatton Trout Lake<br>Hatton, Nr Wragby, Lincs<br>Tel: Wragby 858682<br>On site<br>(Open all year) |
| **Hevingham Lakes** | Norwich | Carp<br>Tench<br>Bream<br>Roach | Hevingham Lakes, Hevingham, Norwich<br>Tel: (060548) 368<br>Permits from Bungalow at entrance |
| **Hickling Broad** | Hickling | Bream<br>Roach<br>Tench<br>Pike | Norfolk Naturalists Trust<br>Warden on site<br>Mainly Boat Fishing<br>Hirer:<br>Martham Ferry Boatyard, Martham<br>W.W. Beale, The Staithe Garage, Hickling<br>Whispering Reeds Boatyard, Hickling |
| **Hill View Trout Lake** | Skegness | Brown Trout<br>Rainbow Trout | Hill View Trout Lake, Skegness<br>Warden's Caravan on site |
| **Hollowell Reservoir** | Northampton | Pike<br>Perch<br>Rudd | Anglian Water<br>Fishing Lodge on site |
| **Horsey Mere** | Horsey | Roach<br>Bream<br>Pike | Nature Reserve<br>Mainly Boat Fishing<br>Permits: Mr Tubby, Staithe Store, Horsey<br>Boat Hire from Local Yards<br>Closed Nov–Feb |
| **Lakeside Caravan Park** | Saxmundham, Suffolk | Carp<br>Bream<br>Roach<br>Tench | Lakeside Caravan Park<br>Saxmundham, Suffolk<br>Permits on site |
| **Lenwade House Lake** | Lenwade, Norfolk | Rainbow Trout | Lenwade House Hotel<br>Gt Witchingham, Norwich<br>Local Angling Shops |
| **Linford Lakes (Ten)** | Milton Keynes | Carp<br>Bream<br>Tench<br>Roach<br>Pike<br>Perch | Linear Fisheries Club<br>Secretary, 23 Cemetery Road,<br>Houghton Regis, Dunstable, Beds<br>Tel: (0582) 867479<br>Local Tackle Shops<br>Site Office |
| **Little Paxton Gravel Pits** | St Neots | Tench<br>Rudd<br>Carp<br>Pike | Redland Angling Scheme<br>Weighbridge Office<br>Bailiff on bank |
| **Loughton Lodge Lake (and Other Waters)** | Milton Keynes | Most Species of Coarse Fish | Milton Keynes Angling Association<br>Secretary, T. Jeans, 6 Bolton Close, Bletchley, Milton Keynes<br>Local Tackle Shops |
| **Maxey Pit** | Peterborough | Mixed Coarse Fish | Peterborough and District Angling Association<br>Local Tackle Shops |
| **Narborough Trout Lakes** | King's Lynn | Rainbow Trout | Narborough Trout Lakes<br>Narborough Mill, King's Lynn,<br>Norfolk Tel: 0760 338005<br>Permits on site |

| Water | Location | Species | Permits |
|---|---|---|---|
| **Ormesby Broad (and Rollesby and Filby Broads)** | Ormesby | Bream<br>Rudd<br>Tench<br>Pike | Boat Only<br>Hirers: G. Skoyles, Old Sportsman Cottage |
| **Oulton Broad** | Oulton | Flounders<br>Mullet<br>Bream<br>Tench | Bank Fishing from:<br>Nicholas Everitt Park<br>Boat Hire from:<br>A. Collins, Tackle Shop, Commodore Road, Lowestoft<br>J. Mallett, Camping Boats, Marsh Road, Oulton Broad |
| **Pitsford Reservoir** | Northampton | Brown Trout<br>Rainbow Trout | Anglian Water<br>Fishing Lodge at Reservoir<br>Tel: (0604) 781350 |
| **Ranworth Broad** | | Roach<br>Bream<br>Tench<br>Pike | Norwich and District Angling Association<br>Boats can be obtained from the Association through Local Tackle Shops |
| **Ravensthorpe Reservoir** | Northampton | Brown Trout<br>Rainbow Trout | Anglian Water<br>Fishing Lodge at Reservoir<br>Tel: 0604 770875 |
| **Ringstead Grange Trout Fishery** | Ringstead<br>Kettering | Rainbow Trout<br>Brown Trout<br>Brook Trout<br>Salmon | Ringstead, Grange Trout Fishery<br>Ringstead, Kettering, Northants<br>Tel: Wellingborough 622960 |
| **Rockells Farm Ponds** | Saffron Walden | Carp<br>Tench<br>Rudd | Rockells Farm<br>Duddenwold End,<br>Saffron Walden<br>Essex<br>Tel: 0763 838053<br>(Accommodation) |
| **Rutland Water** | Oakham, Leics | Brown Trout<br>Rainbow Trout | Anglian Water<br>Fishing Lodge at Reservoir<br>Tel: Empingham (078086) 770<br>(Open all year for Rainbow Trout)<br>Talbot Hotel, New Street, Oundle, Northants |
| **Seckford Hall Lake** | Woodbridge, Suffolk | Rainbow Trout<br>Carp | Seckford Hall Hotel<br>Nr Woodbridge, Suffolk<br>(Open all year) |
| **Sibson Fisheries** | Peterborough | Bream<br>Carp<br>Tench<br>Rudd<br>Rainbow Trout<br>Brown Trout | Sibson Fisheries<br>Office, New Lane, Stibbington<br>Tel: 0780 782621<br>Bailiff, D. Moisey, 51 Church Lane, Stibbington |
| **South Walsham Broad** | South Walsham, Norfolk | Bream<br>Roach<br>Perch<br>Pike | Fleet Dyke and Village Staithe<br>Otherwise mainly Boat Fishing |
| **Swanton Morley Lakes** | East Dereham, Norfolk | Roach<br>Carp<br>Tench<br>Rudd<br>Pike<br>Perch | Outdoor Water Recreation Ltd<br>Lakeview, Old Bury Hill, Dorking, Surrey<br>Mrs V. Marsham, Waterfall Farm, Swanton Morley<br>Local Tackle Shops |

| Water | Location | Species | Permits |
|---|---|---|---|
| **Sywell Reservoir** | Wellingborough | Tench<br>Pike<br>Roach | Wellingborough Nene and District Angling Club<br>Local Tackle Shops |
| **Taswood Lakes** | Norwich | Carp<br>Tench<br>Bream<br>Rudd | Taswood Lakes Fishery<br>Flordon, Norwich<br>Permits at Bungalow |
| **Taverham (Ringland Lakes and River Wensum)** | Old Costessey, Norfolk | Carp<br>Tench<br>Bream<br>Roach<br>Chub | Leisure Sports Angling<br>Huntsman Motor, Caravette Centre and Filling Station, West End, Old Costessey, Norwich, Norfolk<br>Tel: Norwich 742806 |
| **Toft Newton Trout Fishery and Cleatham Trout Fishery** | Market Rasen, Lincolnshire | Rainbow Trout<br>Brown Trout<br>Brook Trout<br>Salmon (stocked) | Toft Newton Reservoir, Toft Next Newton, Market Rasen, Lincolnshire<br>Office on site<br>Tel: 067 37453 |
| **Waveney Valley Lakes** | Harleston | Carp<br>Tench | Waveney Valley Lakes Caravan Park<br>Wortwell, Harleston, Norfolk<br>Shop on site |
| **Withy Pool** | Hitchin, Herts | Large Carp<br>Catfish | K. Maddocks, Withy Pool, Bedford Road, Henlow, Beds<br>Fishing with caravan accommodation |
| **Wroxham Broad** | Wroxham, Norfolk | Pike | Small Permit Fee<br>Boat Hire:<br>E.C. Burton & Sons, Merton, The Rhond, Wroxham<br>Tel: Wroxham 2751 |

## SEA ANGLING

**Skegness to King's Lynn**
The sea wall can produce plenty of action, particularly during the high water period when fish come inshore to feed on worms and other food. Some local anglers use strips of fresh herring as a substitute for worm, although generally speaking lugworms dug locally produce the bulk of the good catches for beach and pier anglers. Sandbanks and extremely shallow water make boat angling in the Skegness area rather difficult. Farther south, at King's Lynn, fishing is rather restricted and apart from river fishing for silver eels and flounders, shore anglers have little opportunity of finding good sport. The boat angler however, can get out from King's Lynn to fish the famed Wash marks for tope and thornback skate. Tope fishing in this area can be extremely good and large catches of these fine fighting fish can be taken during the summer months.

**Hunstanton**
With its sandy beaches and fine pier, Hunstanton can produce some remarkably good catches of flatfish, whiting, silver eels and the occasional cod or codling. Lugworm can be dug locally and the area fishes well in all but a strong north-west wind which, when coupled with the prevailing tide flows, makes fishing impossible. Heacham and Holkham beaches are favourite venues with local and visiting anglers.

**Sheringham**
The rocky shoreline and pier produce good catches of flatfish, whiting and cod. Boat fishing in this area can produce plenty of big bags, although individual fish seldom achieve specimen weights. The noted shore marks of the area are Weybourne, Cley and Salthouse beaches.

**Wells**
The large fishing fleet based here provides ample opportunity for boat fishing and the many channels and holes in the sea bottom can provide excellent tope and skate fishing.

**Cromer**
Like most coastlines the east coast changes considerably throughout its length, with one area providing good flat-fishing, another offering the opportunity of bigger fish. Cromer combines both. Best known for its pier and beach fishing, Cromer is famous for sole and, oddly enough, big tope. More than one 40 lb plus tope have been caught by a beach or pier angler fishing with big baits, and it would seem likely that these big fish come inshore to take advantage of the flatfish shoals that browse over the area. A favourite spot here is the east end of the beach where sandy spots surrounded by rock provide flatfish with food and shelter from marauding predators.
From Cromer round to Great Yarmouth the beaches at Walcott, Bacton, Mundesley, Horsey, Hemsby, Winterton and Caister are all good places to fish. Unfortunately during the holiday season the over-spill from nearby holiday camps can make these beaches too crowded to fish, although night-fishing sessions on any of these beaches can be productive. During the winter months small codling are plentiful and each cast brings the chance of making contact with a 20 lb-plus cod. During various parts of the year whiting, dabs, sole, flounders and good skate can be caught from these beaches.

**Great Yarmouth and Gorleston**
These towns are usually packed with holiday-makers from June to late September. Even so, with nearly seven miles of beach, roughly two miles of quays and three piers, the shore angler has plenty of opportunity to practise his sport. Boat fishing from the harbour or from the beach provides excellent opportunities to avoid holiday crowds and with good fishing at almost any time of the year, the whole area makes an ideal angling base.

**Lowestoft**
This is another excellent centre with good sandy beaches, and two piers providing plenty of scope for local and visiting anglers alike. In the yacht basin close to the harbour entrance it is possible to catch flounders, silver eels, smelt and even good mullet although these latter fish are difficult to catch. Lowestoft, like Yarmouth is noted mainly for its autumn and winter cod fishing. During the autumn and early winter months, huge shoals of prime whiting may also visit the area providing good catches for both boat and shore fisher-men. South of Lowestoft at Pakefield and Kessingland there is deep water close to the shore.

**Southwold**
Southwold boasts a good sandy beach, a short pier and a harbour. Being situated in a bay, the beach is practically tide-free, although at the harbour entrance the tide run is often so strong that it makes fishing well-nigh impossible. Anglers fishing here at slack water are often rewarded with good catches of fine sole. There are also bass in the bay although as a general rule they are far from plentiful. The whole area is capable of yielding bass of exceptional size, but most of these fish are caught accidentally on big baits intended for skate or tope. Occasionally someone fishing with light tackle for flatfish makes contact with a big bass. More often than not this results in a tackle breakage and the loss of the fish.
Farther along, the coast is a rather stony beach until it reaches the estuary of the Alde River. Often busy with holidaymakers, this area fishes well through-out the year. Several small, isolated beaches north of the town fish well during the winter months, particularly for whiting and the occasional big cod.

**Orford**
Situated on the Alde estuary this is a good summer venue for skate fishing but to get to the best grounds it is necessary to cross the river. This can be arranged through the offices of the Harbour Master.

**Felixstowe, Walton-on-the-Naze and Clacton-on-Sea**
These are difficult places to fish during the summer months because of their holiday popularity. All three towns have good piers and beaches which vary from sand to large stones and mud patches. For boat fishing during the summer months, bass and thornback skate are the main species while in the winter months cod and whiting can be caught from beaches and boats alike. Felixstowe produced the original bass record.

**Blackwater and Crouch**
The coast off these rivers

dries out with extensive mud and sandbanks, and is best explored in many boat trips with an experienced fisherman. Alternatively charter trips are available. The estuaries themselves provide some excellent fishing, including bass at the right time of the tide. This area is famous for the development of up-tide boat casting — a method which has already produced a good tope.

**Southend, Canvey Island and the Thames Estuary**
This whole area can provide good summer and winter fishing and a wide variety of fish. Quite apart from the normal flounders, silver eels, cod bass and skate, this section of the Essex coastline has in recent seasons produced a steady stream of more unusual fish. Heavyweight sting-ray can often be encountered and beach and inshore-boat anglers often make contact with good, big smooth hounds. The Thames estuary up as far as Gravesend is now, thanks to a gradual cleaning-up process of the river, producing excellent results. Winter cod and flounder fishing is particularly good and a year or two ago the whole area began to produce excellent haddock catches. These have now diminished again but local anglers feel that the haddock shoals could re-appear at any time to add interest and weight to boat anglers' catches.
The whole of the Thames estuary is wide open for exploration. As yet only a fraction has been discovered and there is a great deal of scope for any angler, particularly those who can get afloat, to discover this fascinating area. The "up-tide" techniques have done a great deal to indicate the potential of this area.

# ACCOMMODATION

## CAMBRIDGESHIRE
### Chatteris

**CROSS KEYS HOTEL & RESTAURANT**
16 Market Hill, Chatteris, Cambridgeshire
Tel: 03543 3036

5 Bedrooms

M LF LP AL

A 16th-century coaching inn. A la carte menu, bar snacks seven days a week, Sunday roast. Children welcome. Oak-beamed lounge with log fires, excellent accommodation including the Cromwell Room with four-poster bed. Coarse fishing, 40ft on River Ouse and 16ft on River Nene. Local trout fishing Gratham and Moreborough, within easy reach of the hotel.

| | B & B |
|---|---|
| | £ |
| High Season | 10.75 |

Supplements: Baby in cot free

## ESSEX
### Saffron Walden

**ROCKELLS FARM**
Duddenhoe End, Saffron Walden, Essex, CB11 4UY
Tel: 0763 838053
Classification not yet known
4 Bedrooms (2 with private bathroom/shower).

M

The farm is an arable farm with a private lake of 3 acres. The lake is in the garden and is stocked with mainly carp, tench and rudd of various sizes which provide excellent fishing. Between Cambridge and London there are plenty of opportunities for sightseeing with Saffron Walden as the nearest town.

| | B & B | Half Board |
|---|---|---|
| | £ | £ |
| High Season | 11.00 | 15.00 |
| Mid Season | 10.00 | 14.00 |
| Low Season | 10.00 | 14.00 |

Children's discounts available
**HS** 1 Jul–30 Sep
**MS** May, Jun, Oct
**LS** Nov–Apr, except Christmas

## LINCOLNSHIRE
### Boston

**NEW ENGLAND HOTEL**
Wide Bargate, Boston, Lincolnshire, PE21 6SH
Tel: 0205 65255

25 Bedrooms (All with private bathroom/shower).

M T LF LP AL HT

A traditional country town hotel with modern accommodation and facilities. Our spacious Boston Carving Table Restaurant is well known for the quality of the roast, a la carte specialities and fresh vegetables. A porter is on duty throughout the night and early morning to serve refreshments for those arriving late or leaving early. Fishing is close at hand either in the 'drains' or Witham, both walking distance. Estuary and sea a little further away.

| | B & B | Half Board |
|---|---|---|
| | £ | £ |
| High Season | 23.50 | 29.00 |
| Low Season | 23.50 | 27.00 |

Children's discounts available
**HS** 1 Apr–2 Nov
**LS** 3 Nov–31 Mar
Supplements: Single room £13.50 midweek

### Bourne

**THE ANGEL HOTEL**
Market Place, Bourne, Lincolnshire, PE10 9AE
Tel: 0778 422346

13 Bedrooms (All with private bathroom/shower).

M LF LP AL HT

The Angel Hotel Centre was formerly a historic coaching inn, restored to retain its old-world atmosphere. All rooms have colour TV and free in-house movies. Copperfield's Restaurant offers a la carte and table d'hote dishes. The courtyard consists of 7 shops, including unisex hairdressers and sports shop. Nearby Rutland Water offers Europe's best trout fishing, wind surfing, and sailing. The Rivers Welland, Witham and Glen offer bream, tench and roach.

| | Bed Only £ | B & B £ | Half Board £ |
|---|---|---|---|
| High Season | 16.00 | 20.00 | 27.00 |

Children's discounts available
Supplements: Single room £4

## Branston

**MOOR LODGE HOTEL**
Branston, Nr Lincoln,
Lincolnshire, LN4 1HU
Tel: 0522 791366

25 Bedrooms (All with private bathroom/shower).

M T LF LP AL

A country hotel situated close to the River Witham and within 30 minutes of Hazelford Weir, Newark Dyke and Winthorne on the River Trent. The hotel is Egon Ronay and Ashley Courtney recommended and is owned and managed by Peter Nannestad who has spent many happy hours fly-fishing for rainbow trout. There are tea/coffee-making facilities and colour TV in all rooms. A cosy bar and restaurant for fishermen's tales.

| | Bed Only £ | B & B £ | Half Board £ |
|---|---|---|---|
| High Season | 15.00 | 18.50 | 23.50 |

Children's discounts available
Supplements: Single room £4.50
Children sharing parents' room – complimentary

## NORFOLK
## Great Yarmouth

**BURLINGTON HOTEL**
North Drive, Great
Yarmouth, Norfolk
Tel: 0493 844568
Classification not yet known
32 Bedrooms (22 with private bathroom/shower).

M T LF LP AL HT

The Burlington Hotel, with its own car park, is a small, friendly hotel with an intimate bar serving English food of the highest standards, which we guarantee you will look forward to after a day in the fresh air. As an added attraction for the family we have a Turkish steam bath and indoor heated swimming pool. Information and all types of bait available from Dave Docwra, a local angler of repute.

| | B & B £ | Half Board £ |
|---|---|---|
| High Season | 32.00 | 44.00 |
| Mid Season | 30.00 | 42.00 |
| Low Season | 28.00 | 38.00 |

Children's discounts available
**HS** 16 Jul–20 Sep
**MS** 23 May–15 Jul, 21 Sep–10 Oct
**LS** Mar–22 May, 11 Oct–10 Nov
Closed 11 Nov–Feb
Supplements: Room with bath/shower & WC £12.00. Single room £6

**STAR HOTEL**
24 Hall Quay,
Great Yarmouth,
Norfolk, NR30 1HG
Tel: 0493 842294

42 Bedrooms (All with private bathroom/shower).

M T LF LP AL HT

This 16th-century building overlooks the quay and the River Yare in the centre of the town. Yarmouth has historical links with fishing and the hotel continues the tradition by offering both sea (dab, skate and dogfish during the summer and cod, whiting and flatfish in the winter) and broads (bream, roach and tench with pike in season) fishing weekends. Boat hire is available plus special rates for clubs or groups.

| | B & B £ |
|---|---|
| High Season | 25.00 |

Children's discounts available
Supplements: The price quoted above: £25 mid week and £23 for weekend B & B

## Norwich

**MAIDS HEAD HOTEL**
Tombland, Norwich,
Norfolk, NR3 1LB
Tel: 0603 761111

80 Bedrooms (All with private bathroom/shower).

M T AL HT

Situated in the heart of historic Norwich, opposite the cathedral and close to the River Wensum. Coarse fishing is available on the Rivers Chet and Yare, in particular Rockland and Surlingham Broads where roach, bream, pike and tench may be caught. The Maids Head provides an ideal base with its 3 bars, restaurant and well-equipped bedrooms.

| | B & B £ | Half Board £ |
|---|---|---|
| High Season | 27.38 | 34.00 |
| Mid Season | 27.38 | 32.00 |
| Low Season | 27.38 | 29.50 |

Children's discounts available
**HS** Sep–Oct
**MS** Nov–Mar
**LS** Apr–Aug
Supplements: Single room £6

## NORTHAMPTONSHIRE
## Oundle

**TALBOT HOTEL**
New Street, Oundle,
Peterborough,
Northamptonshire, PE8 4EA
Tel: 0832 73621

39 Bedrooms (All with private bathroom/shower).

M T

Talbot Hotel, a 17th-century coaching inn situated in the quiet market town of Oundle, Northamptonshire. Bedrooms are comfortably furnished with private bathroom, colour TV and tea/coffee-making facilities. The Restaurant and Lounge Bar featuring log fires, offer relaxing surroundings after your busy day. Rutland Water offers excellent fishing throughout the year and is steadily building a reputation as one of the best fishing lakes in Europe.

| | B & B £ | Half Board £ |
|---|---|---|
| High Season | 41.00 | 31.50 |
| Mid Season | 41.00 | 31.50 |
| Low Season | 41.00 | 28.00 |

Children's discounts available
**HS** Jul–Aug
**MS** Apr–Jun, Sep–Oct
**LS** Nov–Mar
Supplements: £7 per person for Clubroom. Above HB rates are for special weekend breaks

See page 4 for details of symbols

## SUFFOLK Mildenhall

**SMOKE HOUSE INN**
Beck Row, Mildenhall,
Suffolk, IP28 8DH
Tel: 0638 713223

80 Bedrooms (All with private bathroom/shower).

Trout and sea trout fishing on River Wissey, Norfolk and River Lark, Suffolk. Also coarse fishing on River Ouse and lower stretches of Rivers Lark and Wissey. Matches by arrangement. At the Smoke House every room has en-suite facilities, direct-dial telephone, colour TV. The Cocktail Bar adjoins an excellent restaurant where a la carte and table d'hote meals are served until 10.30 pm daily. Two inglenook fireplaces. Lounge Bar. Friendly family atmosphere.

| | B & B £ | Half Board £ |
|---|---|---|
| High Season | 25.00 | 31.00 |

Children's discounts available
Supplements: Single room £12

## Sudbury

**MILL HOTEL**
Walnut Tree Lane, Sudbury,
Suffolk, CO10 6BD
Tel: 0787 75544

47 Bedrooms (All with private bathroom/shower).

The Mill Hotel, which is a 300 year old converted mill that dates back to the 18th century, stands next to the River Stour and holds fishing rights to the adjacent stretch of water. The Meadow Bar overlooks the Mill pool and tranquil water meadow. The mill wheel divides the bar from the restaurant and is still working today and shielded behind plate glass screens and is an unusual and attractive centre piece.

| | B & B £ |
|---|---|
| High Season | 25.00 |

Children's discounts available
Supplements: Single room £35 — price of SB

## Thorpeness

**DOLPHIN INN & RESTAURANT**
Peace Place, Thorpeness,
Nr. Leiston, Suffolk,
IP16 4NB
Tel: 072885 2544

Classification not yet known
17 Bedrooms (9 with private bathroom/shower).

Ideally situated for sea angling (sea 150 yds away). This family-run hotel has a chef proprietor producing excellent food. TV lounge and three bars.

| | B & B £ | Half Board £ |
|---|---|---|
| High Season | 16.50 | 24.50 |
| Mid Season | 15.50 | 23.50 |
| Low Season | 14.00 | 22.00 |

Children's discounts available
**HS** Jun–Aug
**MS** May, Sep
**LS** Oct–Apr
Supplements: Room with bath/shower & WC £2. Single room £3

*Prices in England for Fishing are per person, sharing a double room, per night, including VAT (at the current rate of 15 per cent).*

## Westleton

**THE CROWN AT WESTLETON**
Westleton, Saxmundham,
Suffolk, IP17 3AO
Tel: 072873 273

Classification not yet known
14 Bedrooms (9 with private bathroom/shower).

The Crown at Westleton is set in the centre of the winner yet again of Suffolk's Best Kept Village Competition, opposite the thatched church and a short walk from the village green and duck pond. Only a little further lies the RSPB Minsmere Bird Reserve and the coast at Dunwich is two-and-a-half miles away. Coarse and game fishing are available locally. Aldeburgh, Southwold and Snape Maltings are all within a 10-mile drive.

| | B & B £ | Half Board £ |
|---|---|---|
| High Season | 14.95 | 23.45 |
| Mid Season | 14.95 | 23.45 |
| Low Season | 14.95 | 23.45 |

Children's discounts available
**HS** May–Sept
**MS** Oct–Dec
**LS** Jan–Apr
Closed Christmas Day, Boxing Day
Supplements: Room with bath/shower & WC £2.15. Single room £3.40.

*Sea Angling writer Ken Townley, plus giant ling on Tatler IV*

# THAMES

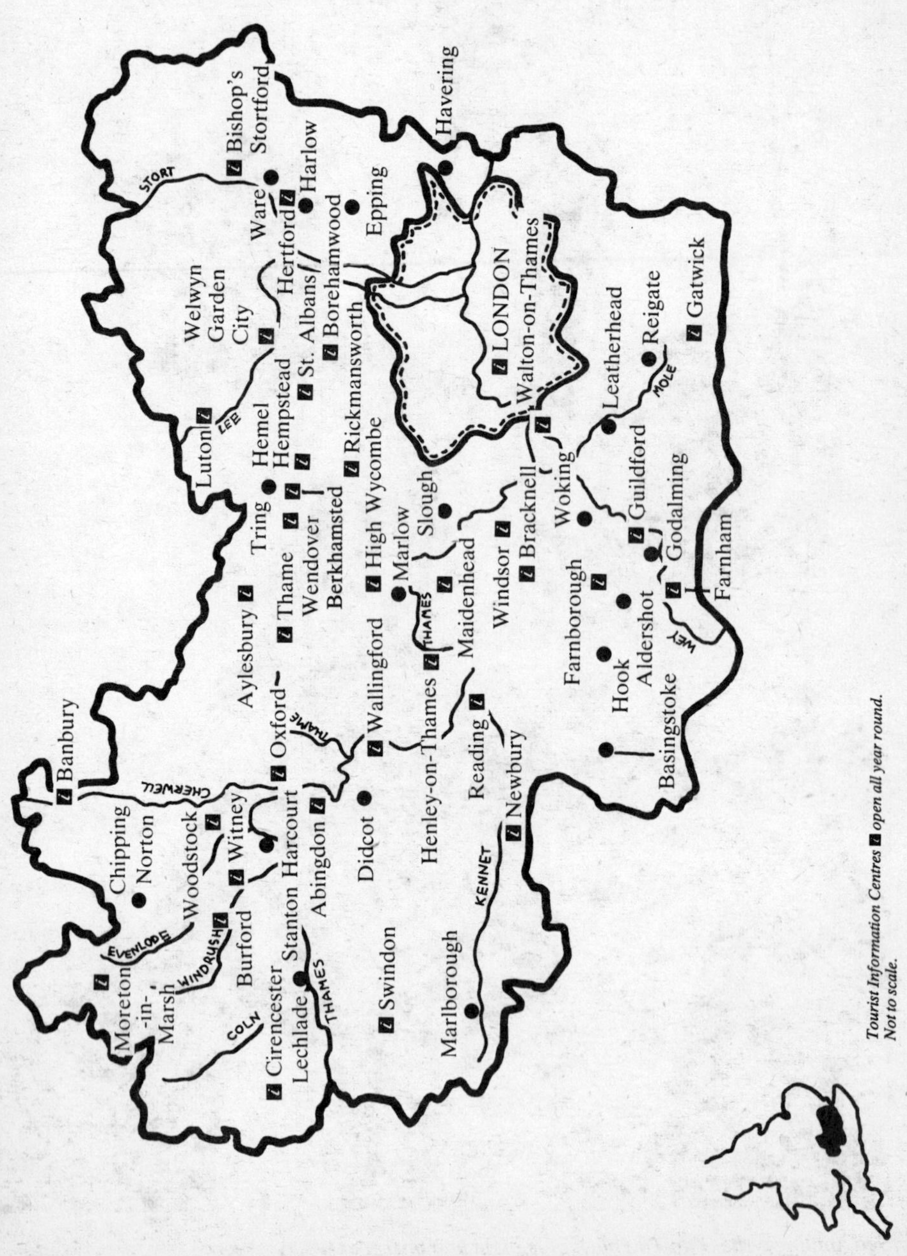


*Tourist Information Centres ▪ open all year round.*
*Not to scale.*

# THAMES

Rising in the limestone folds of the Cotswolds almost within sight of the Bristol Channel, the Thames system provides a transect of lowland England before meeting the tide at London. Most aspects of freshwater fishing are represented – trouting in the spring-fed chalk and limestone streams of the Cotswolds and Chilterns, and coarse fishing for barbel, chub, roach and dace among the water meadows and weir pools of the main river.

Large water supply reservoirs provide excellent trout fishing within minutes of the nation's capital city and ponds, gravel pits and canals provide haunts for carp, tench, bream and roach in leafy hollows or suburban parks.

**Water Authority**
Thames Water, Nugent House,
Vastern Road, Reading RG1 8DB
Tel: (0734) 593391

**East and North Division**
The Grange, Crossbrook Street, Waltham Cross, Herts EN8 8LX

**Central Division**
New River Head, Rosebery Avenue, London EC1R 4TP

**South and West Division**
Denton House, Iffley Turn, Oxford OX4 4HJ

**Fishing Seasons**
Salmon — 1 Apr–30 Sept

Brown Trout — 1 Apr–30 Sept

Rainbow Trout — 1 Apr–30 Sept

Rainbow Trout in Enclosed Waters — No close season

Coarse Fish — 16 Jun–14 Mar

**Thames Water Licence Required**
Full list of distributors from Water Authority

**Regional Tourist Boards**
Thames and Chilterns Tourist Board,
8 Market Place, Abingdon, Oxfordshire
OX14 3UD
Tel: (0235) 22711

London Visitor and Convention Bureau
26 Grosvenor Gardens, London
SW1W 0DU
Tel: 01 730 3450

West Country Tourist Board,
Trinity Court, 37 Southernhay East,
Exeter, Devon EX1 1QS
Tel: (0392) 76351

Southern Tourist Board, Town Hall Centre,
Leigh Road, Eastleigh, Hampshire, SO5 4DE
Tel: (0703) 616027

South East England Tourist Board,
1 Warwick Park, Tunbridge Wells,
Kent, TN2 5TA
Tel: (0892) 40766

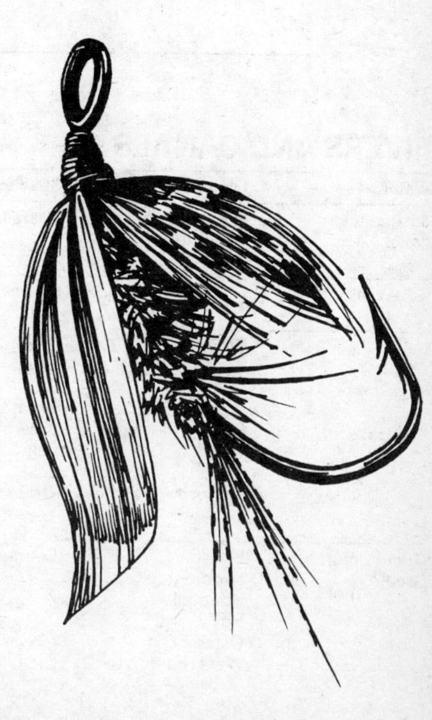

# THAMES ANGLING CLUBS

**Abingdon & Oxford Anglers Alliance**
Roger Bateman, Secretary, 16 The Gap, Marcham, Abingdon, Oxford
**Dartford & District Angling & Preservation Society (DDAPS)**
A. Mingham, Secretary, DDAPS, Lake House, 2 Walnut Tree Avenue, Dartford, Kent DA1 1LJ
**Farnham Angling Society**
R.T. Frost, Secretary, 70 Prince Charles Crescent, Farnborough, Hants GU14 8DL
**Godalming Angling Society**
Secretary, 87 Summers Road, Farncombe, Godalming, Surrey GU7 3BE
**Guildford Angling Society**
Secretary, Gareth Park, 72 Phillips Avenue, Worcester Park, Surrey
**Leatherhead & Distict Angling Society**
R. Boychuk, Secretary, 22 Poplar Avenue, Leatherhead, Surrey
**Lychnobite Angling Society**
Peter D. White, Secretary, 18 Margaret Avenue, St Albans, Herts AL3 5TE
**Marlborough & District Angling Association**
M. Ellis, Secretary, "Failte", Elcot Close, Marlborough, Wiltshire
**Prestwood & District Angling Club**
B. Putt, Secretary, 72 Frances Street, Chesham, Bucks HP5 3ES
**Swindon Isis Angling Club**
Secretary, 53 Arnolds Way, Cirencester, Glos
**The Tring Anglers**
B. Boucher, Secretary, 2 Hivings Park, Chesham, Bucks HP5 2LG
**Wey Navigation Angling Amalgamation**
I. Fraser, Secretary, 4 Elmgrove Road, Weybridge, Surrey KT13 8NZ

## RIVERS AND CANALS

| Water | Location | Species | Permits |
|---|---|---|---|
| **Basingstoke Canal** | Odiham to Weybridge | Coarse Fish | Farnham Angling Society<br>Membership Secretary, Mr M. Borra, The Creel, Station Road, Aldershot |
| **Cherwell** | Oxford | Coarse Fish | Abingdon and Oxford Anglers Alliance<br>Tackle Shops, Oxford and Aylesbury |
| **Coln** | Bibury | Brown Trout<br>Rainbow Trout | Bibury Court Hotel, Bibury<br>Nr Cirencester, Gloucestershire<br>Tel: 028574 337 |
| | Bibury | Brown Trout<br>Rainbow Trout | Swan Hotel, Bibury, Cirencester, Gloucestershire Tel: 028574 204 |
| | Fairford | Trout | Hyperion Hotel, London Street, Fairford, Gloucestershire Tel: 0285 712349 |
| **Grand Union Canal** | London<br>Paddington to Southall<br>Hayes and Osterley<br>West Drayton to Uxbridge<br>Slough<br>Tring | Coarse Fish | London Anglers Association<br>Forest Road Hall, Hervey Park Road, London E17 6LJ<br>Tel: 01 520 7477<br>Bailiffs on the water |

| Water | Location | Species | Permits |
|---|---|---|---|
| **Kennet** | Newbury | Brown Trout<br>Rainbow Trout | Barton Court Fishery<br>Barton Court Farm, Kintbury, Nr Newbury |
| | Newbury | Brown Trout<br>Rainbow Trout | Millwaters Hotel, London Road, Newbury<br>Tel: 0635 49977 |
| **Kennet and Avon Canal** | Marlborough | All Coarse Fish | Marlborough and District Anglers Association<br>Secretary, Mr M. Ellis, "Failte", Elcot Close, Marlborough<br>Day tickets available locally |
| **Lambourne** | Newbury | Brown Trout<br>Rainbow Trout | Millwaters Hotel, London Road, Newbury<br>Tel: 0635 49977 |
| **Lee Navigation Channel** | Broxbourne | Coarse Fish | Redland Angling Scheme<br>Bailiffs on bank |
| | Walthamstow | Coarse Fish | Thames Water<br>Permits at Fishery |
| **Loddon** | Arborfield | Coarse Fish | Farnham Angling Society<br>Membership Secretary, Mr M. Borra, The Creel, Station Road, Aldershot |
| **Newcut** | Walthamstow | Coarse Fish | Thames Water<br>Permit at Fishery |
| **Regents Canal** | London | Coarse Fish | London Anglers Association<br>Forest Road Hall, Hervey Park Road, London E17 6LJ Tel: 01 520 7477 |
| **Stort** | Stanstead Abbotts | Chub<br>Roach<br>Perch<br>Pike | Briggens House Hotel<br>Stanstead Road, Stanstead Abbotts, Nr Ware, Herts Tel: 027 979 2416 |
| **Thame** | Parts | Coarse Fish | Leighton Buzzard Angling Club<br>D. Ayres, 52 Montmore Road, Leighton Buzzard |
| **Thames** | Oxford<br>Abingdon | Coarse Fish | Abingdon and Oxford Anglers Alliance<br>Local Tackle Shops, Oxford, Abingdon, Aylesbury |
| | Wallingford | Coarse Fish | Beetle and Wedge Hotel<br>Ferry Lane, Moulsford, Oxfordshire<br>Tel: 0491 651381/651376 |
| | Cricklade | Coarse Fish | Swindon Isis Angling Club<br>Local Tackle Shops<br>Swindon, South Cerney |
| | Windsor | Chub<br>Pike<br>Roach<br>Dace<br>Trout<br>Barbel<br>Wild Carp | Oakley Court Hotel<br>Windsor Road (A3081), Nr Windsor, Berkshire<br>Tel: 0628 74141 |
| | Shepperton | Coarse Fish | Shepperton Moat House Hotel<br>Felix Lane, Shepperton, Surrey<br>Tel: 0932 241404 |
| | Eton Wick | Coarse Fish | London Anglers Association<br>Forest Road Hall, Hervey Park Road, London E17 6LJ<br>Tel: 01 520 7477 |

| Water | Location | Species | Permits |
|---|---|---|---|
| **Tring Canals** | Tring | Coarse Fish | The Tring Anglers<br>Bailiffs<br>Chiltern Sports, Tring<br>Ayres Supermarket, Tring<br>Amersham Outdoor Sports and Leisure, Amersham |
| **Wey** | Elstead | Coarse Fish | Farnham Angling Society<br>Membership Secretary, Mr M. Borra, The Creel, Station Road, Aldershot |
| | Godalming | Chub<br>Dace<br>Roach<br>Pike<br>Carp<br>Perch | Godalming Angling Society<br>Allchornes Tackle Shop, Godalming |
| | Guildford | Chub | Guildford Angling Society<br>Secretary, Gareth Park, 72 Philips Ave, Worcester Park, Surrey |
| **Wey Navigation Canal** | Weybridge<br>Byfleet<br>Ripley | All Coarse Fish | Wey Navigation Angling Amalgamation<br>Bailiff on Patrol |

# LAKES AND RESERVOIRS

| | | | |
|---|---|---|---|
| **Abbey Grounds Lake** | Cirencester | Trout<br>Pike<br>Roach | Cirencester Town Council<br>Bingham House, 1 Dyer Street, Cirencester<br>Patrol Officer in Grounds |
| **Aldenham Reservoir** | Borehamwood | Coarse Fish | Aldenham Country Park, Park Office, Dagger Lane, Elstree, Herts |
| **Aldermaston Gravel Pits** | Aldermaston | Carp<br>Perch<br>Tench<br>Bream | Leisure Sport Angling<br>Tadley Angling Centre, 33 Reynards Close, Tadley, Hants |
| **Badshot Lea Ponds (and 7 Other Ponds in Area)** | Aldershot | Coarse Fish | Farnham Angling Society<br>Membership Secretary, Mr M. Borra, The Creel, Station Road, Aldershot |
| **Barn Elms Reservoirs Nos 5, 6 and 8** | Hammersmith, London | Brown Trout<br>Rainbow Trout | Thames Water<br>Permits at Reservoir<br>Advance bookings advised<br>Tel: 01 748 3423 |
| **Blenheim Palace Lake** | Woodstock | Tench<br>Coarse Fish | Estate Office, Blenheim Palace, Woodstock, Oxford |
| **Boddington Reservoir** | Banbury | Bream<br>Roach<br>Tench<br>Carp<br>Pike | British Waterways Board<br>Fisheries Officer, Willow Grange, Church Road, Watford (S.A.E.) |
| **Bretons Lake** | Rainham, Essex | Carp<br>Tench<br>Roach<br>Rudd<br>Perch | Bretons Angling<br>Bailiffs on bank |

| Water | Location | Species | Permits |
|---|---|---|---|
| **Brooklands Lake (and Gravel Pits)** | Dartford | Coarse Fish | Dartford and District Angling and Preservation Society<br>Bailiffs on water |
| **California Country Park Lake** | Wokingham | Coarse Fish | Wokingham District Council<br>California Country Park<br>Rangers Office |
| **Christchurch Lake** | Stanton Harcourt | Carp | J.H. Kalicki, ARC Linch Hill Fishery, Stanton Harcourt, Oxford<br>Permits on site |
| **Coate Water Lake** | Swindon | Coarse Fish | Thamesdown Borough Council<br>Coate Water Country Park, Marlborough Road, Swindon<br>Warden on site |
| **Dinton Pastures Country Park Lake** | Reading | Coarse Fish | Wokingham District Council<br>Dinton Pastures Country Park, Reading<br>Rangers Office |
| **Dorchester Complex** | Dorchester-on-Thames | All Coarse Fish Species | Amey Anglers Association<br>J.H. Kalicki, ARC Linch Hill Fishery, Stanton Harcourt, Oxford |
| **Dorchester Lake (and Marlborough Pool)** | Oxford | Coarse Fish | Abingdon and Oxford Anglers Alliance<br>Local Tackle Shops, Oxford, Aylesbury |
| **Fairlands Valley Park Lake** | Stevenage | Most Coarse Fish | Stevenage Borough Council<br>Fairlands Valley Park, Six Hills Way, Stevenage, Herts<br>Permits on site |
| **Farmoor Reservoir** | Farmoor (Oxford) | Brown Trout<br>Rainbow Trout<br>Triploid Trout | Thames Water<br>Permits at Reservoir<br>Boat Bookings Tel: 0865 863033 |
| **Farthings Lake** | Battle | Carp<br>Tench<br>Bream<br>Roach<br>Rudd | Outdoor Water Recreation Ltd<br>Lakeview, Old Bury Hill, Dorking, Surrey<br>Stiles Garage, High Street, Battle<br>Surridge Newsagents, High St, Battle |
| **Hatfield Forest Lakes** | Bishops Stortford | Carp<br>Pike<br>Most Coarse Fish | The National Trust<br>Hatfield Forest, Takeley, Bishops Stortford<br>Warden at lakeside |
| **Hinksey Park Lake** | Oxford | Carp<br>Tench<br>Bream<br>Roach | Oxford City Council<br>Hinksey Park Ticket Office |
| **Hollybush Lake** | Farnborough | Carp<br>Tench<br>Bream<br>Roach<br>Pike<br>Perch | Redland Angling Scheme<br>J and A Newsagents, Hollybush Lane (300 yds from Fishery) |
| **Hooks Marsh** | Waltham Abbey | Bream<br>Tench<br>Roach<br>Pike | Leisure Sport Angling<br>P & B Hall, 44 Highbridge Street, Waltham Abbey |
| **Horcott Complex** | Fairford | All Coarse Fish | Amey Anglers Association<br>J.H. Kalicki, ARC Linch Hill Fishery, Stanton Harcourt, Oxford |

| Water | Location | Species | Permits |
|---|---|---|---|
| **Horseshoe Lake** | Lechlade | Carp<br>Tench<br>Bream<br>Roach | ARC Fisheries<br>'The Paper Shop', Lechlade, Glos |
| **Horton Trout Fishery** | Slough | Rainbow Trout<br>Brown Trout<br>Salmon | Horton Trout Fishery<br>Kingsmead Fish Farms, Stanwell Road, Horton, Slough, Berks Tel: 0753 684858 |
| **Kings Weir Fishery** | Broxbourne | Tench<br>Roach<br>Bream<br>Pike | Redland Angling Scheme<br>Bailiff on bank |
| **Latimer Park Lakes** | Chesham | Brown Trout<br>Rainbow Trout | Latimer Park Lakes, Latimer, Chesham, Bucks<br>Tel: 02404 2391 |
| **Linch Hill Fishery** | Witney<br>Abingdon<br>Oxford | Coarse Fish<br>Trout | Harcourt Arms Hotel<br>Harcourt Arms, Oxon OX8 1RF |
| **Lower Moor Fishery** | Cirencester | Brown Trout<br>Rainbow Trout | Geoff Raines<br>Lower Moor Fishery, Oaksey, Malmesbury, Wiltshire |
| **Mitcham Common Ponds** | Mitcham, Surrey | Carp<br>Tench<br>Pike | London Borough of Merton<br>Local Fishing Tackle Shops |
| **Mychett Mere** | Farnborough | Coarse Fish | Amey Anglers Association<br>Arc Linch Hill Fishery, Stanton Harcourt, Oxford |
| **Newbury Trout Lakes** | Newbury | Rainbow Trout | Newbury Trout Lakes<br>Lower Farm, Burysbank Road, Newbury, Berks<br>Cabin at Fishery |
| **No. 1 Lake** | South Cerney | Carp<br>Tench<br>Rudd<br>Bream<br>Crucian Carp<br>Pike | Swindon Isis Angling Club<br>Local Tackle Shops in South Cerney |
| **Old Bury Hill Lake** | Dorking | Tench<br>Carp<br>Pike<br>Bream<br>Zander | Outdoor Water Recreation Limited<br>'Lakeview', Old Bury Hill, Westcott, Nr Dorking, Surrey<br>Tel: 0306 883621 |
| **Queen Mother Trout Fishery** | Slough | Brown Trout<br>Rainbow Trout | Queen Mother Trout Fishery, Horton Road, Horton, Slough, Berks<br>Tel: 0753 683605 |
| **Rainbow Lake Trout Fishery** | Cirencester | Brown Trout<br>Rainbow Trout<br>Salmon | Rainbow Lake Trout Fishery<br>Wildmoorway Lane, South Cerney, Glos |
| **Roughgrounds Farm Lake** | Lechlade | Carp | ARC Fisheries<br>The Paper Shop, Lechlade, Glos |
| **Ruislip Lido** | Ruislip | Rudd<br>Tench<br>Bream<br>Roach<br>Pike | London Borough of Hillingdon<br>The Manager, Ruislip Lido, Reservoir Road, Ruislip |

| Water | Location | Species | Permits |
|---|---|---|---|
| **Savay Gravel Pit** | Denham, West London | Carp<br>Tench<br>Bream<br>Roach<br>Pike<br>Perch | Redland Angling Scheme<br>Peverill's Newsagent, Harefield<br>Balfours Newsagent, Denham |
| **Shermanbury Place Fishery (Lake and River Adur)** | Henfield, Sussex | Most Coarse Fish<br>Trout | Outdoor Water Recreation Limited<br>Bailiff on bank |
| **Stoneacres Lake** | Stanton Harcourt | Rainbow Trout<br>Coarse Fish | Arc Linch Hill Fishery<br>Stanton Harcourt<br>Permits on site |
| **Sundridge Lakes** | Sevenoaks | Carp<br>Roach<br>Coarse Fish | Rod and Line Ltd<br>Geoffrey Bucknall, 70–72 Loampit Vale, Lewisham Tel: 01 852 1421<br>(Season Tickets only) |
| **Theale Complex** | Reading | All Coarse Fish | Amey Anglers Association<br>ARC Linch Hill Fishery, Stanton Harcourt, Oxon |
| **Tring Reservoirs** | Tring | Catfish<br>Bream<br>Tench<br>Pike<br>Roach | Mr B. Double, Reservoir House, Watery Lane, Marsworth, Nr Tring, Herts<br>Tel: 044 282 2379<br>Bailiff on bank |
| **Walthamstow No. 1, No. 2 and No. 3** | Walthamstow, London | Coarse Fish | Thames Water<br>Permits at Reservoir Complex |
| **Walthamstow No. 4/No. 5** | Walthamstow, London | Brown Trout<br>Rainbow Trout<br>Pike (Winter) | Thames Water<br>Permits at Reservoir<br>Tel: 01 808 1527 |
| **Wellington Country Park Lake** | Reading, Basingstoke | Tench<br>Chub<br>Rudd<br>Roach<br>Carp | Wellington Country Park<br>Riseley, Reading, Berks<br>Permits at Reception |
| **West Warwick Reservoir** | Walthamstow, London | Carp | Thames Water<br>Permits at Reservoir Complex |
| **Wraysbury Complex** | Wraysbury | All Coarse Fish | Amey Anglers Association<br>ARC Linch Hill Fishery, Stanton Harcourt, Oxon |
| **Wraysbury Gravel Pits** | Wraysbury | Carp<br>Pike<br>Bream<br>Tench | Leisure Sport Angling<br>Wraysbury Newsagents, High St, Wraysbury<br>Davies Angling, 47 Church Street, Staines<br>(Permits in advance) |
| **Wroughton Reservoir** | Wroughton, Swindon | Trout | Thames Water<br>Peter's Pet Supplies, 6–8 St Johns Road, Wroughton, Nr Swindon, Wilts |

# ACCOMMODATION

## BERKSHIRE
### Newbury

**MILLWATERS HOTEL**
London Road, Newbury,
Berkshire, RG13 2BY
Tel: 0635 49977

17 Bedrooms (All with private bathroom/shower).

M T LF LP AL HT

A delightful, listed Georgian country house in 8 acres of mature gardens. 2 famous chalk rivers, The Lambourn and Kennet flow through the grounds providing game and coarse fishing throughout the year (brown and rainbow trout, grayling, chub). Arrangements also with lakes nearby. Tuition provided certain weekends. Resident proprietors offer personal service. Lakeside bar. Traditional English and country French cuisine served in Barn Restaurant.

| | Bed Only £ | B & B £ | Half Board £ |
|---|---|---|---|
| High Season | 27.00 | 30.25 | 38.25 |
| Mid Season | 24.25 | 27.50 | 35.50 |
| Low Season | 21.75 | 25.00 | 33.00 |

Children's discounts available
**HS** 17 Apr–30 Sep
**MS** 1 Oct–31 Dec
**LS** Jan–16 Apr
Supplements: Single room £7

## GLOUCESTERSHIRE
### Bibury

**BIBURY COURT HOTEL**
Bibury, Nr. Cirencester,
Gloucestershire, GL7 5NT
Tel: 028574 337

16 Bedrooms (15 with private bathroom/shower).

M T LF LP AL HT

Bibury Court is a Jacobean house in six acres of garden through which the River Coln flows. Guests (two) may fish the garden stretch for brown/rainbow trout. Game fishing at Cotswold Water Park (fifteen minutes), Horshoe Lake, Rainbow Lake, Churn Pool Manor Brook Lake (TWA licence required). Coarse fishing, Ashton Keynes Angling Club, South Cerney Angling Club, Amey Road Stone Co., Claydon Park Lake. Day tickets on site. Tackle D.J. Sports, Cirencester.

| | B & B £ |
|---|---|
| High Season | 42.00 |

Closed Christmas

**SWAN HOTEL**
Bibury, Cirencester,
Gloucestershire, GL7 5NW
Tel: 028574 204

23 Bedrooms (All with private bathroom/shower).

M T LP AL HT

A 17th-century Cotswold stone coaching inn situated on the banks of the River Coln. The hotel has been tastefully modernised throughout. All rooms en-suite, direct-dial telephone and colour TV. An elegant Georgian restaurant serving varied and interesting menus. A comfortable bar, and lounges with log fires in winter. Own adjacent stretch of well stocked fishing offering rainbow and brown trout with some grayling. Fishing restricted to residents and is free of charge.

| | B & B £ | Half Board £ |
|---|---|---|
| High Season | 26.25 | 37.50 |

Children's discounts available
Supplements: Single room £4.25

## HERTFORDSHIRE
### Stanstead Abbotts

**BRIGGENS HOUSE HOTEL**
Stanstead Road,
Stanstead Abbotts, Nr. Ware,
Hertfordshire, SG12 8LD
Tel: 027979 2416

58 Bedrooms (All with private bathroom/shower).

M T LF LP AL

A magnificent country mansion, surrounded by a 45-acre estate, Briggens House Hotel is a unique blend of tradition and charm reflecting all that's fine in a country house hotel. The Briggens House has the advantage of having the River Stort running through its grounds. Fish known to be in the river are chubb, perch, roach, eels and pike. In addition there are a number of alternative fishing grounds in the locality.

| | B & B £ | Half Board £ |
|---|---|---|
| High Season | 33.00 | 45.25 |

Children's discounts available
Supplements: Single room £16.50

## OXFORDSHIRE
### Banbury

**CROMWELL LODGE HOTEL**
North Bar, Banbury,
Oxfordshire, OX16 0TB
Tel: 0295 59781

32 Bedrooms (All with private bathroom/shower).

M T LF

All 32 bedrooms have private bathroom, colour TV, radio alarm and tea/coffee-making facilities. Family-owned hotel in the centre of Banbury with large private garden and patio, yet within 10 minutes walk of coarse fishing waters. Lounge bar with log fire. Restaurant offering varied and mouthwatering menus, summer barbeques daily. Packed lunches available. Dogs are accepted.

| | B & B £ | Half Board £ |
|---|---|---|
| High Season | 22.00 | 30.95 |
| Low Season | 20.00 | 28.95 |

Children's discounts available.
**HS** from 1st May 1987
**LS** 1 Oct 86–30 Apr 87
Supplements: Single room £10

*Prices in England for Fishing are per person, sharing a double room, per night, including VAT (at the current rate of 15 per cent). Check prices when you book and mention England for Fishing.*

## Stanton Harcourt

**HARCOURT ARMS HOTEL**
Stanton Harcourt,
Oxfordshire, OX8 1RJ
Tel: 0865 882192
Classification not yet known
16 Bedrooms (10 with private bathroom/shower).

Harcourt Arms Hotel is half-a-mile from Linch Hill Fishery where some excellent coarse and game fishing can be enjoyed. Stoneacres Lake in the fishery has both trout and coarse fishing, whilst the Willow Pool is stocked only with trout in excess of 2lbs. Rods are available for hire at Harcourt Arms. The River Thames at Bablockhythe is 2 miles distant. Farmoor Reservoir is 5 miles away.

| | B & B £ |
|---|---|
| High Season | 22.25 |

Supplements: Single room rate £29.50. Double room rate £44.50

## WILTSHIRE Lacock

**THE RED LION**
High Street, Lacock, Nr. Chippenham, Wiltshire, SN15 2LQ
Tel: 024973 456
Listed
3 Bedrooms (1 with private bathroom/shower).

The Red Lion is in the centre of the famous picturesque National Trust village of Lacock. It is a traditional inn with no juke box or fruit machine, but serving beer from the wood and baking its own bread. We only have 3 bedrooms. The Bristol Avon runs through the village offering superb coarse fishing. There are many good trout lakes locally and day ticket still waters.

| | B & B £ |
|---|---|
| High Season | 15.00 |

Children's discounts available.
Supplements: Room with bath/shower & WC £5. Single room £7

## Marlborough

**THE CROWN HOTEL**
Everleigh, Marlborough, Wiltshire, SN8 3EY
Tel: 026485 223
6 Bedrooms (2 with private bathroom/shower).

A 'fishing family'-run country hotel supplying local licences, flies, leaders and advice on many local stillwaters and chalkstreams. Casting tuition and practice on hotel lawn. Frequented by many local fishermen and river keepers plus English fly team. Gargantuan breakfast, no plastic pots or portion control. For further description see 'Camra Bed and Breakfast Guide'. Adjacent Salisbury, Stonehenge for wife.

| | B & B £ |
|---|---|
| Mid Season | 14.50 |

Children's discounts available.
Supplements: Room with bath/shower & WC £2. Single room £1.50

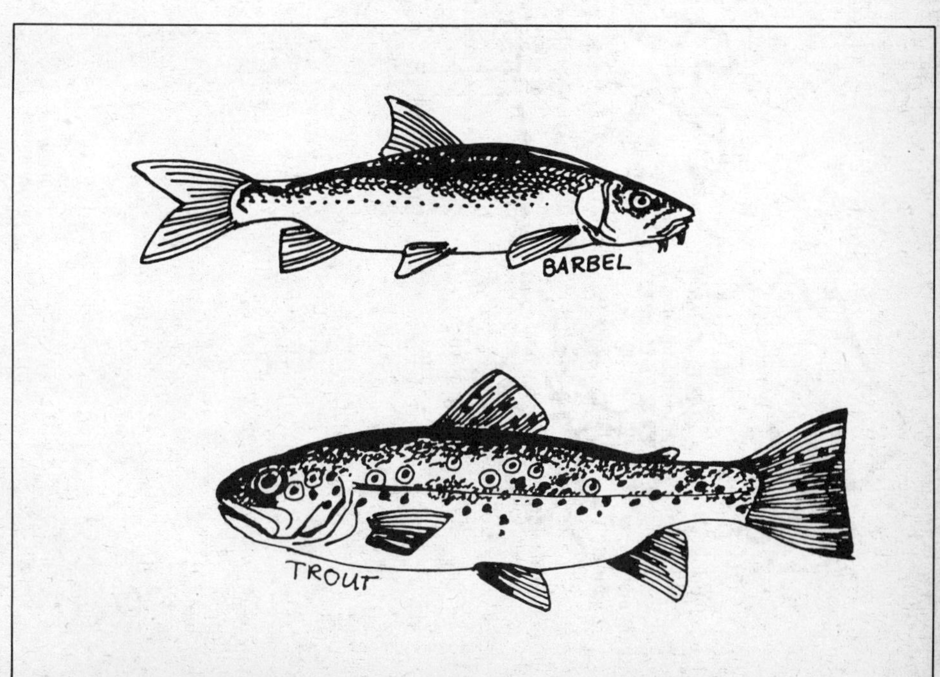


See page 4 for details of symbols

# SOUTHERN

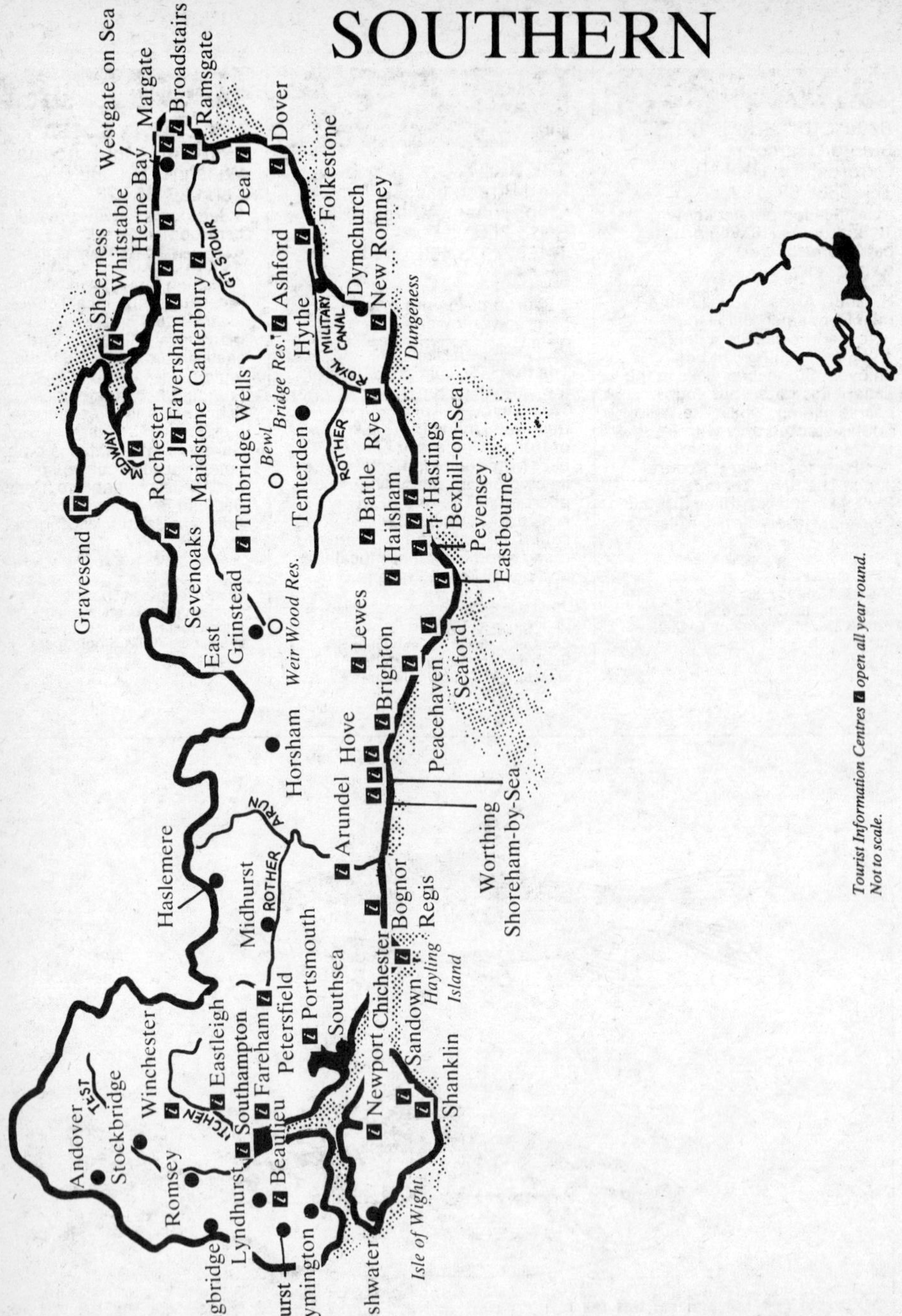

Andover
Stockbridge
Winchester
Romsey
Fordingbridge
Lyndhurst
Southampton
Eastleigh
Fareham
Beaulieu
Brockenhurst
Lymington
Petersfield
Portsmouth
Southsea
Freshwater
Newport
Chichester
Isle of Wight
Sandown
Shanklin
Hayling Island
Bognor Regis
TEST
ITCHEN
Haslemere
Midhurst
ROTHER
ARUN
Arundel
Horsham
Worthing
Shoreham-by-Sea
Hove
Brighton
Lewes
Peacehaven
Seaford
East Grinstead
Weir Wood Res.
Sevenoaks
Gravesend
MEDWAY
Rochester
Maidstone
Tunbridge Wells
Bewl Bridge Res.
Tenterden
Hailsham
Battle
Eastbourne
Pevensey
Bexhill-on-Sea
Hastings
Rye
ROTHER
ROYAL MILITARY CANAL
Dungeness
New Romney
Dymchurch
Hythe
Ashford
Folkestone
Dover
Deal
GT STOUR
Canterbury
Faversham
Sheerness
Whitstable
Herne Bay
Westgate on Sea
Margate
Broadstairs
Ramsgate

*Tourist Information Centres* ▪ *open all year round.*
*Not to scale.*

# SOUTHERN

From the chalk ridges of the North and South Downs and from the limestone plateau of Hampshire rise springs of clear water which produce some of the world's greatest trout streams — the Test and the Itchen — closely preserved as classic fly fishing waters. The same clear springs give rise to a new generation of small stillwater trout fisheries, famed for the same qualities of growing trout. Once they leave the chalk uplands and wend across the vales, the streams are well-stocked with most species of coarse fish and some have runs of migratory trout and salmon as well. Many of the ponds and gravel pits are famed for carp and tench.

**Water Authority**

Southern Water
**Headquarters**
Guildbourne House, Chatsworth Road, Worthing, West Sussex
Tel: (0903) 205252

**Hampshire and Isle of Wight Division**
Southern Water
Otterbourne, Winchester, Hampshire
Tel: (0962) 714585

**Sussex Division**
Southern Water
Falmer, Brighton, East Sussex
Tel: (0273) 606766

**Kent Division**
Southern Water
Luton House, Capstone Road, Chatham, Kent Tel: (0634) 46655

**Fishing Seasons**

Salmon — 17 Jan–2 Oct

Sea Trout — 1 May–31 Oct

Trout (inc. Rainbow Trout) — 3 Apr–31 Oct

Rainbow Trout — No close season (in enclosed waters containing only Rainbow Trout)

Coarse Fish — 16 Jun–14 Mar

**Southern Water Licence Required**

**Regional Tourist Boards**
South East England Tourist Board, 1 Warwick Park, Tunbridge Wells, Kent TN2 5TA Tel: (0892) 40766

Southern Tourist Board, Town Hall Centre, Leigh Road, Eastleigh, Hampshire SO5 4DE
Tel: (0703) 616027

# SOUTHERN ANGLING CLUBS

**Andover Angling Club**
Robin Adcock, Secretary, Flat 2, Bridge House, 154 Junction Road, Andover, Hants SP10 3JF
**Bishops Waltham Anglers Club**
Mrs M. Creese, Secretary, 8 St Andrews Green, Meonstoke, Southampton SO3 1NG
**The Maidstone Victory & Medway Angling Preservation Society**
J. Perkins, Secretary, 33 Hackney Road, Maidstone, Kent ME16 8LN
**Petersfield & District Angling Club**
Secretary, 12 Heather Road, Petersfield, Hants GU31 4HE
**Rother Angling Club**
Mrs E. Smithers, Secretary, "North Bank", June Lane, Midhurst, W. Sussex GU29 9EL
**Southern Anglers**
Trevor Irons, Secretary, 7 Nelson Crescent, Horndean, Portsmouth, Hants PO8 9LZ

# RIVERS

| Water | Location | Species | Permits |
|---|---|---|---|
| **Arun** | Arundel | Coarse Fish | Sussex County Angling Association<br>George and Dragon, Burpham<br>Shepherd, 10 High St, Arundel |
| | Arundel | Pike<br>Perch<br>Roach<br>Sea Trout | Southern Water<br>Free Fishing<br>(Rod licence required) |
| | Worthing | Coarse Fish<br>Sea Trout | Worthing and District Piscatorial Society<br>Ken Denman Ltd, 2 Marine Place, Worthing<br>Lagoon Tackle Shop, 327 Kingsway, Hove |
| **Itchen** | Southampton | Coarse Fish | Public Fishing, Left Bank Only<br>Between Woodmill and Mawsbridge |
| | Winchester<br>(The Weirs) | Coarse Fish | Winchester City Council<br>Public Fishing |
| | Alresford | Brown Trout | Jack Sheppard<br>Chalk Stream Flyfishers, 52b West Street,<br>Alresford, Hampshire<br>SO24 9AV Tel: 096 273 4864 |
| | Various Beats | Coarse<br>Trout<br>Salmon | "Fishings to Let Ltd"<br>The Rod Box, 52 St Georges Street,<br>Winchester Tel: 0962 61561 |
| | Winchester | Trout | The Royal Hotel, St Peter Street, Winchester,<br>Hampshire Tel: 0962 53468 |
| **Medway** | Maidstone | Coarse Fish | Maidstone Victory Angling and Preservation<br>Society<br>Local Tackle Shops |
| | Yalding Sluice | Coarse Fish | Free Fishing<br>200 Metres South Bank, Upstream |
| | Yalding | Coarse Fish | Free Fishing<br>The Lees, South Bank |
| | East Peckham | Coarse Fish | Permits — Local Tackle Shops |
| **Moors Stream** | Bishop's Waltham | Rainbow Trout<br>Grayling<br>Roach<br>Rudd | Bishops Waltham Anglers Club<br>Secretary, Mrs M. Creese, 8 St Andrews<br>Close, Meonstoke, Southampton<br>Tel: 0489 877664 |
| **Rother (Kent)** | Rye | Coarse Fish | Southern Water<br>Free Fishing from Roadside<br>Bank between Iden and Scots Float |
| | Rye | Coarse Fish | Rye and District Angling Society<br>Robins Tackle Shop |
| | Peasmarsh | Coarse Fish | Flackley Ash Hotel<br>Peasmarsh, Nr Rye, East Sussex |
| **Rother (Sussex)** | Midhurst | Dace<br>Roach<br>Grayling<br>Carp<br>Bream | Rother Angling Club<br>Rice Bros, West St, Midhurst<br>News Shop, North St, Midhurst<br>Rother Inn, Lutener Road, Easebourne,<br>Midhurst |
| | Rogate | Trout<br>Grayling<br>Dace<br>Chub | Southern Anglers<br>Wyndam Arms, Rogate |

| Water | Location | Species | Permits |
|---|---|---|---|
| **Rother (Sussex) contd.** | Midhurst | Trout<br>Pike<br>Chub<br>Roach | Southdowns Hotel and Restaurant<br>Rogate, Petersfield<br>Tel: 073 080 521/763 |
| | Various Beats | Coarse Fish | Clive Vale Angling Club<br>Secretary, Mr B. Towner, 9 Leyvis Road, St Leonards on Sea, East Sussex |
| **Royal Military Canal** | Ashford | Coarse Fish | Ashford and District Angling Club<br>Secretary, Mrs B. Thomsett, c/o Ashford Sports, 14 North Street, Ashford |
| **Stour** | Canterbury | Coarse Fish | Canterbury and District A.A.<br>Secretary, N. Stringer, Riversdale, Mill Road, Sturry, Kent<br>Club Bailiff |
| **Test** | Nr Winchester | Trout | The Royal Hotel<br>St Peter Street, Winchester, Hampshire<br>Tel: 0962 53468 |
| | Stockbridge | Brown Trout<br>Rainbow Trout | Greyhound Inn<br>High Street, Stockbridge, Hants |
| | Winchester | Brown Trout<br>Rainbow Trout | "Fishing to Let Ltd"<br>The Rod Box, 52 St Georges Street, Winchester |

# LAKES AND RESERVOIRS

| Water | Location | Species | Permits |
|---|---|---|---|
| **Ashby Farm Reservoirs** | Ashford | Carp<br>Tench<br>Chub<br>Roach<br>Bream<br>Pike | Ashby Farms Ltd<br>The Buss Barn, Fairfield Road, Appledore, Ashford, Kent<br>Self Catering Accommodation |
| **Avington Trout Fishery** | Avington | Rainbow Trout<br>Brown Trout | Avington Trout Fishery<br>Avington, Nr Winchester<br>(Open all year)<br>Tel: 096278 312 |
| **Bayham Lake Trout Fishery** | Tunbridge Wells | Brown Trout<br>Rainbow Trout | Bayham Lake Trout Fishery<br>Bayham Abbey, Lamberhurst, Tunbridge Wells, Kent<br>Tel: 0892 890276 |
| **Bewl Water** | Lamberhurst | Brown Trout<br>Rainbow Trout | The Manager, Bewl Water<br>Fishing Lodge at Reservoir<br>Tel: 0892 890352 |
| **Cadmans Pool** | Lyndhurst | Carp<br>Tench<br>Rudd | Forestry Commission<br>Queens House, Lyndhurst, Hants<br>Tel: 042 128 3141<br>Sports and Tackle Shops in Lyndhurst, Lymington, Christchurch, Bournemouth |
| **Chalk Springs Fishery** | Arundel | Rainbow Trout<br>Brown Trout | Jonathan Glover<br>Chalk Springs Fishery, Park Bottom, Arundel<br>Tel: Arundel 883742 |
| **Fen Place Mill** | East Grinstead | Brown Trout<br>Rainbow Trout | Fen Place Mill Estate<br>J.A. Anderson, High St, East Grinstead |

| Water | Location | Species | Permits |
|---|---|---|---|
| **Foxcotte Lake** | Andover | Carp<br>Tench<br>Roach<br>Bream<br>Rudd<br>Dace<br>Grayling | Andover Angling Club<br>Charlton Newsmarket, Charlton<br>John Eadies Sports, Andover<br>Challis Gas, Andover |
| **Furnace Brook Trout Fishery** | Heathfield | Rainbow Trout | Furnace Brook Trout Farm and Fishery<br>Trolliloes, Cowbeech, Near Herstmonceux, Hailsham, East Sussex Tel: 0435 830298 |
| **Gravetye Lake** | East Grinstead | Trout | Gravetye Manor Hotel and Country Club<br>Nr East Grinstead, West Sussex<br>Tel: 0342 810567<br>Hotel Guests and Members Only |
| **Hatchet Pond** | Lymington | Bream<br>Rudd<br>Pike<br>Tench | Forestry Commission<br>The Queen's House, Lyndhurst<br>Tel: 042 128 3141<br>Local Tackle and Sports Shops in Lyndhurst, Lymington, Christchurch, Bournemouth |
| **Heath Lake** | Petersfield | Carp<br>Bream<br>Rudd | Petersfield and District A.C.<br>Bailiff on the bank |
| **Inn on the Lake** | Gravesend | Coarse Fish | Inn on the Lake<br>A2, Shorne, Gravesend, Kent<br>Tel: 047482 3333 |
| **Island Fish Farm and Meadow Lakes** | Brighstone (Isle of Wight) | Carp<br>Roach<br>Trout | Island Fish Farm and Meadow Lakes<br>Nr Yafford Mill, Brighstone, Isle of Wight<br>Tel: 0983 740941 |
| **Leigh Park Gardens Lake** | Havant | Carp<br>Tench<br>Roach<br>Rudd<br>Pike<br>Eels | Southern Anglers<br>Leigh Park Garden Farm, Trail, Havant |
| **Leominstead Trout Fishery** | Lyndhurst | Trout | Leominstead Lakes<br>Emery Down, Lyndhurst<br>Tel: Lyndhurst 2610 |
| **Little Hemingfold Farm Lake** | Battle | Rainbow Trout | Little Hemingfold Farm, Telham, Battle, East Sussex Tel: 04246 2910 |
| **Lythe Hill Hotel Pond** | Haslemere | Carp<br>Tench<br>Rudd | Lythe Hill Hotel<br>Petworth Road, Haslemere, Surrey<br>Allchornes, Godalming, Surrey |
| **Mopley Farm Trout Fishery** | Southampton | Brown Trout<br>Rainbow Trout | Mopley Farm Trout Fishery<br>Mopley Farm, Mopley Road, Blackfield, Southampton<br>Accommodation |
| **'Newells' Specimen Carp and Coarse Fishery** | Horsham | Carp<br>Tench<br>Crucian Carp<br>Rudd<br>Pike | 'Newells' Specimen Carp and Coarse Fishery<br>Permit at Lakeside<br>(Day visitor to be accompanied by season ticket holder) |
| **Rooksbury Mill Trout Fishery** | Andover | Brown Trout<br>Rainbow Trout | Rooksbury Mill Trout Fishery<br>Rooksbury Road, Andover, Hants<br>Tel: 0264 52921 |

| Water | Location | Species | Permits |
|---|---|---|---|
| **Blagdon Reservoir** | Bristol | Brown Trout<br>Rainbow Trout | Bristol Waterworks Company<br>Fishing Lodge<br>Self Service Kiosks |
| **Cameley Lakes** | Bristol | Brown Trout<br>Rainbow Trout | John Harris<br>Cameley Lakes, Temple Cloud |
| **Cheddar Reservoir** | Cheddar | Carp<br>Bream<br>Pike<br>Eels | Cheddar Angling Club<br>Crossroads Filling Station,<br>Shipham Cross Roads, Cheddar<br>Veals Fishing Tackle, 61 Old Market Street, Bristol<br>Broadway House Caravan Park,<br>Axbridge Road, Cheddar |
| **Chew Valley Reservoir** | Bristol | Brown Trout<br>Rainbow Trout | Bristol Waterworks Company<br>Fishing Lodge<br>Self Service Kiosks |
| **Clatworthy Reservoir** | Taunton | Brown Trout<br>Rainbow Trout | Wessex Water<br>Reg Deer, Reservoir Ranger<br>Tel: 0984 23549 |
| **Damerham Fisheries** | Fordingbridge | Trout | Damerham Fisheries, Damerham, S. End,<br>Fordingbridge Tel: 072 53441 |
| **Durleigh Reservoir** | Bridgwater | Rainbow Trout | Wessex Water<br>Bob Jones, Reservoir Ranger<br>Tel: 0278 424786 |
| **Flowers Farm Lake** | Sherborne | Brown Trout<br>Rainbow Trout | Flowers Farm, Hilfield, Nr Cerne Abbas, Dorset<br>Tel: 03003 351 |
| **Hawkridge Reservoir** | Bridgwater | Brown Trout<br>Rainbow Trout | Wessex Water<br>King Square, Bridgwater<br>Tel: 0278 457333 ext 314 |
| **Hucklesbrook Trout Lake** | Fordingbridge | Brown Trout<br>Rainbow Trout<br><br>Roach<br>Perch<br>(1987) | Hucklesbrook Angling<br>Hucklesbrook, Ringwood Road,<br>Nr Fordingbridge, Hants<br>Tel: 0425 54957 |
| **Langford Fisheries** | Salisbury | Brown Trout<br>Rainbow Trout | Langford Fisheries<br>Steeple Langford, Salisbury, Wilts<br>Tel: 0722 790770 |
| **Longleat Lakes** | Warminster | Carp<br>Tench<br>Bream<br>Roach | Water Bailiff<br>Longleat House, Warminster, Wiltshire<br>Tel: 0985 215082 |
| **Otterhead Lakes** | Churchinford | Brown Trout<br>Rainbow Trout | Wessex Water<br>King Square, Bridgwater<br>Tel: 0278 457333 ext 314 |
| **Pallington Lakes (3) (and River Frome)** | Dorchester | Chub<br>Tench<br>Carp<br>Roach<br>Bream<br>Trout | B. Clarke<br>Pallington Lakes, Pallington, Dorchester<br>Tel: Puddletown 8141 |
| **Rockbourne Trout Fishery (6 Lakes and Chalkstream)** | Fordingbridge | Brown Trout<br>Rainbow Trout | Tony Hern<br>Rockbourne Trout Fisheries Ltd<br>Sandleheath, Fordingbridge, Hants<br>Tel: 07253 603 |

| Water | Location | Species | Permits |
|---|---|---|---|
| **Sutton Bingham Reservoir** | Yeovil | Brown Trout<br>Rainbow Trout | Wessex Water<br>Peter Hill, Reservoir Ranger<br>Tel: 0935 872389 |
| **Tolpuddle Trout Fishery** | Tolpuddle | Brown Trout<br>Rainbow Trout | Richard Slocock<br>Tolpuddle Trout Fishery and Wessex Fly Fishing<br>Lawrence's Farm, Tolpuddle, Dorchester, Dorset Tel: 030584 460 |
| **Tucking Mill** | Midford<br>Nr Bath | Carp<br>Tench<br>Bream<br>Rudd<br>Roach<br>Chubb | Kingswood Disabled Angling Club<br>Secretary, Mr G. Thompson, 1 Honey Hill Road, Kingswood, Bristol<br>Disabled Anglers and Helpers Only |

# SEA ANGLING

## South Coast

### Christchurch to Poole

At Mudeford the combined estuaries of the Hampshire Avon and Dorset Stour flow out to sea through a remarkably narrow estuary mouth. The combined force of two heavy rivers meeting the sea causes a strong tidal flow and the 'run' at Mudeford has long been noted as a dangerous piece of water. Anglers using small boats in this area are well-advised to confine their fishing activities to the miles of protected water inside Christchurch Harbour. This is no real handicap for bass, mullet and flounders abound within the confines of the harbour and its adjacent saltwater creeks. Grey mullet are particularly common and the favourite local method is to spin for these elusive fish using a totally localised baited-spoon rig. Christchurch mullet, find the flashing appeal of a tiny spoon irresistible and provided the single hook is baited with a tiny scrap of ragworm the fish will chase and snatch at the spoon until they become firmly hooked. Mullet spinning here is essentially a light tackle sport.

Mullet can also be caught on float tackle baited with bread or harbour ragworm. Once again this is a light-tackle sport and most local experts use roach-style tackle. The technique is to trot the baited hook down alongside the main flow of river water. The mullet shoals tend to gather just out of the main current. By using plenty of bread-based groundbait it does not take long to get the fish feeding avidly. Bass and flounders are usually taken on leger tackle baited with ragworm.

Shore anglers fishing at Stanpit often catch big bass and good-sized flounders on leger tackle. The quay wall at Mudeford is worth fishing, particularly after dark when bass, flounders and the occasional conger eel can be caught.

### Hengistbury Head

Hengistbury Head is a favourite shore-fishing resort with local sea-angling clubs. Regular beach fishing competitions are held in this area and fair catches of mixed bass, flatfish, and pouting are commonly made. A great attraction is the long groyne that juts out to sea. By walking out on this groyne it is possible to fish into quite deep water. For the angler interested in big fish, the groyne can fish fairly well for conger eels and, in the winter, the occasional cod. Bass, mullet, small wrasse and flatfish can also be caught along the entire length of the groyne.

### Southbourne

Southbourne Pier fishes consistently well for flatfish, bass, mullet, mackerel and garfish and the occasional winter cod. Most of the fish are caught by casting well out from the pier. Big mullet, bass and the odd fair-sized conger can be caught round the pier piles and it does not do to concentrate entirely on distance casting.

Southbourne's beaches, like most in the area, tend to be rather featureless but they do fish well for flatfish and school bass. For the offshore angler, Southbourne Rough is well worth a try. This is an area of rough ground situated a mile or so off the pier. During the summer the rough is a good mark for bream, pouting, conger and skate; during the winter months, it is a good place to catch cod. Fish to 42 lb have been caught in this area and the average size of rod-caught cod is 16 to 20 lb. These big cod mainly fall to whole imported Californian squid.

**Bournemouth**
Bournemouth Pier is the big attraction with local and visiting anglers. This pier often fishes extremely well for flatfish and bass. Float fishing with mackerel-strip bait also produce big catches of mackerel and garfish during the summer months. Rowing boats can be hired from the adjacent beach and, as small boat fishing a mile or so offshore can be very good, these are well worth considering. Bournemouth Bay is particularly good for plaice fishing, the technique being to drift with the tide using a baited-spoon or leger rig to attract the fish.
In the summer months, daytime fishing from Bournemouth Beach is practically impossible. After dark, however, the beaches are clear of bathers and can be used for fishing purposes. Flatfish and bass are the only two types of fish you can expect on a regular basis while beach fishing in this area and, as a rule, most of the fish caught tend to be on the small side.

**Poole Harbour**
Poole Harbour, with its 96 square miles of coastline, is the second largest natural harbour in the world and as such it is bound to attract anglers. At one time plaice were the favourite local species and in past years many huge plaice were caught from various marks round Brownsea Island. Unfortunately over-fishing by anglers and commercial fishermen seem to have virtually wiped out big plaice stocks, although the odd outsized fish can still be caught. Anglers fishing the quay at Poole catch flounders, small plaice and good bass. At Hamworthy, light leger and spinning tackle regularly accounts for big bass and at the mouth of Poole Harbour good catches of small bass and flatfish are commonplace. From the boat-angling point of view, anywhere in the harbour is capable of producing good fishing, although most anglers concentrate on marks round Brownsea Island where flatfish, bass, and pouting can be caught. Bass fishing around the mouth of Poole Harbour can provide exciting fishing. Offshore marks are good for skate, tope, conger, black bream and a variety of lesser species. Light tackle bass-enthusiasts can arrange trips to the Training Bank grounds which in recent seasons have produced immense catches of huge bass.

*Colin Holder with 17lb cod caught off Mudeford*

**Swanage to Weymouth**
Beyond Poole the coastline changes character considerably. High cliffs interspersed with small sheltered beaches provide ample scope for the shore fisherman and dinghy angler alike, with a wide variety of fish available from most marks.

Beyond the cliffs of Studland, Swanage Bay opens up to provide a wealth of good fishing. Shore anglers fishing this area can expect to catch bass, conger, pouting, dab, plaice and mullet. Swanage Pier can fish well at times, particularly for mullet and mackerel. Swanage Bay itself is good for boat fishing. Small-boat anglers fishing this bay catch thornback ray, tope, pollack, conger, pouting, dogfish, various flatfish, bass and black bream.

The best bait in this area seems to be ragworm or fish and squid strip-baits. Heavyweight tope often come into Swanage Bay and many anglers boat-fishing in the bay have been smashed up by these hard-fighting little sharks which can weigh up to 50 lb.

**Kimmeridge**

Anglers fishing this stretch of the Dorset coastline often bypass some tremendous fishing areas which lie directly between Swanage and Weymouth.

Kimmeridge is a typical example of an overlooked fishing ground. Situated some five miles from Corfe Village, Kimmeridge Bay is controlled by a local estate which charges a toll fee for parking and fishing. The bay consists of numerous ledges of flat rock which run straight out from the beach. At first sight these ledges and the comparatively shallow water of the bay appear to offer little opportunity for angling. Examine any of the local rock pools, however, and you will quickly discover that the bay is alive with shellfish, shrimps, prawns, crabs and tiny rock fish. It is a natural, well-stocked larder which is more than capable of providing large predatory fish with an ample and easily obtainable supply of live food.

Tope, conger, bass, pollack and some monster mullet use Kimmeridge Bay as a feeding ground and anglers who are prepared to put in time and thought can really get to grips with some big fish in this shallow and sheltered bay. Boat fishing off Kimmeridge can be very good indeed. The whole area is alive with fish of many kinds, including a plentiful supply of beautiful, big black bream. Apart from these bream, which tend to be fussy feeders, Kimmeridge is the sort of place where big baits pay off handsomely. Whole mackerel or pouting is more likely to catch fish than a fillet or fish strip-bait. Tope, conger and good-sized skate abound in this area and all three tend to prefer one big meal rather than a whole series of snacks.

**Weymouth**

Long-established as a top boat-fishing site, Weymouth and its surrounding area is also something of a shore angler's paradise. Always a popular holiday resort, Weymouth's town beach is virtually unfishable during the summer months, but the stone pier at the harbour mouth is well worth trying, particularly for conger eels. Float-fishing from the pier head sometimes produces good mixed bags of fish, mackerel and pollack being the main species encountered. Rock fishing enthusiasts should head for nearby Portland Bill. For the less adventurous, there are plenty of places round the Portland Lighthouse which provide easy-to-get-at, safe casting positions. The flat ledge adjacent to Pulpit Rock is a popular mark. This broad, easily accessible ledge allows the angler to float or bottom fish in absolute comfort and yet still stand every chance of catching some good-sized fish. This is a favourite venue with local anglers and visitors alike. Close to a good car park, easy to walk to and simple to fish, Pulpit Rock and its adjoining ledge is as good a place to start as any round Portland. Bass, conger, wrasse and pollack are the mainstay of Portland's rock fishing. Mackerel, garfish, bull huss and mullet can be caught all round Portland Bill. Between Portland and Weymouth the road passes over a narrow neck of water known as the Fleet. This runs up behind Chesil Beach and is a good place for flatfish and the occasional monster bass. In periods of rough weather, when beach and rock fishing is virtually impossible, the Fleet provides comfortable, often rewarding fishing.

**Chesil Bank**

Eighteen miles of steep-to shingle make up the famed Chesil Bank. A long-established shore angling hot-spot, the bank can produce a wide variety of fish, some of which grow to a vast size. This is one of the few beaches in the British Isles where you might well hook a shark. Chesil Bank is a year-round venue; conger, skate, tope, flatfish and

mackerel make up the bulk of the summer catches, while winter anglers find big cod, whiting and hefty spurdog. Chesil Bank once held the British spurdog record. Summer or winter, Chesil Beach is essentially a big-fish site. Knowledgeable anglers invariably fish here with fairly heavy tackle and big baits. Huge tope and conger are commonly hooked along the beach and monster monkfish are very occasionally encountered. Night fishing produces the best results, but the beach can fish well during the daytime, particularly after a storm when the water is coloured by clouds of disturbed sand. At times like this, bass and flatfish often bite freely and the angler who is prepared to use big baits and wait patiently for a bite can often finish up the day with a nice big thornback ray or two to show for his efforts.
Practically any section of Chesil Beach is worth fishing, although it is difficult to gain access to much of the beach. Favourite, easily-reached venues like Seatown, Eype, Abbotsbury, Burton, Beadstock and West Bexington are often heavily fished. During the summer months Chesil Bank Beach is noted for its productive mackerel fishing. Vast shoals of these fast moving fish sweep right inshore in search of whitebait and many anglers fish the bank specifically for mackerel.
The coastline at Bridport is really part of the Chesil Bank, but it is possible to fish from the walls of West Bay harbour. This again is a good place for mackerel and all the other species of fish that frequent Chesil Bank.
It is possible to launch small boats at many points along Chesil Bank. Dinghy fishermen do very well in this area, for, by using a boat, it is possible to fish many highly-productive marks which, while not far offshore, are still well beyond casting range of the beach. By boat fishing it is possible to catch pollack, black bream and one or two other species of fish which are rarely encountered by anglers fishing from the Chesil Bank. Great care should be taken when boat fishing at any point off Chesil, for this is an exposed coastline which can become extremely dangerous very quickly. Keep an eye on the weather and wind strength and do not take silly chances and you will not come to much harm. Ignore the signs and you could easily be in serious, trouble very quickly.

## North Coast

### Minehead

Facing directly out into the Bristol Channel, Minehead should fish better than it does, but ultra-fast tides and fairly shallow water make this section of coastline rather bad for anglers. On occasions, good-sized conger, bass and flatfish are caught from Minehead Harbour Wall, Dunster Beach, Madbrain Beach or the horribly-named Gasworks Beach. From time to time immense conger eels are washed up along this coastline. In all probability these dead or dying giants come drifting inshore from one of the many wrecks which litter the Bristol Channel. Some of these eels weigh up to 100 lbs. Small-boat fishing off Minehead is very difficult. Raging tides make it unsafe in anything other than perfect conditions.
Charter boats fishing offshore grounds take good catches of prime thornback skate, bull huss, cod, tope, coner and sea bream. The best tackle for boat fishing is a single hooking running leger baited with fish or squid. For shore fishing worm or crab baits should be employed.

### Watchet

Similar in many ways to Minehead, Watchet and its adjacent coastline is seldom very productive. Tides are exceptionally fierce and amateur boatmen are advised to take great care at all times. Shore fishing at Blue Anchor Beach and St Audrie's Bay can produce flatfish and small bass. Good sized lugworm can be dug at Blue Anchor Bay and isolated pockets of big ragworm can be found off Watchet Harbour.

### Bridgwater and Weston-super-Mare

There is comparatively good shore fishing all the way along this section of coastline, Burnham-on-Sea town beach, with Hinkley Reef, River Parrett estuary, Brean Down, the toll road from Weston to Sand Bay all worth a try. This is mainly bass, flatfish and silver eel territory and the best baits to use are ragworm and lugworm. At times the silver eel fishing can be very good, particularly during the late summer and early autumn period. Silver eels tend to bite freely provided the bait is anchored hard on the bottom. For the pier anglers, the old pier at Weston, Knightstone Harbour and the Stolford to Hinkley Sea Wall make good stations.

Small boat fishing is fairly good, mackerel, skate, flat-fish, cod, conger and tope being caught. Bristol itself is hardly worth considering from the fishing point of view.

Boat fishing in the Bristol Channel is seldom very good, although good fish do occasionally occur. Strong tides and coloured water make fishing difficult at the best of times.

# ACCOMMODATION

## AVON
### Chelwood

**CHELWOOD HOUSE**
Chelwood, Avon, BS18 4NH
Tel: 07618 730
Classification not yet known
9 Bedrooms (All with private bathroom/shower).

M LF LP AL

For the discerning angler, not only does he have the opportunity to fish in two of the finest trout lakes in the country, Chew Valley and Blagdon, but also we offer comfortable accommodation in a gracious house where the chef-patron takes delight in producing gourmet meals. For the angling 'widow' Chelwood House is within easy reach of 3 famous cities: Bath, Bristol and Wells.

| | B & B £ | Half Board £ |
|---|---|---|
| High Season | 25.00 | 40.00 |

Closed Jan
Supplements: Single room £10.

### Weston-super-Mare

**THE CARRINGTON HOTEL AND HARVEST INN**
28 Knightstone Road, Weston-super-Mare, Avon, BS23 2AN
Tel: 0934 26621
18 Bedrooms (8 with private bathroom/shower).

M T

The Carrington Hotel and Harvest Inn Restaurant is situated in the best position on the seafront between the Grand Pier and Marine Lake, almost immediately next door to the Winter Gardens. We are open all year. The hotel offers a friendly atmosphere with all the comfort and amenities that one associates with a family-run hotel.

| | Bed Only £ | B & B £ | Half Board £ |
|---|---|---|---|
| Mid Season | 10.00 | 12.50 | 15.00 |

Children's discounts available
Supplements: Room with bath/shower & WC £1 per person

## DORSET
### Corfe Castle

**MORTONS HOUSE HOTEL**
East Street, Corfe Castle, Dorset, BH20 5EE
Tel: 0929 480988
7 Bedrooms (All with private bathroom/shower).

M T LF LP AL

An Elizabethan house in the centre of the historic village of Corfe Castle with views of the castle and Purbeck Hills from the garden and terrace. A wide variety of fishing in the area including the well known Frome at Wareham. Superb walking, wildlife sanctuaries, good beaches and historic buildings all within easy reach. BR main line services at Wareham with transport by car to the hotel.

| | B & B £ | Half Board £ |
|---|---|---|
| High Season | 27.50 | 37.00 |
| Low Season | 20.00 | 29.50 |

**HS** 1 May–30 Sep
**LS** 1 Oct–30 Apr
Supplements: Single room £10. LS breaks, HS breaks, 6 or 7 days, weekend breaks throughout year

### Dorchester

**THE MANOR HOTEL**
Beach Road, West Bexington, Dorchester, Dorset, DT2 9DF
Tel: 0308 897616
10 Bedrooms (All with private bathroom/shower).

M T

A 17th-century manor house 500 yards from Chesil Beach. Panoramic views of unspoilt Dorset coast from most bedrooms. Excellent reputation for cuisine and service. Three real ales in character cellar bar. Log fires. The Chesil Beach is renowned for onshore fishing. 5 miles away there is sea fishing and boat hire at West Bay. Coarse fishing is 15 miles away at Pallington Lakes, Puddletown.

| | B & B £ | Half Board £ |
|---|---|---|
| High Season | 19.95 | 29.95 |
| Mid Season | 19.00 | 28.95 |
| Low Season | 18.00 | 27.95 |

Children's discounts available
**HS** 1 Jul–30 Sep
**MS** 1 Mar–30 Jun
**LS** 1 Oct–28 Feb

### Poole

**FAIRLIGHT HOTEL**
1 Golf Links Road, Broadstone, Poole, Dorset, BH18 8BE
Tel: 0202 694316
10 Bedrooms (7 with private bathroom/shower).

M LF LP AL

Private, family-run, licensed hotel in its own grounds. Close to Rivers Stour, Avon, Frome, Piddle, Test, Itchen and Broadlands lakes. Poole, Bournemouth, Christchurch and coast a few miles away. Comfortable lounge, colour TV, cosy bar, full central heating and open fires in winter. Excellent meals freshly prepared by resident proprietors. A warm welcome and friendly atmosphere assured. Day tickets available River Stour.

| | B & B £ | Half Board £ |
|---|---|---|
| High Season | 12.00 | 21.00 |

Children's discounts available
Closed 20 Dec–4 Jan
Supplements: Room with bath/shower & WC £2. Single room £4. For 3–6 nights supplement is £1, 1–2 nights £2

**HAVEN HOTEL**
Sandbands, Poole, Dorset, BH13 7QL
Tel: 0202 707333

80 Bedrooms (All with private bathroom/shower).

In an idyllic setting, standing at the very edge of the sea, overlooking Bournemouth Bay, Shell Bay, Brownsea Island and the Purbeck Hills. Sea fish off the hotel's terrace or explore the excellent fishing grounds of Poole Harbour & Bay. After a day's fishing relax in the hotel's unique leisure centre complete with spa pools, steam room, sauna, solarium, gymnasium and squash court, or just relax in the sun lounges.

| | B & B £ | Half Board £ |
|---|---|---|
| High Season | 30.00 | 39.00 |
| Low Season | 25.00 | 34.00 |

Children's discounts available
**HS** 23 May–4 Sep
**LS** 1 Jan–22 May, 5 Sep–31 Dec

## Swanage

**DURLSTON COURT HOTEL**
Park Road, Swanage, Dorset, BH19 2AE
Tel: 0929 422430
55 Bedrooms (21 with private bathroom/shower).

Durlston Court Hotel is situated in South Swanage overlooking the bay, Purbeck Hills and the harbour. The 55 bedromed hotel still retains a friendly atmosphere where guests can relax and enjoy good food and wine. Games room, outdoor swimming pool, pub, 3 bars, snacks and 2 restaurants. Hire of equipment, boats, including night fishing, bait and freezer space all organised. Special club/group packages available.

| | B & B £ | Half Board £ |
|---|---|---|
| High Season | 17.50 | 25.00 |
| Mid Season | 17.00 | 24.00 |
| Low Season | 15.00 | 22.50 |

**HS** Jul–Aug **MS** Apr–Jun
**LS** Sep–Mar
Open Christmas and New Year
Supplements: Single room £2.50, guaranteed sea view £2.50 per room

# SOMERSET

## Cheddar

**CLIFF HOTEL**
Cheddar Gorge, Cheddar, Somerset, BS27 3QL
Tel: 0934 742346

22 Bedrooms (5 with private bathroom/shower).

The heart of the Mendip Hills with waterfalls in tropical bird garden. Close to Cheddar and Blagdon lakes. Durleigh/Hawkridge for game, or King Sedgemoor Drain, Huntspill Cripps. Axe, Hixham, Yeo, Brue Keww for coarse. Weston, Burnham, Kilvets for sea. Good home cooking in friendly family-owned and run hotel with two bars, restaurant, wine bar. TV lounge overlooking lake and waterfall. Apply for your free brochure, also details of available fishing.

| | B & B £ | Half Board £ |
|---|---|---|
| High Season | 12.00 | 16.50 |
| Low Season | | 15.50 |

Children's discounts available
**LS** Mar–May, Sep–Nov
Closed 1 Jan–28 Feb
Supplements: Room with bath/shower & WC £1.50

## Dulverton

**CARNARVON ARMS HOTEL**
Brushford, Dulverton, Somerset, TA22 9AE
Tel: 0398 23302

26 Bedrooms (23 with private bathroom/shower).

The Carnarvon Arms has some of the finest salmon and trout fishing in the West Country, offering 7½ miles on rivers Exe, Barle and charming Haddeo tributary which tumbles through ancient woodland from Wimbleball Lake — some 15 minutes drive. The lovely atmosphere of this hotel, run by family and friendly local service, is ideal for family holidays, overseas visitors as well as the dedicated fisherman.

| | Bed Only £ | B & B £ | Half Board £ |
|---|---|---|---|
| High Season | 18.00 | 25.00 | 33.00 |
| Mid Season | 15.00 | 22.00 | 30.00 |
| Low Season | 13.00 | 20.00 | 28.00 |

Children's discounts available
**HS** Aug–Sep **MS** May–Jul, Oct
**LS** Nov–Apr
Closed Feb
Supplements: Single room £3

## Wookey

**GLENCOT HOUSE**
Glencot Lane, Wookey Hole, Nr. Wells, Somerset, BA5 1BH
Tel: 0749 77160
10 Bedrooms (5 with private bathroom/shower).

Glencot House is set in 18 acres with river frontage and offers good food and service in peaceful, elegant surroundings. Private fishing within the grounds is available, and Chew Valley Lake and Weston Super Mare are a short drive away. All rooms have TV, telephone and tea/coffee-making facilities. Indoor jet stream pool, sauna and exercise room. Snooker room and bar.

| | B & B £ | Half Board £ |
|---|---|---|
| High Season | 17.50 | 29.00 |

Children's discounts available

**MANOR FARM**
Worth, Wookey, Wells, Somerset, BA5 1LW
Tel: 0749 73428
6 Bedrooms

A 17th-century farmhouse offering homely, clean accommodation and every comfort assured. All rooms with hot and cold water and TV. Visitors lounge with colour TV. Ample home cooking. Manor Farm is in a beautiful rural setting close to the Mendip Hills with picturesque shallow river running through it with wild ducks and geese. Within walking distance from restaurant and pub. Within 8 miles of 6 excellent fishing locations.

| | Bed Only £ | B & B £ | Half Board £ |
|---|---|---|---|
| High Season | 5.00 | 7.00 | 11.00 |

Children's discounts available

See page 4 for details of symbols

# SOUTH-WEST

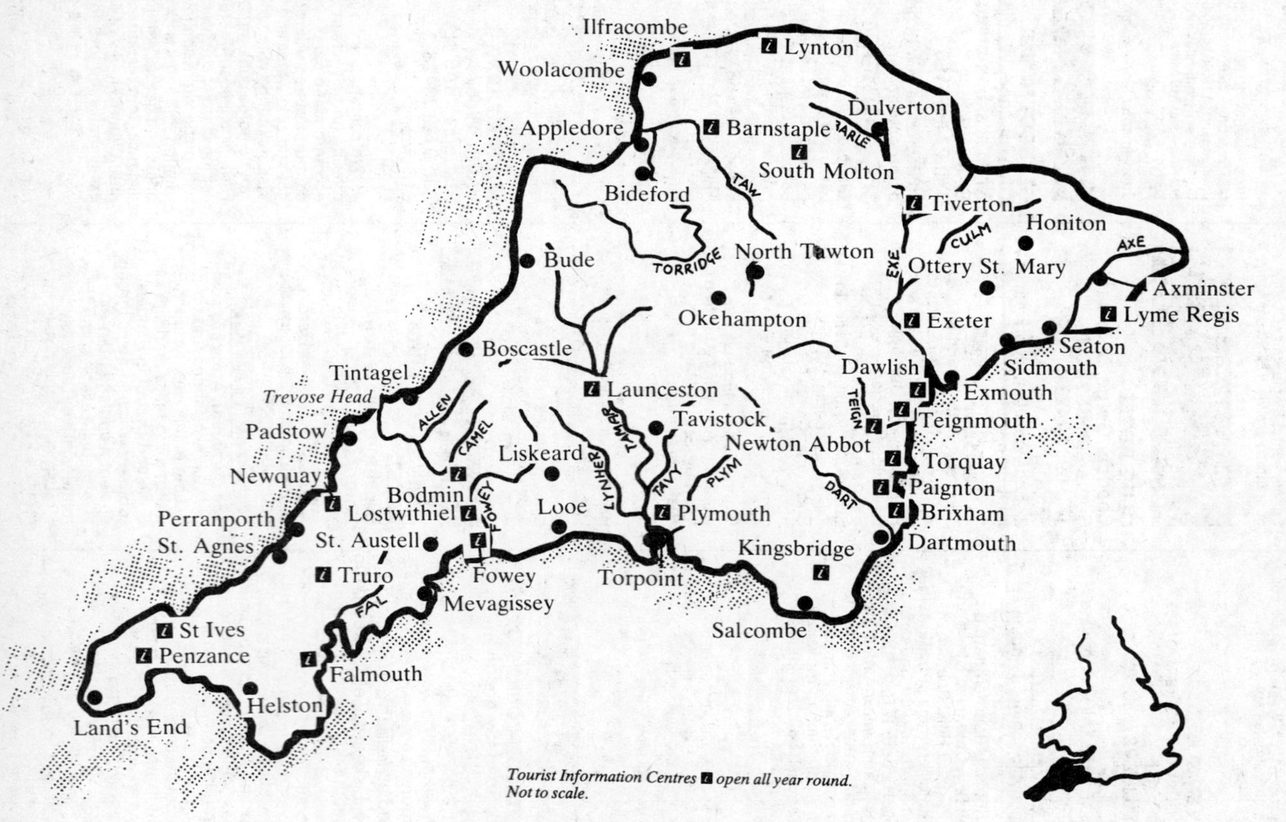

Ilfracombe
Lynton
Woolacombe
Dulverton
Appledore
Barnstaple
BARLE
South Molton
Bideford
TAW
Tiverton
Honiton
CULM
AXE
Bude
TORRIDGE
North Tawton
EXE
Ottery St. Mary
Axminster
Lyme Regis
Okehampton
Exeter
Seaton
Boscastle
Dawlish
Sidmouth
Tintagel
Trevose Head
Launceston
Exmouth
ALLEN
TAMAR
Tavistock
TEIGN
Teignmouth
Padstow
CAMEL
Newton Abbot
Liskeard
LYNHER
Torquay
TAVY
PLYM
Newquay
Bodmin
FOWEY
Paignton
DART
Lostwithiel
Looe
Plymouth
Brixham
Perranporth
St. Agnes
St. Austell
Dartmouth
Kingsbridge
Truro
Fowey
Torpoint
Mevagissey
FAL
St Ives
Salcombe
Penzance
Falmouth
Helston
Land's End
Tourist Information Centres open all year round.
Not to scale.

# SOUTH WEST

The high moorland masses of Dartmoor, Exmoor and Bodmin Moor gather the moist Atlantic winds and channel the rains down curling trout streams through buzzard-haunted valleys to the Bristol and the English Channels. Spates bring up the salmon and sea trout — "peel" in local dialect — and the visiting angler has been welcomed in hotels and inns throughout the region for more than 100 years. Numerous small and secret ponds and lakes hold prime carp and tench while the many water-supply reservoirs provide first-class stillwater trout fishing.

**Water Authority**

South West Water, Peninsula House, Rydon Lane, Exeter EX2 7HR
Tel: (0392) 219666

**Ranger Service**

There are five Recreation Rangers controlling recreational activities at SWW's various sites.

Ranger (West Cornwall) is Bob Evans, based at Little Argal Farm, Budock, Penryn. Tel: Penryn (0326) 72544.

Ranger (East Cornwall) is Reg England, based at Tregarrick Lodge, Siblyback Lake, Liskeard. Tel: Liskeard (0579) 42266.

Ranger (North West Devon) is Ken Spalding, based at Sparrapark Kilkhampton, Bude. Tel: Kilkhampton (028 882) 262.

Ranger (Exmoor) is based at Hill Farm, Brompton Regis, Dulverton.
Tel: Brompton Regis (039 87) 372.

Ranger (Dartmoor) is Bob Lunk. Contact Recreation Office for details of address.

**Fishing Seasons**

Salmon
- Avon
  - River Avon — 15 Apr–30 Nov (E)
  - River Erme — 15 Mar–31 Oct
- Axe
  - Rivers: Axe, Lim, Otter, Sid — 15 Mar–31 Oct
- Camel
  - River Camel — 1 Apr–15 Dec
- Dart
  - River Dart — 1 Feb–30 Sept (E)
- Exe
  - River Exe — 14 Feb–30 Sept
- Fowey
  - Rivers: Fowey, Looe — 1 Apr–15 Dec
- Tamar and Plym
  - Rivers: Tamar, Tavy, Lynher — 1 Mar–14 Oct
  - River Plym — 1 Apr–15 Dec
  - River Yealm — 1 Apr–15 Dec (E)
- Taw and Torridge
  - Rivers: Taw, Torridge — 1 Mar–30 Sept
  - River Lyn — 1 Feb–31 Oct
- Teign
  - River Teign — 1 Feb–30 Sept

Migratory Trout
- Avon
  - River Avon — 15 Apr–30 Sept
  - River Erme — 15 Mar–30 Sept
- Axe
  - Rivers: Axe, Lim, Otter, Sid — 15 Apr–31 Oct
- Camel
  - Rivers: Camel, Gannel, Menalhyl, Valency — 1 Apr–30 Sept
- Dart
  - River Dart — 15 Mar–30 Sept
- Exe
  - River Exe — 15 Mar–30 Sept
- Fowey
  - Rivers: Fowey, Looe, Seaton, Tresillian — 1 Apr–30 Sept
- Tamar and Plym
  - Rivers: Tamar, Lynher, Plym, Tavy, Yealm — 3 Mar–30 Sept
- Taw and Torridge
  - Rivers: Taw, Torridge, Lyn — 15 Mar–30 Sept

Teign
Rivers: Teign, Bovey — 15 Mar–12 Oct

Brown Trout
Entire Region
Rivers: Camel, Fowey — 1 Apr–30 Sept
Other Rivers and Streams — 15 Mar–30 Sept
All Other Waters — 15 Mar–12 Oct

Rainbow Trout (Entire Region) — No close season

Coarse Fish (Entire Region) — No close season

As part of the Authority's Strategy on Salmon Cropping, the season on some rivers has been changed experimentally and is indicated with an E.

NOTE: Some waters are not open for the full duration of the season, anglers are advised to check with the fishery owner if in doubt.

**Regional Tourist Board**
West Country Tourist Board,
Trinity Court, 37 Southernhay East,
Exeter, Devon EX1 1QS
Tel: (0392) 76351

# SOUTH WEST ANGLING CLUBS

**Avon Fishing Association**
Secretary, 19 Stella Road, Preston, Paignton, S. Devon
**Bodmin Angling Association**
R. Burrows, Secretary, 26 Meadow Place, Bodmin
**Bude Angling Association**
Lt Cdr S.F.W. Blackall, R.N., Hon. Secretary/Treasurer, 5 Ward Close, Stratton, Bude, Cornwall EX23 9BB
**Bude Canal Angling Association**
D. Read, Secretary, 15 Victoria Road, Bude, Cornwall EX23 8RJ
**Launceston Anglers Association**
John Fraser, Secretary, 11 Duke Street, St Stephens, Launceston, Cornwall
**Liskeard & District Angling Club**
O.G. Gilbert, Secretary, 11 Richmond Road, Pelynt, Looe, Cornwall PL13 2NH
**Lostwithiel Fishing Association**
J.H. Hooper, Treasurer, 4 Reeds Park, Lostwithiel, Cornwall PL22 0HF
**Lower Teign Fishing Association**
P.M. Knibbs, Hon. Secretary, Tapley Cottage, Barclays Bank Corner, Teignmouth
**Newton Abbot Fishing Association**
David Horder, Secretary, 22 Mount Pleasant Road, Newton Abbot, Devon TQ12 1AS
**Plymouth & District Freshwater Angling Association**
D.L. Owen, Secretary, 39 Burnett Road, Crownhill, Plymouth PL6 5BH
**R.A.B.I. Angling Club**
Treasurer, 224 Westfield, Plympton, Plymouth PL7 3EW
**Tavy Walkham & Plym Fishing Club**
Mrs J.P. Smalley, Secretary, Haytown, Sampford Spiney, Yelverton, Devon PL20 7QT
**The Upper Teign Fishing Association**
The Anglers Rest, Fingle Bridge, Drewsteignton, Exeter EX6 6PW
**Tiverton & District Angling Club**
Malcolm Trump, Canal Liaison Officer, 20 Beech Close, Willand, Tiverton, Devon
**Torridge Fly Fishing Club**
Secretary, 4 Merryfield Road, Bideford East, N. Devon EX39 4BX
**Wistlandpound Fly-Fishing Club**
A.F. Lovemore, Secretary, The Old Forge, 113b East Street, South Molton, N. Devon EX36 3DB

# RIVERS AND CANALS

| Water | Location | Species | Permits |
|---|---|---|---|
| **Allen** | Wadebridge | Sea Trout<br>Trout | Wadebridge Angling Association<br>Appleton and Cragg, 1 Egloshayle Road,<br>Wadebridge |
| **Avon** | Kingsbridge | Salmon<br>Sea Trout<br>Trout | Avon Fishing Association<br>Mr O'Neil, 55 Church St, Kingsbridge<br>Mr Tomlinson, Post Office, Loddiswell |
| **Axe** | Lyme Regis | Salmon<br>Trout | The George Hotel, Residents Only<br>Axminster, Devon EX13 5DW<br>Tel: 0297 32209 |
| **Barle** | Dulverton | Salmon<br>Brown Trout | Tarr Steps Hotel<br>Hawkridge, Dulverton, Somerset<br>Carnarvon Arms Hotel, Brushford<br>Dulverton Tel: (0398) 23302 |
| **Bude Canal** | Bude | Carp<br>Tench<br>Roach<br>Rudd<br>Dace<br>Eels | Bude Canal Angling Association<br>Local Tourist Information Centre<br>Sampsons Boat House<br>On the Canal Bank |
| **Camel** | Wadebridge | Salmon<br>Sea Trout<br>Trout | Wadebridge and District Angling Association<br>Appleton and Cragg, 1 Egloshayne Road,<br>Wadebridge |
| | Bodmin | Salmon<br>Sea Trout<br>Trout | Liskeard and District Angling Club<br>Treasurer, T. Sobey, Trevartha Farm, Liskeard<br>Local Sports and Tackle Shops |
| **Carey** | Lifton | Salmon<br>Sea Trout<br>Trout | Arundell Arms Hotel<br>Lifton, Devon<br>Tel: (0566) 84666 |
| | Launceston | Salmon<br>Sea Trout<br>Trout | Launceston Anglers Association<br>Tony Kennedy, Tackle and Gun Shop, Church<br>Street, Launceston<br>Jeffries Sports, The Arcade, Launceston |
| **Claw** | Holsworthy | Brown Trout<br>Grayling | Bude Angling Association<br>DIY Centre, The Square, Holsworthy<br>Ray Beare Sports, Belle Vue, Bude |
| **Culm** | Cullompton | Brown Trout | Craddock Estate<br>The Old Parsonage, Uffculme,<br>Cullompton, Devon Tel: 0884 40205 |
| **Dart** | Totnes | Salmon<br>Sea Trout<br>Trout | Dart Angling Association<br>Sports Shops in Totnes, Buckfastleigh,<br>Newton Abbot, Torquay |
| | Ashburton | Salmon<br>Sea Trout | Holne Chase Hotel, Tavistock Road<br>Ashburton, Devon Tel: 03643 471 |
| **Deer** | Holsworthy | Brown<br>Trout | Bude Angling Association<br>DIY Centre, The Square, Holsworthy<br>Ray Beare Sports, Belle Vue, Bude |
| **Exe** | Exeter | Salmon | South West Water<br>Exeter Angling Centre, Smythen Street, Off<br>City Arcade, Fore Street, Exeter |
| | Dulverton | Salmon<br>Trout | Carnarvon Arms Hotel, Brushford<br>Dulverton, Somerset Tel: (0398) 23302 |

| Water | Location | Species | Permits |
|---|---|---|---|
| **Fowey** | Lostwithiel | Salmon<br>Sea Trout<br>Trout | Lostwithiel Fishing Association<br>Four Ways Autos, Lostwithiel<br>Bodmin Trading, Bodmin<br>Angling Centre, St Austell |
| | Liskeard | Salmon<br>Sea Trout<br>Trout | Liskeard and District Angling Club<br>Treasurer, T. Sobey, Trevartha Farm, Liskeard<br>Local Sports and Tackle Shops |
| | Liskeard | Salmon<br>Sea Trout, Trout | Rivermead Farm<br>Twowaterstoot, Liskeard |
| | Bodmin | Salmon<br>Sea Trout<br>Trout | Bodmin Angling Association<br>Secretary, R. Burrows, 26 Meadow Place, Bodmin |
| **Grand Western Canal** | Tiverton | Tench<br>Bream<br>Carp<br>Roach<br>Rudd<br>Pike | Tiverton and District Angling Club<br>Country Sports, William Street, Tiverton<br>Tiverton Sports and Leisure, Market Precinct, Tiverton<br>Membership Secretary, Eric Priest<br>Tel: 0884 252574 |
| **Lyd** | Lifton | Salmon<br>Sea Trout<br>Trout | Arundell Arms Hotel<br>Lifton, Devon<br>Tel: (0566) 84666 |
| **Lyn** | Watersmeet<br>Glenthorne | Salmon<br>Trout | South West Water<br>Coombe Park Lodge, Hillsford Bridge, Lynton<br>Lower Bourne House, High Street, Porlock<br>Pet Shop, Lee Road, Lynton<br>Pilesports, 1 Harbour Lights, Lynmouth |
| | Lynmouth | Salmon<br>Sea Trout<br>Trout | Rising Sun Hotel<br>The Harbour, Lynmouth, Devon |
| **Lynher** | Near Liskeard | Salmon<br>Trout | Liskeard and District Angling Club<br>T. Sobey, Trevartha Farm, Liskeard<br>Local Tackle and Sports Shops |
| **Otter** | Honiton | Trout | Coombe House Hotel<br>Gittisham, Nr Honiton, Devon<br>Hotel Guests Only |
| | Honiton | Trout | Deer Park Hotel, Buckerell Village<br>Honiton, Devon<br>Tel: 0404 2064 |
| **Ottery** | (Parts) | Salmon<br>Sea Trout<br>Trout | Launceston Anglers Association<br>Tackle and Gun Shop, Church Street, Launceston<br>Jeffries Sports, The Arcade, Launceston |
| **Plym** | Plymouth | Salmon<br>Sea Trout<br>Trout | Plymouth and District Freshwater Angling Association<br>D.K. Sports (Tackle Shop), Vauxhall Street, Plymouth |
| | Yelverton | Salmon<br>Sea Trout<br>Trout | Tavy, Walkham and Plym Fishing Club<br>Rock Stores, Yelverton |
| **Tamar** | Lifton | Salmon<br>Sea Trout<br>Trout | Arundel Arms Hotel<br>Lifton, Devon<br>Tel: (0566) 84666 |

| Water | Location | Species | Permits |
|---|---|---|---|
| **Tamar** contd. | Launceston | Salmon<br>Sea Trout<br>Trout | Launceston Anglers Association<br>Tackle and Gun Shop, Church Street, Launceston<br>Jeffries Sports, The Arcade, Launceston |
| | Holsworthy | Brown Trout | Bude Angling Association<br>DIY Centre, The Square, Holsworthy, Devon<br>Ray Beare Sports, Belle Vue, Bude |
| | Launceston | | E.J. Broad<br>Lower Dutson Farm, Launceston<br>Farm Guests Only |
| **Tavy** | Tavistock | Salmon<br>Sea Trout<br>Trout | Tavy, Walkham and Plym Fishing Club<br>Barkell's, Duke St, Tavistock<br>The Keep, Brook St, Tavistock |
| **Taw** | Chumleigh | Salmon<br>Sea Trout<br>Trout | Fox and Hounds Hotel<br>Eggesford, Chumleigh, Devon<br>Tel: (0769) 80345/80262 |
| **Teign** | Newton Abbot | Salmon<br>Sea Trout | Lower Teign Fishing Association<br>Percy Hodge (Sports) Ltd, Queen Street, Newton Abbot<br>Tel: Newton Abbot 54923 |
| | Chagford | Salmon<br>Sea Trout<br>Trout | Upper Teign Fishing Association<br>The Anglers Rest, Drewsteignton<br>Exeter Angling Centre, Fore Street, Exeter<br>Bowdens, The Square, Chagford<br>Drum Sports, Courtenay Street, Newton Abbot<br>Local Hotels<br>Gidleigh Park Hotel & Restaurant |
| **Thrushel** | Lifton | Salmon<br>Sea Trout<br>Trout | Arundell Arms Hotel, Lifton, Devon<br>Tel: (0566) 84666 |
| **Torridge** | Torrington (Riversdale Beat) | Salmon<br>Sea Trout<br>Trout | Riversdale, Weare Gifford, Bideford |
| | Hatherleigh | | Half Moon Inn<br>Sheepwash, Devon |
| | Torrington (Little Warham) | | Little Warham House<br>Beaford, Winkleigh, North Devon<br>(Self Catering Accommodation) |
| | Holsworthy | | Woodford Bridge Hotel<br>Milton Damerel, North Devon |
| | Meeth | Salmon<br>Sea Trout | Friars Hele Farm, Meeth,<br>Okehampton, Devon Tel: 0837 810282 |
| **Torridge (and Other Rivers)** | Torrington | Salmon<br>Sea Trout<br>Wild Brown Trout | West of England Fisheries<br>West of England Centre of Game Angling,<br>Caynton Street, Torrington, Devon<br>Tel: 0805 23256 |
| **Walkham** | Tavistock | Salmon<br>Sea Trout<br>Trout | Tavy, Walkham and Plym Fishing Club<br>Barkells, Duke St, Tavistock<br>The Keep, Brook St, Tavistock<br>Rock Stores, Yelverton |

# LAKES AND RESERVOIRS

| Water | Location | Species | Permits |
|---|---|---|---|
| **Alder Lake** | Okehampton | Carp<br>Tench<br>Bream<br>Trout<br>Roach | Alder Farm Chalets<br>Lewdown, Okehampton, Devon<br>Tel: Lewdown 444<br>(Self Catering Accommodation) |
| **Argal Reservoir** | Falmouth | Rainbow Trout | South West Water<br>Self Service on Site |
| **Avon Dam** | South Brent | Brown Trout<br>Brook Trout | South West Water<br>Free of Charge |
| **Badham Farm** | St Keyne | Carp<br>Tench<br>Rudd | Badham Farm, St Keyne, Liskeard, Cornwall<br>Tel: 0579 43572 (Accommodation) |
| **Blakewell Fisheries** | Barnstaple | Brown Trout<br>Rainbow Trout | Blakewell Fisheries<br>Muddiford, Barnstaple<br>(Open all year) |
| **Burrator Reservoir** | Yelverton | Brown Trout<br>Rainbow Trout | South West Water<br>The Rock Hotel, Yelverton |
| **Choone Farm** | Penzance | Carp<br>Tench<br>Perch<br>Rudd | Choone Farm<br>St Buryan, Penzance<br>Tel: (0736) 810220<br>Quay Shop, Penzance<br>(Self Catering Accommodation) |
| **College Reservoir** | Falmouth | Carp<br>Tench<br>Bream<br>Roach | South West Water<br>Self Service from Neighbouring Argal Reservoir |
| **Colliford Reservoir** | St Neot | Brown Trout | South West Water<br>Self Service at Reservoir |
| **Coombe Lands Coarse Fishery** | Cullompton | All Types Coarse Fish | Billingsmoor Farm<br>Butterleigh, Cullompton, Devon |
| **Crowdy Reservoir** | Camelford | Brown Trout<br>Rainbow Trout | South West Water<br>Self Service at Reservoir |
| **Darracott Reservoir** | Torrington | Carp<br>Tench<br>Bream<br>Roach<br>Rudd | South West Water<br>"Fisherman's Retreat", 7 South Street, Torrington<br>Tel: (08052) 22040 |
| **Dutson Water** | Launceston | Carp<br>Tench<br>Golden Tench<br>Rudd<br>Roach | Lower Dutson Farm<br>Launceston<br>Tel: (0566) 2607<br>(Open all year) |
| **East Batsworthy Fishery** | Tiverton | Rainbow Trout | East Batsworthy Fishery<br>Rackenford, Tiverton |
| **Exe Valley Fishery** | Dulverton | Trout | Exe Valley Fishery Ltd<br>Exbridge, Dulverton |
| **Fernworthy Reservoir** | Chagford | Brown Trout<br>Rainbow Trout | South West Water<br>Self Service at Reservoir<br>Gidleigh Park Hotel and Restaurant, Chagford |

| Water | Location | Species | Permits |
|---|---|---|---|
| **Gammaton Reservoirs** | Bideford | Brown Trout<br>Rainbow Trout | Torridge Fly Fishing Club<br>Gales Sports, 3–5 Mill Street, Bideford, Devon |
| **Golden Lake Fisheries (5 Lakes)** | Okehampton | Carp<br>Golden Tench<br>Golden Orfe<br>Trout | Angler's Paradise Holidays<br>The Gables, Winsford, Halwill, Beaworthy, Devon EX21 5XT<br>(Open all year) |
| **Hollies Trout Farm** | Honiton<br>Cullompton | Trout<br>Carp<br>Tench<br>Roach<br>Rudd<br>Bream | Hollies Trout Farm<br>Sports Shop, Cullompton<br>(Open all year) |
| **Jennetts Reservoir** | Bideford | Carp<br>Tench | South West Water<br>The Tackle Box, Unit 5, Kings Shopping Centre, Cooper Street, Bideford<br>Tel: (02372) 70043 |
| **Kennick and Tottiford Reservoirs** | Bovey Tracey | Brown Trout<br>Rainbow Trout | South West Water |
| **Lithiack Lake** | St Germans (Cornwall) | Carp<br>Tench<br>Bream<br>Roach<br>Rudd<br>Perch | R.A.B.I. Angling Club<br>Clive's Tackle and Bait, Ebrington Street, Plymouth<br>Tel: Plymouth 228940 |
| **Lower Slade Reservoir** | Ilfracombe | Carp<br>Tench<br>Bream<br>Roach | South West Water<br>Slade Post Office, Lee Road, Slade<br>Tel: (0271) 62257 |
| **Lower Tamar Reservoir** | Holsworthy | Carp<br>Tench<br>Bream<br>Dace | South West Water<br>Self Service on Site |
| **Meldon Reservoir** | Okehampton | Brown Trout<br>Rainbow Trout | South West Water<br>Free of Charge |
| **Mill Leat Trout Fishery (and River Fishing)** | Holsworthy | Rainbow Trout<br>(Brown Trout in River) | Mill Leat Trout Fishery<br>Thornbury, Holsworthy, Devon<br>'DIY' Centre, 25 The Square, Holsworthy |
| **Newhouse Fishery** | Totnes | Rainbow Trout<br>Brown Trout | Newhouse Farm<br>Moreleigh, Totnes, Devon<br>(Open all year) |
| **Old Mill Reservoir** | Dartmouth | Carp<br>Tench<br>Roach | South West Water<br>"Sportsman's Rendezvous", 16 Fairfax Place, Dartmouth<br>Tel: (080 43) 3509 day<br>(080 421) 282 eves |
| **Oxenleaze Farm Coarse Fishery** | Wiveliscombe | Carp<br>Tench | Oxenleaze Farm Caravans<br>Chipstable, Wiveliscombe, Somerset<br>Tel: (0984) 23427<br>Free to Residents<br>Open all year |

| Water | Location | Species | Permits |
|---|---|---|---|
| **Porth Reservoir** | Newquay | Rainbow Trout | South West Water<br>Self Service at Reservoir<br>Contact Ranger for Boats<br>Tel: (0326) 72544 |
| **Preston Ponds** | Kingsteignton | Carp<br>Tench<br>Roach<br>Rudd | Newton Abbot Fishing Association<br>Local Tackle Shops |
| **Rackerhayes Ponds** | Kingsteignton | Tench<br>Carp<br>Roach<br>Pike<br>Eels<br>Rudd | Newton Abbot Fishing Association<br>Local Tackle Shops |
| **Retallack Waters** | St Columb | Carp<br>Tench<br>Bream<br>Roach<br>Rudd | Retallack Park<br>St Columb, Cornwall<br>Tel: (0637) 880174<br>At Shop/Cafe at Car Park<br>(Open all year) |
| **St Tinney Farm** | Camelford | Brown Trout<br>Rainbow Trout<br>Carp<br>Tench<br>Rudd | St Tinney Farm Holidays<br>Otterham, Camelford, Cornwall PL32 9TA<br>Free Fishing, Restricted to Residents of Caravans/Tents on Farm |
| **Shillamill Lakes** | Looe | Carp<br>Tench<br>Crucian Carp<br>Roach<br>Rudd | Shillamill Lakes<br>Lanreath, Looe, Cornwall<br>Tel: 0503 20271<br>Shop on site<br>Self Service Unit<br>(Open all year) |
| **Siblyback Reservoir** | Liskeard | Brown Trout<br>Rainbow Trout | South West Water<br>Self Service at Reservoir |
| **Slapton Ley** | Kingsbridge | Pike<br>Perch<br>Roach<br>Rudd<br>Eel | Slapton Ley Field Centre<br>Slapton, Nr Kingsbridge, South Devon<br>Tel: Kingsbridge 580466<br>Boat Fishing Only<br>(Open all year) |
| **South Farm Holidays** | Cullompton | Carp<br>Tench<br>Roach | South Farm<br>Blackborough, Cullompton, Devon<br>Free Fishing for Self Catering Guests Only |
| **Spurtham Fishery (and River Fishing)** | Upottery | Rainbow Trout | Spurtham Fishery Ltd<br>Spurtham Farm, Upottery, Nr Honiton<br>Tel: Upottery 209 |
| **Squabmoor Reservoir** | Exmouth | Carp<br>Tench<br>Bream<br>Roach | South West Water<br>Knowle Post Office<br>The Tackle Shop, Exmouth<br>Exeter Angling Centre, Fore Street, Exeter<br>(Open all year) |
| **Stafford Moor Fishery** | Winkleigh | Rainbow Trout<br>Brown Trout | Stafford Moor Fishery<br>Dolton, Winkleigh, North Devon EX19 8RQ<br>Tel: Dolton 360/371/363<br>(Pay Pond open all year) |
| **Stithians Reservoir** | Redruth | Brown Trout<br>Rainbow Trout | South West Water<br>Golden Lion Inn, Menhenon |

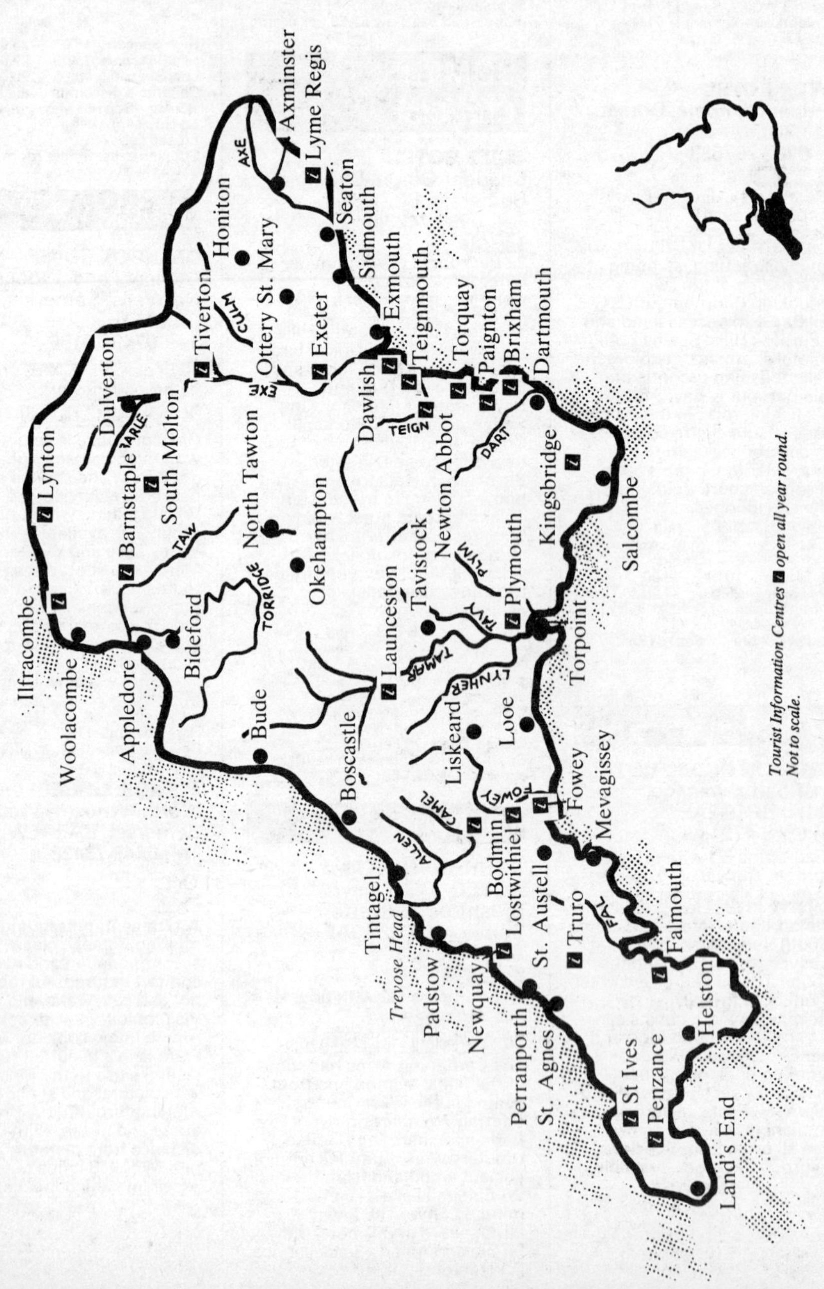

Axminster
Lyme Regis
Seaton
Honiton
Sidmouth
Ottery St. Mary
Exmouth
Tiverton
Exeter
Teignmouth
Torquay
Paignton
Brixham
Dartmouth
Dulverton
Dawlish
Newton Abbot
Kingsbridge
Salcombe
Lynton
Barnstaple
South Molton
North Tawton
Okehampton
Tavistock
Plymouth
Torpoint
Ilfracombe
Woolacombe
Appledore
Bideford
Launceston
Bude
Boscastle
Liskeard
Looe
Fowey
Mevagissey
Bodmin
Lostwithiel
St. Austell
Truro
Falmouth
Tintagel
Trevose Head
Padstow
Newquay
Perranporth
St. Agnes
St Ives
Penzance
Helston
Land's End
AXE
CULM
EXE
BARLE
TAW
TORRIDGE
TEIGN
DART
PLYM
TAVY
TAMAR
LYNHER
CAMEL
ALLEN
FOWEY
FAL
Tourist Information Centres open all year round.
Not to scale.

| Water | Location | Species | Permits |
|---|---|---|---|
| **Stone Lake** | Okehampton | Carp<br>Tench<br>Bream<br>Roach<br>Rudd<br>Perch | Stone Farm<br>Bridestowe, Okehampton, Devon EX20 4NR<br>(Open all year)<br>Bed and Breakfast mid-May to mid-September |
| **Stout Trout Fishery** | Cullompton | Rainbow Trout | Billingmoor Farm<br>Butterleigh, Cullompton, Devon EX15 1PQ<br>(Open all year) |
| **Tin Deen** | Penzance | Carp<br>Roach<br>Rudd | G.J. Laity and Son<br>Bostrase Farm, Goldsithney,<br>Penzance Tel: (073 676) 3486 |
| **Trewcreek Lakes** | St Austell | Carp<br>Tench<br>Roach<br>Rudd<br>Crucian Carp | Trewcreek Farm Holiday Park<br>Hewaswater, St Austell, Cornwall |
| **Upper Slade Reservoir** | Ilfracombe | Rainbow Trout | South West Water<br>Slade Post Office, Lee Road, Ilfracombe<br>Tel: (0271) 62257<br>(Limited to 12 Permits)<br>(Open all year) |
| **Upper Tamar Reservoir** | Holsworthy | Rainbow Trout<br>Brown Trout | South West Water<br>Self Service at Reservoir |
| **Venford Reservoir** | Ashburton | Brown Trout<br>Brook Trout | South West Water<br>Free of Charge |
| **Wimbleball Reservoir** | Dulverton | Brown Trout<br>Rainbow Trout | South West Water<br>Self Service at Reservoir<br>Bookable in advance from Ranger |
| **Wistlandpound Reservoir** | South Molton | Trout | South West Water<br>Wistlandpound Fly Fishing Club<br>Self Service at Reservoir |
| **Woodlay Farm Lakes** | Cornwall | Carp<br>Tench<br>Crucian Carp<br>Roach | Woodlay Holidays, Cornwall<br>Tel: (0503) 20221 (08406) 563<br>Free Fishing Restricted to Holiday Guests Only<br>(Open all year) |

# SEA ANGLING

### Lyme Regis

The harbour at Lyme Regis tends to dry out at low water but adjacent beaches are fishable at most states of the tide. The entire area is good for bass fishing. Church Beach, Church Cliff Beach and Western Beach are the favourite local venues. They produce conger, bass, skate, wrasse, flatfish, mullet and the occasional good-sized tope. Boat fishing in Lyme Regis is generally quite good, skate being extremely common at most times of the year.

### Seaton

Noted for its big bass, Seaton Beach is well worth a visit. One of the best places to fish is at the estuary of the River Axe. This is often thick with shoaling mullet and anyone who likes mullet fishing will be well advised to try their luck here. Bass, and flatfish also run into this narrow waterway and at various times some pretty hefty bass have been caught in this area. Boat fishing off Seaton is good. Skate, conger, bream, dogfish, pollack, mackerel and garfish are plentiful. This is quite a good area to dinghy fish, although the rather steep shingle beach can make launching and beaching a boat difficult in all but calm seas.

**South Devon Coast**

Most anglers who visit this area automatically gravitate towards Brixham. During the past decade Brixham has become a sort of Mecca for boat fishermen from all over the British Isles and also from the Continent. Most of these anglers come for the wreck-fishing. Due to the amount of publicity given to these huge catches, few anglers realise that the south coast of Devon can offer a wide variety of good shore and inshore fishing. The whole stretch of rugged coastline is more than capable of giving good fishing, albeit with mini-monsters.

Big wrasse and bass abound and there are many places where the shore and inshore dinghy fisherman can expect to catch conger eels of up to, and possibly just over, 40 lbs. Do not make the mistake of underestimating, or in any way overlooking, the fine fishing potential of this rich and varied coastline.

**Exmouth to Plymouth**

**Exmouth**

A popular holiday resort, Exmouth has good fishing. School bass and flounders are very common in this area, particularly from Bull Hill Bank and Shelley Gut. Orcombe Point Beach and Rocks provide good mixed fishing for conger, bass, wrasse, flatfish, dogfish and the very occasional tope. Night fishing from the old jetty and Exmouth Pier can provide good sport, particularly with small conger eels. Dangerous tides make small boat fishing difficult, although offshore marks can produce good mixed catches.

**Teignmouth**

This is basically a flatfish and bass area. Local anglers fish the river a great deal using live sand eels as bass bait and ragworm for flatfish. Small boat fishing within the river mouth can produce splendid catches of big plaice and medium sized bass. Grey mullet are also very common in the river, although few anglers fish for them. During the winter months good catches of big flounders can be made from marks in the river. A rolling leger or baited spoon is the best terminal rig to use for these fish.

**Torquay**

The most noted mark in the Torquay area is Hope's Nose, a peninsula which can be reached via the Marine Drive. Hope's Nose is one of those all round marks which constantly produces surprise catches. In past seasons the Nose has produced award-winning wrasse, plaice, conger, bass and even oddities like angler fish.

It is also a favourite mackerel fishing station and can usually be relied upon to produce good bags of prime mackerel to float and spinning tackle. Anglers who have plenty of time and patience to spare will be well advised to try for grey mullet around the Nose, for at times huge shoals come into this area to feed.

Apart from Hope's Nose, Watcombe, Anstey's Cove and Abbey Sands are well worth fishing. All are capable of producing mixed fishing, although Hope's Nose is by far the best shore station in the area. Torquay Harbour provides plenty of pier jetty fishing. These spots are good for flatfish, mackerel, garfish, bass, mullet and fair-sized conger eels. Dinghy fishing off Torquay is generally good.

**Brixham**

Quite apart from the excellence of its offshore boat fishing grounds, Brixham yields good catches to the shore fisherman and inshore dinghy angler. The most popular shore fishing venue is the breakwater. This spot is often used for club and interclub competitions. Big wrasse are often caught from the breakwater in quantity and at one time many competitions were won with this species.

During the summer months the holiday crowds make most of the local beaches unfishable. At night, however, most beaches fish well for a wide variety of species. Night fishing sessions on the breakwater produce catches of conger and the usual spate of monster-conger stories. In most cases these stories are factual. Apart from wrasse and conger, the breakwater also produces pouting, mackerel, mullet, garfish, pollack and the usual flatfish. Anglers wishing to boat-fish can either launch their own craft or hire small boats by the hour, half-day or day from the beach at St Mary's Bay. Small-boat fishing in the Brixham area is good. Quite apart from the species encountered by the shore angler, it is possible to catch tope, monkfish, skate and even the odd cod while inshore boat fishing. A running leger employing one or at the most two hooks is the best terminal rig to use. There are some very hefty wrasse to be had in the Brixham area and the best way of catching these big fish is to employ the one bait that most big wrasse just cannot refuse — a prawn. Offshore marks produce a variety of big fish. Wreck fishing is particularly productive for conger, ling, cod, pollack and coalfish.

*A fine plaice — Dartmouth*

**Dartmouth**
Now primarily a wreck-fishing centre, Dartmouth is also capable of producing good shore and inshore boat fishing. Nearby Slapton Sands, Blackpool Sands and Compass Cove provide the beach enthusiast with plenty of scope, while the quay and harbour wall give directly on to the Dart Estuary. This estuary is something of a fish haven; a worm, crab or fish bait cast well out into the tidal stream will normally catch fish fairly quickly. Flounders are very common in the Dart, as too are bass and thornback skate. The thornback skate are particularly interesting. They are fairly plentiful, grow to a reasonable size and provide good sport on beach casting tackle. Peeler crab is the best bait for these fish, although mackerel fillets can also be effective. Boat fishing within the Dart estuary can be very productive; bass are often encountered in fair numbers and a light leger baited with sand-eel or ragworm is the best way of catching these fine fish. Over the nearby Bank good catches of big plaice and turbot are made.

**Salcombe**
Salcombe is a good bass fishing station. The various beaches provide ample opportunity for shore casting, with ragworm as the best local bait. Apart from bass, Salcombe and its surrounding coastline fishes well for wrasse, conger, skate, flatfish, mackerel and pollack. Inshore boat fishing can be good. Live sand-eels make the best bait but, at a pinch, elongated slivers of mackerel, cut to resemble a sand-eel, will catch plenty of good fish.

Boat fishermen at Salcombe often catch a bonus fish in the shape of a huge turbot. The grounds off Salcombe are in fact ideally suited for turbot and many of these succulent flatfish fall to baits intended for bass. At Downderry there is plenty of scope for all styles of rock fishing and I have had some good pollack in this area on artificial lures.

**Plymouth to Mevagissey**

**Plymouth**
The shore fishing marks to head for in this area are Bolt Tail, to the east of Plymouth, Stoke Point and Rame Head, on the mouth of the Yealm. The beautiful Yealm estuary is a good area to dig worm bait and the river mouth itself is a fine place to fish. Like most estuaries, the Yealm produces a good selection of fish species. Plaice, and during the winter, heavyweight flounders are often caught in fair quantities and for the angler with bigger fish in mind, running leger tackle baited with fish strip or sand-eel bait will attract good-sized thornback skate and some really hefty specimen small-eyed ray. There is always the chance of breaking the existing rod-caught record for the species, for very big small-eyed ray are known to use the Yealm area as a feeding ground. Unlike thornback ray, which tend to be out-and-out scavengers, the small eyed ray is a comparatively fussy eater. The best bait for this species is a really fresh, large sand-eel.

**Rame Head**
This headland, one of the biggest natural projections in the English Channel, provides an excellent base for all kinds of rock-fishing expeditions. Big wrasse are common off the Rame and good pollack, bass and conger can also be caught. At many points on this coastline the rocks drop sheer away into very deep water. Many rock gullies hold a fair depth of water even at low tide, and will produce surprisingly larger conger.
Conger eels are by nature a rock-living species and the tumbled granite rocks off the Devon, and particularly the Cornish, coastlines provide them with ample shelter and a superabundant food supply in the shape of wrasse, pollack, crabs and worms.

**Looe**
Traditional home of the Cornish shark fleet and the Shark Club, Looe has plenty to offer the angler. For those who like to ring the changes as much as possible, Looe is an ideal base. Float fishing from the Banjo Pier will produce mackerel, pollack, and wrasse, while in the river mouth it is possible to bottom fish for flounders and the odd plaice. To add spice to a holiday, it is not a bad idea to have a day out on a Looe sharking boat or book a seat on a charter boat that specialises in reef fishing. Weather permitting, many of these reef-fishing boats operate over marks situated near the Eddystone Lighthouse. This is a most exciting area to fish. Anglers who own their own boats and have a reasonable amount of sea experience might well like to try their hand at bass fishing off the Eddystone Reef.

**Fowey**
Fowey has long since been noted for its bass fishing and it is usually possible to hire a self-drive boat to take full advantage of the bass marks within the river itself as well as out in the open sea.
Fowey bass specialists normally use live sand eels as bait, although for the reef marks outside the river, artificial eels have proved to be highly effective. The estuary of the Fowey offers immense possibilities for all sorts of fishing, although bass are the most sought-after species.
Apart from its magnificent bass fishing, Fowey River holds a wide variety of sport fish. Conger, some being of prodigious size, lurk round the quays, jetties and river marks and the river is often thick with good-sized thornback skate. Small boat anglers often tie up to the huge buoys below the china clay jetties and it is from these mid-river marks that the main skate catches are made.
To catch consistently in the Fowey the best bait to use is soft-back or peeler crabs. These moulting crabs can be collected at low water from under weed-covered rocks. The foreshore below the jetty at Goulant is an ideal crab-collecting area, although at a pinch almost any likely section of foreshore will do. For the angler who prefers a more active style of fishing, flounder and plaice provide the ideal targets. These interesting, active flatfish can be caught either from the shore or from a boat. The

most killing technique for both fish is to spin with a very large baited spoon rig. The stretch of the river known as Sawmills is the best place for big 'flatties' and it is from this point approximately midway between Golant and Fowey, that many immense specimen flounders have been taken. The grey mullet is very common in the Fowey River, vast shoals being present throughout the summer and early autumn months. Few anglers try to catch these elusive fish.

**Par**
Situated between Fowey and St Austell, Par offers plenty of beach fishing for plaice, bass and the occasional sole. Bass fishing can be very good at times, particularly after a gale when the water has been churned up to a soup-like consistency. Similar in many ways is the beach at Pentewan nearer to Mevagissey. I have had excellent catches of smallish bass from this beach and during the early part of the year some good-sized plaice in the bay make a welcome addition to the day's fishing. Ragworm can be dug at Pentewan and local anglers often dig over the beach to get white ragworm, an absolutely deadly fish-catcher.

**Mevagissey**
Long-famous as a holiday and fishing centre, Mevagissey is nowadays one of the major wreck-fishing and shark-fishing ports in the West Country and big boats leave the port daily, bound for distant-water wrecks. Not all the fishing round Mevagissey has to be done from big boats — the whole of the bay area offers ample opportunity for small-boat fishermen to try their luck. Good catches of pollack, conger, mackerel, garfish, dog-fish and wrasse can be taken at various points round the bay. The rocks adjacent to the headland at Chapel Point are often thick with fair-sized pollack which can be caught on feathers or on ragworm. Worm bait used in this area invariably produces some big wrasse to add interest to the day's fishing. Self-drive boats can be hired in the outer harbour.
For the shore fishing enthusiast, Mevagissey and its adjacent beaches can provide tremendous fishing. To the east and only reachable by a long walk up past the coastguard station, lie two very isolated beaches, Big Polstreath and Little Polstreath. These are divided by a spear-point of rock which in turn is split. The outer end of this natural barrier is a good place to fish on a falling tide but care must be taken to move back as the tide begins to rise, otherwise it is possible to get cut off completely from the shore. Polstreath can on occasion produce a wide variety of fish. Bass, including some very big fish, often frequent this beach and, on the rocky extremities of either beach, wrasse and pollack can usually be caught in quantity.
Lighthouse Quay and the Island Quay on the east side of the harbour-entrance provide plenty of scope for the shore fisherman. Float-fishing for mackerel and garfish is a favourite style of angling from the Lighthouse Quay, strips of fresh mackerel and garfish making the best bait. Similar tactics using worm baits on either the Lighthouse Quay or the Island Quay produce wrasse in plenty and the occasional pollack and big bass. Both quays have produced bass and pollack of over 10 lbs, often caught by anglers who have been fishing for mackerel.
The quays at Mevagissey provide good bottom-fishing, particularly for conger eels. In years gone by the Lighthouse Quay has produced conger of over 70 lb on heavy handline tackle, and rod and line anglers have taken conger to 50 lb from this same quay.
Apart from the fish already mentioned, many other species of fish can occasionally be caught round the quay walls. Red bream, dog-fish, John Dory, horse mackerel, mullet, plaice, big wrasse and many smaller species as well. The Lighthouse Quay, facing the open sea, can also spring the occasional surprise. One lucky angler fishing a light, single-hook nylon paternoster rig struck at a gentle bite and found himself firmly attached to a monster turbot. This fish surprisingly enough was played out and gaffed on extremely light line. Later it officially tipped the scales at a fraction over 18 lb. Yet another angler, bottom fishing for conger, hooked a heavy, but slow-moving, fish, which subsequently turned out to be a 43 lb monkfish.
Over the hill from

Mevagissey, the tiny beach at Port Mellon Cove can provide some fair fishing for small bass and the occasional conger. This beach is a good place to rake for live sand-eels. Port Mellon is also useful as a place to leave a car before starting the long walk out to the magnificent rock gullies round Chapel Point. This is a favourite headland with wrasse anglers for the many, often easily accessible rock gullies around Chapel Point can, if fished properly, produce immense catches of big wrasse. The best ways to fish this area for wrasse are to float-fish or paternoster a hard-backed crab bait in the deeper gullies. Anglers who prefer to catch other fish will find spinning for pollack and the occasional bass most rewarding. Between Chapel Point and the massive loom of the Dodman Point lies a wealth of good fishing. Rock-fishing enthusiasts are well advised to explore the entire area, for pollack, wrasse, bass and conger are common in all the deeper gullies and light float-fishing from ledges which face directly out to sea will produce mackerel and big garfish as well.
Off Gorran Haven there is plenty to interest the small-boat angler. The varied nature of the sea bed in this area provides a rich feeding ground for many kinds of fish. Offshore, the stark Gwineas Rock is worth trying on calm days for bass and big pollack.
Bottom-fishing throughout the bay will produce dog-fish, skate, conger, bull huss, wrasse, tope, pollack and red bream. Spinning or trolling is often used here to take big bass, mackerel, garfish and pollack. The bass and pollack normally fall to red-gill eels trolled well behind the boat.

**Mevagissey, to Falmouth**
Between Mevagissey and Falmouth miles of craggy indented coastline provide a wealth of almost untapped fishing: beaches, bays, coves and rock gullies proliferate in a wild confusion. This is wrasse, bass and big conger country. Almost any part of this coastline fishes well and much of its potential is at best barely scratched by local and visiting fishermen. This is a coastline which can produce surprise catches. More than one monster angler-fish has been taken by shore fishermen here and at times, particularly in the late autumn, some very hefty conger move inshore to feed within casting range of the rocks. Much of this coastline is controlled by the National Trust and most of the sea shore is accessible by public footpaths.
However, many good fishing spots are quite a hike from the nearest car park and many involve awkward scrambles down fairly steep cliffs. Because of these natural hazards, much of the fishing is unexploited. Anglers who do not mind a walk and a scramble will discover many hot-spot sites that rarely get fished more than once a season.

**Falmouth**
Basically a boat-fishing centre, Falmouth and its adjacent harbour area offers little for the shore fisherman, the only exception being mullet. Mullet can be taken in Penryn Harbour, or from the Customs House Quay or the Prince of Wales Pier.
Boat fishing inside Falmouth harbour can be quite good, flatfish, bass and the occasional skate being the most common species encountered.

**Penzance**
Penzance has a great deal to offer the shore fisherman. For miles on either side of the town there are plenty of good shore fishing venues. Penzance is an ideal point from which to reach both the south and north coast fishing grounds. Treen, Sennen Cove, Logan Rocks, Eastern Green, St Michael's Mount, Porth Curna and Looe Bar are just a very few of the many productive fishing spots that are situated within striking range. Most of these spots are easily reached, but there are dozens of less accessible places, all of which can provide good fishing with either beach-casting, float-fishing or spinning tackle. Bait can be dug on most of the beaches in the Penzance area. Lugworm is the favourite local bait. Sand-eels can be raked at Sennen Cove.

**Newquay**
Newquay and its adjacent area have a great deal to offer the visiting angler. The north coast of Cornwall is good for bass fishing and Newquay's adjacent beaches provide ample scope for shore casting. The beaches to head for are Great Western, Fistral, Watergate, Towan, Tolcarne, Porth, Lusty Glaze, Crantock and Whipsiderry. Apart from these spots there is plenty of

rock fishing available, but be careful: big seas are common and to avoid serious accidents due to high tides or freak wave patterns, the rock angler should only fish in calm weather and even then he must keep an eye on tide flow and wave action.
Most local anglers travel to Trevose Head for serious rock fishing. Trevose Head is noted for wrasse, tope and small-eyed ray. The tope and small-eyed ray are normally caught on leger tackle baited with fresh sand-eel. The big wrasse fall mainly to worm or crab bait. Trevose Head can easily produce tope and small-eyed ray in excess of the present record sizes.
The north and south quays of Newquay Harbour are worth fishing, particularly for mackerel, bass, garfish, mullet, conger and wrasse.
Small-boat fishing is not to be recommended anywhere round Newquay or, for that matter, anywhere along the north Cornish coastline which faces directly out into the Atlantic. Bad tides and heavy seas are extremely common and unless you are a very experienced boat-handler with intimate knowledge of this rugged coastline it is very easy to get into serious trouble very quickly indeed.

**Bude**
Bude is another good fishing centre. Beaches like Widemouth Bay, Summerleaze Beach, Sandy Mouth and Crooklets Beach are all good for catching bass and flatfish. The breakwater at Summerleaze is worth a try, although it seldom fishes as well as the beaches.
Boat fishing off Bude is often difficult, although by picking the right conditions and keeping a weather eye open it is possible to go afloat. Boat fishermen anchoring or drifting over local inshore marks take mackerel, garfish, pollack, bass, flatfish, conger eels, tope, wrasse and pouting. Best baits are again live or freshly-killed sandeels. If these are unobtainable, strips of fillets of mackerel make a good substitute. For shore fishing, ragworm, lugworm and peeler crab make the best baits. North of Bude the coastline becomes increasingly rugged, providing ample scope for a wide variety of fishing possibilities. Local boats operating along this coastline take immense catches of large porbeagle shark, fish weighing over 200 lb being relatively common.

**Bideford and Appledore**
Both these ports now provide charter boat services which concentrate mainly on porbeagle shark fishing. At times these sharks are so numerous over the inshore grounds that they can make a considerable and dangerous nuisance of themselves to dinghy and small boat anglers. A favourite trick of the local shark population is to snatch at mackerel or pollack which have been hooked by boat fishing anglers. The shark are so persistent that at times anglers are forced to stop fishing and go back to port to avoid the fish-stealing porbeagle. Naturally, a big shark, hooked from a small boat, can be a nasty customer to deal with and few anglers care to match tackle and strength with these giants from the confines of a small boat.
Quite apart from shark, the Bideford-Appledore area is basically a good fishing locality. There is good shore fishing, particularly for bass and flatfish. Favourite local stations are Greysand, the estuary of the River Torridge near the iron railway bridge. For the pier or harbour angler Bideford Quay is well worth a visit. Apart from the fish already mentioned, the offshore grounds yield skate, tope, conger, ling, black and red bream, dog-fish, pouting and the occasional cod.

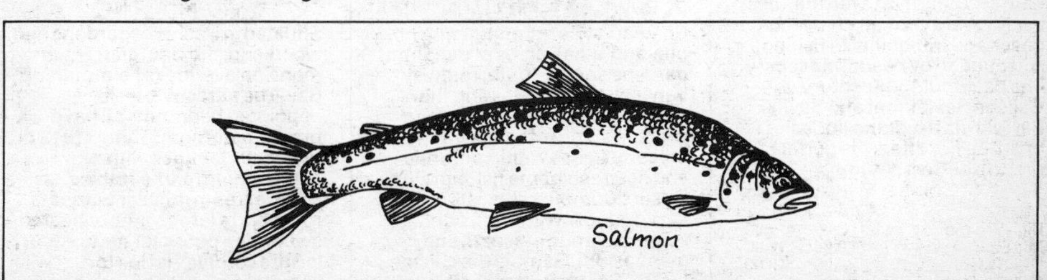
Salmon

# ACCOMMODATION

## CORNWALL
### Bude

**BURN COURT HOTEL**
Burn View, Bude, Cornwall, EX23 8DB
Tel: 0288 2872

35 Bedrooms (22 with private bathroom/shower).

M T LF LP HT

The hotel adjoins the quiet little town and is only 100 yards from the Downs and a short walk to the Summerleaze and Crooklets beaches. All shops and facilities are within a few minutes walk. Burn Court Hotel is under the personal supervision of the resident proprietors. All 35 rooms are centrally heated. Radio/intercom and tea/coffee-making facilities in all rooms. RAC two-star and Ashley Courtenay recommended.

| | Bed Only £ | B&B £ | Half Board £ |
|---|---|---|---|
| High Season | 20.00 | 28.00 | 36.00 |
| Mid Season | 18.00 | 26.00 | 32.00 |
| Low Season | 16.00 | 24.00 | 30.00 |

Children's discounts available
**HS** Jul–Aug **MS** May, Jun, Sep
**LS** Oct–Apr
Supplements: Room with bath/shower & WC £1 per person per night

**THE TREE INN HOTEL**
Fore Street, Stratton, Bude, Cornwall, EX23 9DA
Tel: 0288 2038/2931
7 Bedrooms

M T LF LP AL HT

This unique, historical and charming old inn offers the warmth, comfort and facilities you are looking for. Whatever your fishing needs they are all here and only five to ten minutes away where you can enjoy the peace and tranquility of fishing surrounded by beautiful scenery. The beautiful 13th-century Galleon Restaurant and Beville Bar with its flagstone floor and open log fire offers the perfect end to a perfect day.

| | Bed only £ | B & B £ |
|---|---|---|
| High Season | 9.00 | 11.00 |
| Mid Season | 9.00 | 11.00 |
| Low Season | 8.00 | 10.00 |

Children's discounts available
**HS** Jul–Sep **MS** Apr–Jun
**LS** Oct–Mar
Supplements: Half Board prices on request

### Falmouth

**BUDOCK VEAN HOTEL**
Mawnan Smith, Falmouth, Cornwall, TR11 5LG
Tel: 0326 250288

53 Bedrooms (All with private bathroom/shower).

M T LF LP AL HT

This country house hotel is set in 65 acres of subtropical gardens on the picturesque Helford River and offers many cosy traditional charms as well as the modern comforts that are the hallmark of a top class hotel. The hotel is within easy reach of the sea as well as the Argall and Stithians reservoirs which both offer game fishing. There is also a 9-hole golf course, indoor swimming pool, tennis courts and private foreshore.

| | Bed Only £ | B&B £ | Half Board £ |
|---|---|---|---|
| High Season | 33.50 | 38.50 | 48.50 |
| Mid Season | 27.50 | 32.50 | 42.50 |
| Low Season | 20.75 | 25.75 | 35.75 |

Children's discounts available
**HS** 29 Jun–28 Sep
**MS** Mar–28 Jun
**LS** 29 Sep–5 Jan, excl Christmas
Closed Jan–Feb
Supplements: Single room £1.50. £3 per day for dogs

**GREEN LAWNS HOTEL**
Western Terrace, Falmouth, Cornwall, TR11 4QJ
Tel: 0326 312734

41 Bedrooms (39 with private bathroom/shower).

M T LF LP AL HT

Chateau-style hotel standing in one-and-a-half acres of delightful gardens, facing south, midway between the beaches and the town. First-class fly fishing and coarse fishing is found within 2 miles, beaches within one mile and deep sea/game fishing. Our Leisure Complex consists of a large indoor swimming pool, sauna, solarium, jacuzzi, and gymnasium. Sample the cuisine in 'The Garras Restaurant', renowned for local seafood, steaks and chef's specialities.

| | B&B £ | Half Board £ |
|---|---|---|
| High Season | 24.00 | 34.00 |
| Low Season | 19.00 | 29.00 |

Children's discounts available
**HS** Jun–Sep
**LS** Oct–May
Supplements: Single room £8

**HOTEL ST. MICHAELS**
Gyllyngvase Beach, Seafront, Falmouth, Cornwall, TR11 4NB
Tel: 0326 312707

75 Bedrooms (All with private bathroom/shower).

M T LP AL

A hotel for all seasons where winter really is warmer. All year round wreck fishing and coarse fishing at nearby College and Argal Reservoirs (10 minutes drive). All rooms have private bathroom, colour TV, telephone and tea/coffee-making facilities. Renowned for excellent cuisine. Indoor pool, sauna, solarium, jacuzzi, trimnasium, tennis, squash and watersports.

| | B&B £ | Half Board £ |
|---|---|---|
| High Season | 31.00 | 43.00 |
| Mid Season | 29.00 | 41.00 |
| Low Season | 27.00 | 39.00 |

Children's discounts available
**HS** 24 May–26 Sep
**MS** 1 Apr–23 May, 27 Sep–31 Oct
**LS** 1 Nov–31 Mar
Supplements: Single room £4

**PENMERE MANOR HOTEL**
Mongleath Road, Falmouth, Cornwall, TR11 4PN
Tel: 0326 314545

33 Bedrooms (All with private bathroom/shower).

M T LP

Situated in 5 acres of gardens and woodland, the Georgian mansion overlooks Falmouth Bay. The attractive, well-appointed bedrooms all have private bathroom. There are two residents' lounges with compendium games tables, a snooker room, a cellar games room and a large outdoor heated swimming pool. Our new indoor leisure complex is due for completion in 1987.

| | B & B | Half Board |
|---|---|---|
| | £ | £ |
| High Season | 26.00 | 35.75 |
| Mid Season | 24.00 | 31.25 |
| Low Season | 22.00 | 30.50 |

Children's discounts available
**HS** 22 May–22 Oct **MS** 27 Mar–21 May
**LS** 23 Oct–26 Mar Closed 19 Dec–27 Dec
Supplements: Double or twin room occupancy by single £10 per night

## Gunnislake

**HINGSTON HOUSE**
St. Ann's Chapel, Gunnislake, Cornwall, PL18 9BE
Tel: 0822 832468

8 Bedrooms (2 with private bathroom/shower).

M T LF LP AL HT

Beautiful country house in lovely grounds with spectacular views of Tamar Valley. Central heating, tea/coffee-making facilities in all rooms, licensed bar with 'Snug', spacious sitting room, each with log fires in winter months. Ample storage space for fishing tackle. Personal service by owners includes excellent home cooking using own and local produce. Central for Tamar, Sibleyback, Burratoh and Crowdy Lakes; sea fishing from Plymouth or north coast.

| | B & B | Half Board |
|---|---|---|
| | £ | £ |
| High Season | 11.50 | 18.50 |

Children's discounts available

## Hayle

**GLENCOE HOUSE HOTEL**
Churchtown Road, Gwithian, Nr. Hayle, Cornwall, TR27 5BX
Tel: 0736 752216

11 Bedrooms (All with private bathroom/shower).

M T LF LP AL HT

When it comes to fishing we've got the lot. Beach casting, with direct access to St. Ives Bay, deep sea, wrecking or trolling and coarse, there is no close season in Cornwall. We are a friendly, relaxed hotel on outskirts of picturesque village. Superb cuisine with extensive a la carte and table d'hote menus. Full central heating, cosy bar, 2 four-poster beds, heated indoor swimming pool and very good service. Any 5 nights £135 including dinner, breakfast and VAT.

| | B & B | Half Board |
|---|---|---|
| | £ | £ |
| High Season | 23.00 | 29.00 |
| Mid Season | 22.00 | 28.00 |
| Low Season | 21.00 | 24.00 |

Children's discounts available
**HS** mid Jul–mid Sep
**MS** mid May–mid Jul
**LS** mid Sep–mid May
Supplements: Single room £4.50

## Helston

**TREGILDRY HOTEL**
Gillan, Manaccan, Helston, Cornwall, TR12 6HG
Tel: 032623 378

11 Bedrooms (7 with private bathroom/shower).

M T LF HT

Situated overlooking Falmouth Bay. Large and small boats available for deep sea, wreck and off shore fishing. Family-run hotel. Warm, comfortable bedrooms, many en-suite. Guide recommended for food. Away from crowds. Many coastal walks. Party bookings up to 20 persons.

| | B & B | Half Board |
|---|---|---|
| | £ | £ |
| High Season | 25.00 | 30.00 |
| Mid Season | 20.00 | 25.00 |
| Low Season | 18.00 | 22.00 |

Children's discounts available
**HS** 11 Jul–31 Aug **MS** Jun, Sep
**LS** Apr, May, Oct Closed 1 Nov–Easter
Supplements: Room with bath/shower & WC £2. Single room £5

## Liskeard

**BADHAM FARM**
St. Keyne, Liskeard, Cornwall, PL14 4RW Tel: 0579 43572

5 Bedrooms (1 with private bathroom/shower).

M T LF LP AL

At Badham Farm in the peaceful Looe Valley, near Looe, we have a choice of accommodation for your fishing holiday: 4 luxury self-catering cottages/ apartments or B & B in our guest house. Guests may use our new coarse fishing lake, stocked with carp, tench, rudd etc. Tennis court, putting green, laundry, games room, play area, pets' paddock, parking, licensed lounge bar in farmhouse where meals/snacks are available. Personal attention.

| | B & B | Half Board |
|---|---|---|
| | £ | £ |
| High Season | 12.50 | 19.50 |
| Low Season | 11.50 | 18.50 |

Children's discounts available
**HS** Jul, Aug **LS** Mar–Jun, Sep–Dec
Closed Jan–Feb

## Looe

**POLRAEN COUNTRY HOUSE HOTEL** Sandplace, Nr. Looe, Cornwall, PL13 1PJ
Tel: 05036 3956

5 Bedrooms (All with private bathroom/shower).

M LF LP AL HT

This fully licensed, country house hotel situated in 2½ acres of landscaped gardens is set in the peaceful Looe Valley two miles from Looe and within easy reach of all major towns in Cornwall. All rooms have private bathroom and there is a wealth of home cooked food.

| | B & B | Half Board |
|---|---|---|
| | £ | £ |
| High Season | 17.00 | 25.00 |
| Mid Season | 16.00 | 24.00 |
| Low Season | 15.00 | 23.00 |

Children's discounts available
**HS** Apr–Oct **MS** Jan–Mar
**LS** Nov–Dec

## Lostwithiel

**CAROTEL**
19 Castle Hill, Lostwithiel, Cornwall PL22 0DD
Tel: 0208 872223

32 Bedrooms (All with private bathroom/shower).

M T LP AL HT

The Carotel is ideally situated in Lostwithiel which is on the River Fowey for salmon/trout fishing. The River Tamar is only 30 minutes drive away. South west water have many reservoirs within easy drive and there is coarse fishing nearby at Shillamill Lakes. Excellent sea-fishing centres of Fowey, Looe and Mevagissey are close by. All facilities can be arranged in advance to make a varied and memorable holiday.

| | Bed Only | B & B | Half Board |
|---|---|---|---|
| | £ | £ | £ |
| High Season | 15.00 | 17.00 | 22.50 |
| Mid Season | 13.00 | 15.00 | 20.50 |
| Low Season | 10.00 | 12.00 | 15.50 |

Children's discounts available
**HS** Jun–Sep **MS** Apr, May, Oct
**LS** Nov–Mar
Supplements: Single room £5.

See page 4 for details of symbols

## Mevagissey

**TREMARNE HOTEL**
Polkirt, Mevagissey, St. Austell, Cornwall, PL26 6UY
Tel: 0726 842213

14 Bedrooms (All with private bathroom/shower).

M T LF HT

Ashley Courtenay recommended, AA, RAC two-star hotel, situated in the delightful Cornish fishing village of Mevagissey. A comfortable hotel with all bedrooms en-suite. Colour TV, radio and tea-making facilities in all rooms. Outdoor heated swimming pool open from mid May to mid September. Reservation can be made for wreck or shark fishing from the hotel either by charter or individual bookings.

| | B & B £ | Half Board £ |
|---|---|---|
| High Season | 17.00 | 25.00 |

Children's discounts available from 5 years
**HS** 23 May–30 Sep
**LS** 1 Apr–22 May, Oct
Closed Nov–Mar
Supplements: Single room £3

## Mousehole

**OLD COASTGUARD HOTEL**
Mousehole, Penzance, Cornwall, TR19 6PR
Tel: 0736 731222
12 Bedrooms (All with private bathroom/shower).

T LF LP AL HT

The Old Coastguard Hotel is situated in a secluded cove, off Mounts Bay, in the quaint old fishing village of Mousehole. The views to be enjoyed are said to be the finest on the south west coast. The hotel gardens have a private entrance to the beach where sun and rock bathing can be enjoyed. Fishing, including shark fishing, is excellent, and sea trips can be arranged.
Children's discounts available
Terms on application

## Newquay

**BAY HOTEL**
Esplanade Road, Pentire, Newquay, Cornwall, TR7 1PT
Tel: 0637 872988

100 Bedrooms (74 with private bathroom/shower).

M LP AL HT

A friendly, family-run hotel overlooking the cliffs and sands of Fistral Bay. Situated 1 mile from town centre and ideally located for those with a passion for rock or long line fishing. All rooms have tea/coffee-making facilities, radio and intercom. Lift to all floors. Games room. Separate TV lounge. Full central heating. 9-hole putting green. Regular entertainment. Own Buttery/snack bar.

| | B & B £ | Half Board £ |
|---|---|---|
| High Season | 13.00 | 20.00 |
| Mid Season | 12.50 | 19.50 |
| Low Season | 12.00 | 19.00 |

Children's discounts available
**HS** 12 Jul–16 Aug
**MS** Jun–11 Jul, 17 Aug–13 Sep
**LS** Mar–May, 14 Sep–Oct
Closed Nov–end Feb
Supplements: Room with bath/shower & WC £2.50. Prices quoted above are the lowest rates available

**TREGURRIAN HOTEL**
Watergate Bay, Newquay, Cornwall, TR8 4AB
Tel: 0637 860280

28 Bedrooms (20 with private bathroom/shower).

M T LF LP AL HT

Best of both worlds—keep your family happy in a two-star hotel only 100 yards from a sandy beach and all the sea fishing you want, yet within easy reach of rainbow fly fishing at Porth and Penryn. College reservoir provides the best carp coarse fishing. Heated pool, games rooms, excellent food. Licensed with comprehensive, modestly priced wine list. Most rooms en-suite, all with heaters, radio, and tea/coffee-making facilities.

| | B & B £ | Half Board £ |
|---|---|---|
| High Season | 14.00 | 22.00 |
| Low Season | 10.00 | 14.00 |

Children's discounts available
**HS** mid Jul–end Aug
**MS** Jun–mid Jul, Sep **LS** May, late Sep Closed Oct–Apr
Supplements: Room with shower & WC £2. Single room with shower & WC +10%. Sea view 45p/£1

## Padstow

**TREGLOS HOTEL**
Constantine Bay, Padstow, Cornwall, PL28 8JH
Tel: 0841 520727

44 Bedrooms (All with private bathroom/shower).

M T LF LP AL HT

Treglos is run as a country house—small enough to give personal attention with a standard of service which is becoming increasingly rare—by a friendly and attentive staff who are well known to those guests who return year after year. The outstanding restaurant specialises in local fresh seafood, home grown vegetables and homemade desserts with Cornish cream. We can offer local fishing—sea, estuary, river and reservoir.

| | Half Board £ |
|---|---|
| High Season | 34.00 |
| Mid Season | 31.00 |
| Low Season | 27.00 |

Children's discounts available
**HS** 17 Jul–25 Sep
**MS** 24 Apr–16 Jul, 26 Sep–9 Oct
**LS** 12 Mar–23 Apr, 10 Oct–3 Nov
Closed 4 Nov–11 Mar
Supplements: Single room £1.50 per night. Balcony £1.50 per person per night

## Penzance

**ALEXANDRA HOTEL**
Alexandra Terrace, Seafront, Penzance, Cornwall, TR18 4NX
Tel: 0736 62644

21 Bedrooms (10 with private bathroom/shower).

M T LF LP HT

Between Penzance and Newlyn Harbour, the hotel is situated on the seafront in Penzance. Coin operated laundrette and free ironing facilities.

| | B&B £ | Half Board £ |
|---|---|---|
| High Season | 13.00 | 19.50 |
| Mid Season | 12.00 | 18.50 |
| Low Season | 11.00 | 17.50 |

Children's discounts available
**HS** 19 Jul–31 Aug
**MS** 1 Jun–18 Jul, 1–30 Sep
**LS** 1 Jan–31 May, 10 Oct–31 Dec
Supplements: Room with bath/shower & WC £2

## Rock

**THE MARINERS MOTEL**
Slipway, Rock, Nr. Wadebridge, Cornwall, PL27 6LD
Tel: 020886 2312

16 Bedrooms (All with private bathroom/shower).

M T LF LP AL HT

The motel is on waters edge with panoramic views over the Camel Estuary, which has good bass, flatfish and salmon fishing in season. Deep sea, shark and wreck fishing. Maybe you would like to try your hand at sailing, windsurfing, surfing, water skiing, cliff walking, golf, or just eating, drinking and relaxing for those who just wish to unwind. All rooms have colour TV, radio, fridge, and tea/coffee-making facilities.

| | B & B £ | Half Board £ |
|---|---|---|
| High Season | 20.00 | 28.00 |
| Low Season | 15.00 | 23.00 |

Children's discounts available
**HS** 12 Jun–13 Sep **LS** 14 Sep–11 Jun
Supplements: Single room £3

## St Agnes

**TREVAUNANCE POINT HOTEL**
Trevaunance Cove, St. Agnes, Cornwall, TR5 0RZ
Tel: 087255 3235

10 Bedrooms (5 with private bathroom/shower).

M T LF

Trevaunance Point Hotel, as its name suggests, stands sentinel upon a headland guarding the seaborne approaches to a sheltered, sandy cove. Fishing from beach or rocks abound with bass and mullet amongst our specialities. Tuition available. Boat fishing by arrangement weather permitting. The hotel is small with centuries of history and an ambiance to match. Ships timbered rooms, open log fires and candlelit cuisine. Abundance of fresh food including fish!

| | B & B £ | Half Board £ |
|---|---|---|
| High Season | 20.00 | 31.00 |
| Mid Season | 19.00 | 30.00 |
| Low Season | 18.00 | 29.00 |

Children's discounts available
**HS** Jun–Oct **MS** Apr–May
**LS** Nov–Mar (except Christmas)
Supplements: Room with bath/shower & WC £5. Single room £15.

## St Mawes

**IDLE ROCKS HOTEL**
St. Mawes, Truro, Cornwall
TR2 5AN Tel: 0326 270771

24 Bedrooms (All with private bathroom/shower).

M T LF LP AL HT

Alongside the water in delightful roseland peninsular, overlooking the famous yachting harbour. Bedrooms have colour TV, radio and tea/coffee-making facilities. Well-known for Anglo-continental cuisine, especially seafood and locally caught fish; an ideal haven to relax after a long day fishing. St. Mawes and nearby Falmouth offer sea fishing for mackerel, bass, turbot and conger. Good freshwater fishing in two well-stocked local reservoirs and the River Fal.

| | Bed Only £ | B & B £ | Half Board £ |
|---|---|---|---|
| High Season | | | 38.00 |
| Mid Season | | | 35.00 |
| Low Season | | | 32.00 |

Children's discounts available
**HS** May–Sep **MS** 1–22 Oct
**LS** 2–30 Apr Closed 23 Oct–1 Apr



See page 4 for details of symbols

## Truro

**THE LUGGER HOTEL**
Portloe, Nr. Truro, Cornwall, TR2 5RD
Tel: 0872 501322

20 Bedrooms (All with private bathroom/shower).

M T LF LP AL HT

Once a 17th-century inn frequented by smugglers, now a cosy, welcoming hotel renowned for its good food and wines, specialising in seafood and locally caught fish. Situated at the water edge in a picturesque fishing cove. Bedrooms have radio, TV and tea/coffee-making facilities. Sea fishing is at nearby St. Mawes and Mevagissey for ray, turbot, conger, mackerel and bass. Freshwater fishing in River Fal and two excellent reservoirs just a short drive away.

| | Half Board £ |
|---|---|
| High Season | 37.50 |
| Mid Season | 33.50 |
| Low Season | 32.00 |

**HS** 1 May–30 Sep
**MS** 1 Oct–10 Nov
**LS** 12 Mar–30 Apr
Closed 10 Nov–11 Mar

## DEVON
## Ashburton

**HOLNE CHASE HOTEL**
Tavistock Road, Ashburton, Devon, TQ13 7NS
Tel: 03643 471

14 Bedrooms (All with private bathroom/shower).

M T LP AL

Holne Chase is a particularly peaceful hotel (member of Relais du Silence) in the Dartmoor National Park. The hotel has about a mile of salmon/sea trout fishing on the River Dart within the hotel grounds plus access to Duchy of Cornwall water (salmon/sea trout, brown trout) and S.W.W.A. Reservoirs. Hotel and Duchy waters fly only. Season March–September.

| | B & B £ | Half Board £ |
|---|---|---|
| High Season | 30.00 | 40.00 |
| Low Season | 25.00 | 35.00 |

Children's discounts available
**HS** Easter–mid Oct **LS** mid Oct–Easter
Supplements: Single room 50%

## Axminster

**GEORGE HOTEL**
Victoria Place, Axminster, Devon, EX14 5DW
Tel: 0297 32209

11 Bedrooms (All with private bathroom/shower).

M T LF LP AL HT

A historic 17th-century inn, 5 miles inland from Lyme Regis. 11 beautifully appointed rooms, all with colour TV, tea/coffee-making facilities, central heating and double glazing. Full restaurant, lounge and public bars, also residents' lounge. Private fishing on approx. 4 miles of river available to residents. Sea fishing from Lyme Regis.

| | B & B £ | Half Board £ |
|---|---|---|
| High Season | 15.00 | 22.00 |

Children's discounts available
Supplements: Single room charge £20. Suite (including 4 poster bed) £5

## Brixham

**QUAYSIDE HOTEL**
King Street, Brixham, Devon, TQ5 9TJ
Tel: 08045 55751

30 Bedrooms (All with private bathroom/shower).

M T HT

Ingeniously converted 17th/18th-century fishermen's cottages and now a warm, friendly and comfortable three-star hotel which overlooks one of the most picturesque and interesting fishing and yachting harbours in the South West. Within a short radius you have a choice of fishing for salmon and trout in the River Dart, coarse fishing and of course sea angling from the hotel which offers superb cuisine with local seafood, and lively bars.

| | B & B £ | Half Board £ |
|---|---|---|
| High Season | 22.00 | 31.50 |
| Mid Season | 20.00 | 29.50 |
| Low Season | 18.00 | 26.00 |

Children's discounts available
**HS** 22 Jul–30 Sep **LS** 1 Nov–31 Mar
**MS** 1 Apr–21 Jul, 1 Oct–31 Oct
Supplements: Room with bath/shower & WC £5. Single room £7. Harbour view £5. Christmas, New Year, Easter and Whit Bank Holidays

## Chagford

**GLENDARAH HOUSE**
Lower Street, Chagford, Devon, TQ13 8BZ
Tel: 06473 3270

8 Bedrooms (1 with private bathroom/shower).

M T LF LP AL

Dartmoor offers the angler an unrivalled choice of fishing — game or coarse, stillwater or stream. Glendarah House is ideally situated for easy access to all moorland streams and reservoirs. It is noted for its friendly atmosphere, comfortable accommodation, and its good food and wine. We will supply packed lunches and fill your coffee flask. There is ample parking. Magnificent views.

| | Bed Only £ | B & B £ | Half Board £ |
|---|---|---|---|
| High Season | 6.25 | 10.00 | 16.50 |

Children's discounts available
Closed Jan–Feb
Supplements: Room with bath/shower & WC £2

**MILL END HOUSE**
Sandypark, Chagford, Nr. Newton Abbot, Devon, TQ13 8JN
Tel: 06473 2282

17 Bedrooms (All with private bathroom/shower).

M LP AL

The hotel is set in its own beautiful gardens on the banks of the River Teign where the local fishing association offers approximately 12 miles of brown trout fishing. Salmon and sea trout are available on a limited basis. Reservoir fishing available. AA and RAC three-star, ETB 4 crowns. Egon Ronay and Ashley Courtenay recommended.

| | B & B £ | Half Board £ |
|---|---|---|
| High Season | 30.00 | 37.50 |
| Mid Season | 28.00 | 35.00 |
| Low Season | 25.00 | 33.00 |

Children's discounts available
**HS** Easter, 2 May–25 Oct
**MS** 1 Apr–1 May (ex Easter)
**LS** 26 Oct–31 Mar
Closed 18 Dec–28 Dec
Supplements: Single room 25%

## Honiton

**THE DEER PARK HOTEL**
Buckerell Village, Honiton,
Devon, EX14 0PG
Tel: 0404 2064

29 Bedrooms (All with private bathroom/shower).

M T LF LP AL HT

Original hunting lodge for Kings of England. Built in 1721, a Georgian manor standing in 34 acres with fishing on the River Otter. 3 miles of river, 5 miles of bank. 8 beats. Bag limit (2½ brace) brown only. Also small 2 acre lake in grounds (rainbow as well).

| | B & B £ | Half Board £ |
|---|---|---|
| High Season | 30.00 | 40.00 |

Children's discounts available

## Ilfracombe

**MARANTHA HOTEL**
Torrs Park, Ilfracombe,
Devon, EX34 8AY
Tel: 0271 63245

23 Bedrooms (9 with private bathroom/shower).

M LF LP AL HT

Our friendly, family-run hotel is the ideal base for a great fishing holiday. We offer our guests comfortable (fully centrally heated) accommodation, an excellent varied menu and personal service in a pleasant relaxed atmosphere. We have a spacious bar, TV/video lounge and games/pool room. All bedrooms with tea/coffee-making facilities. Within easy reach of first class fishing of every type. Arrangements made in advance if required.

| | Bed Only £ | B & B £ | Half Board £ |
|---|---|---|---|
| High Season | 11.50 | 11.50 | 15.50 |
| Mid Season | 10.50 | 10.50 | 14.50 |
| Low Season | 9.00 | 9.00 | 13.00 |

Children's discounts available
**HS** 1 Jul–31 Aug
**MS** May, Jun, Sep
**LS** 1 Oct–30 Apr
Supplements: Room with shower & WC £1.50

**SANDY COVE HOTEL**
Combe Martin Bay,
Berrynarbor, Nr. Ilfracombe,
North Devon, EX34 9SR
Tel: 027188 2243

34 Bedrooms (All with private bathroom/shower).

M T LP AL HT

The hotel owns its own beach. Fish in peace and quiet from the rocks or arrangements can be made with local fishermen for boat sea fishing. Sea fishing festival at Ilfracombe during August. Game fishing at Wistland Pound, coarse fishing at Slade and Mill Park. The hotel stands in 20 acres of beach/cliff/gardens, woods. Outdoor swimming pool, sunbed, sauna, whirlpool, gym equipment. All rooms en-suite with colour TV, radio, and direct-dial telephone.

| | B & B £ | Half Board £ |
|---|---|---|
| High Season | 22.43 | 33.35 |
| Mid Season | 20.99 | 32.20 |
| Low Season | 18.11 | 31.05 |

Children's discounts available
**HS** 23 Jul–7 Sep
**MS** 1 Jul–22 Jul, 8 Sep–30 Sep
**LS** 1 Oct–30 Jun
Supplements: Rooms with sea view and other improvements — phone for tariffs

## Lifton

**LIFTON COTTAGE HOTEL**
Lifton, Devon, PL16 0DR
Tel: 0566 84439

12 Bedrooms (5 with private bathroom/shower).

M LF LP AL

The hotel is a 300-year old listed building, situated between Dartmoor and Bodmin Moor, close to the River Tamar and its many tributaries. Fishing for trout and salmon can be arranged with the Launceston Angling Club, and local coarse fishing lakes are available. We are a small, friendly, family-run hotel with a good restaurant, cosy bar and ample parking. Colour TV and tea/coffee-making facilities in all rooms.

| | B & B £ | Half Board £ |
|---|---|---|
| High Season | 13.00 | 20.25 |

Children's discounts available
Supplements: Room with bath/shower & WC £3

## Lynton

**CASTLE HILL HOUSE HOTEL**
Castle Hill, Lynton, Devon,
EX35 6JA
Tel: 0598 52291

9 Bedrooms (All with private bathroom/shower).

M T LF LP AL HT

Quality small hotel with excellent reputation for fine food. Extensive breakfast till 11am. Friendly and welcoming atmosphere. All rooms have en suite bathrooms, colour TV, clock radio, hairdryer, tea-making facilities and electric blankets. Drying room, laundry and ironing facilities. Open fires and candlelit dining. All this in easy reach of sea fishing from Lynmouth, the East Lyn for salmon and trout and the well-stocked Wistland Pound Reservoir. Taste of Exmoor.

| | Bed Only £ | B & B £ | Half Board £ |
|---|---|---|---|
| High Season | 13.00 | 19.00 | 27.00 |
| Mid Season | 13.00 | 18.00 | 26.00 |
| Low Season | 13.00 | 18.00 | 25.00 |

Children's discounts available
**HS** 1 Jul–21 Sep
**MS** 10–30 Jun, 22 Sep–15 Oct
**LS** 1 Mar–9 Jun, 16 Oct–17 Nov
Closed 18 Nov–28 Feb
Supplements: Single room £5 High Season only
Bargain breaks available.

**SEAWOOD HOTEL**
North Walk Drive, Lynton,
Devon, EX35 6HJ
Tel: 0598 52272
Classification not yet known
12 Bedrooms (All with private bathroom/shower).

M T LF LP AL

The River Lyn is half-a-mile from the hotel: excellent salmon season 1986. Several well-stocked reservoirs few miles distant. Boats available at Lynmouth for sea angling. Information from Bernard Peacock, proprietor/chef/keen salmon fisherman, his locally caught salmon feature on menu. Great pride in cooking and service – we try to provide the extra care, personal attention and friendly atmosphere which often completes a perfect holiday.

| | B & B £ | Half Board £ |
|---|---|---|
| High Season | 98.00 | 145.00 |
| Mid Season | 94.00 | 140.00 |
| Low Season | 82.00 | 128.00 |

Children's discounts available
**HS** 18 Jul–18 Sep
**MS** 23 May–17 Jul
**LS** up to 22 May, After 19 Sep
Closed Mid Nov–Mid Mar
Supplements: Four-poster bed 50p. Dog 50p. Single room £1.

See page 4 for details of symbols

## North Tawton

**THE WHITE HART**
Fore Street, North Tawton,
Devon, EX20 2DT
Tel: 083782 473
3 Bedrooms.

10 first class trout stillwaters and 4 trout and salmon rivers coupled with a friendly, comfortable country pub. Modern, well-equipped accommodation with excellent food. Personal advice on where and how to fish, concessionary permits, local pattern flies, tuition, fly tying instruction and own stretch of small river make this probably 'the best value for money' holiday you can take.

| | B & B | Half Board |
|---|---|---|
| | £ | £ |
| High Season | 10.50 | 13.50 |
| Mid Season | 9.00 | 12.00 |
| Low Season | 8.00 | 11.00 |

**HS** May–Sep
**MS** Mar, Apr, Oct
**LS** Nov–Feb
Supplements: Single room £2

## Okehampton

**FRIARS HELE FARM**
Meeth, Okehampton,
Devon, EX20 3QB
Tel: 0837 810282
3 Bedrooms (2 with private bathroom/shower).

A farmhouse situated in a beautiful position overlooking woodlands and the Torridge Valley. A mile of private salmon and sea trout fishing is available at the farm. A warm welcome awaits, every comfort assured. Attractive menus. Scenic views. Everything to make your holiday a happy one.

| | B & B | Half Board |
|---|---|---|
| | £ | £ |
| High Season | 10.00 | 14.00 |

Children's discounts available
Closed Nov–Feb

**POLTIMORE HOUSE**
South Zeal, Okehampton,
Devon, EX20 2PD
Tel: 0837 840209
7 Bedrooms (4 with private bathroom/shower).

A thatched country guest house on the northern edge of Dartmoor with some of the best game fishing in the West Country available nearby. The principle rivers for salmon, sea-trout and browns are Teign, Taw, Torridge, Dart and Tamar. Nearby are Fernworthy, Kennick and Stafford Moor still-waters. Warm and cosy atmosphere with blazing log fires and traditional home-cooking. Awarded the British Tourist Authority's Commendation for the eleventh successive year.

| | B & B | Half Board |
|---|---|---|
| | £ | £ |
| High Season | 13.00 | 19.50 |
| Low Season | 11.00 | 17.50 |

**HS** Apr–Oct **LS** Nov–Mar
Supplements: Room with bath/shower & WC £2.50

## Ottery St Mary

**FLUXTON FARM HOTEL**
Ottery St. Mary, Devon,
EX11 1RJ
Tel: 040481 2818
10 Bedrooms (3 with private bathroom/shower).

16th-century Devon longhouse, formerly a farm and now a small and comfortable hotel set in lovely countryside with splendid views. Large gardens with stream and trout pond. 2 lounges, both with colour TV, one non-smoking. Small, separate bar. Beamed, candlelit restaurant serving excellent home cooked food using local fresh produce. Full central heating. Tennis court. Friendly relaxed atmosphere with your comfort our main concern.

| | B & B | Half Board |
|---|---|---|
| | £ | £ |
| High Season | 15.00 | 21.50 |
| Mid Season | 13.50 | 19.50 |
| Low Season | 12.50 | 17.50 |

Children's discounts available
**HS** 1 Jul–7 Sep **MS** May, Jun, Sep
**LS** Oct–Apr
Supplements: Room with bath/shower £1

*Prices in England for Fishing are per person, sharing a double room, per night, including VAT (at the current rate of 15 per cent).*

## Paignton

**NEW BARN FARM**
Totnes Road,
Collaton St. Mary,
Paignton, Devon,
TQ4 7PT
Tel: 0803 553602
3 Bedrooms (1 with private bathroom/shower).

Set in 64 acres, the farm has panoramic south Devonshire views. Half-a-mile off A385 Paignton-Totnes road. 2 miles from Paignton and sea. Home produce. Coarse fishing, fly fishing and fun fishing. Trout pools available at our fishing centre, situated in a unique valley below the farmhouse. Dartmoor, reservoir and river fishing 20 minutes drive. S.A.E. for brochure or telephone.

| | B & B | Half Board |
|---|---|---|
| | £ | £ |
| High Season | 8.50 | 12.50 |
| Low Season | 6.50 | 11.00 |

Children's discounts available
**HS** Whitsun–mid Sep
**LS** Mar–Whitsun, mid Sep onwards
Closed Dec–Feb
Supplements: £2 extra if twin room used as single. Dinner £6.50 per head
Children half price under 11 years

## Plymouth

**NEW CONTINENTAL HOTEL**
Millbay Road, Plymouth,
Devon, PL1 3LD
Tel: 0752 220782
76 Bedrooms (All with private bathroom/shower).

A family-run and owned three-star hotel, refurbished to a high standard. All bedrooms have private bathroom, TV, radio, tea-coffee-making facilities, in-house films. New Wine Bar opened for lunch and evening meals. Private car park. 5 minutes away from city centre and Barbican areas.

| | B & B | Half Board |
|---|---|---|
| | £ | £ |
| High Season | 24.00 | 40.00 |
| Mid Season | 24.00 | 30.00 |

Children's discounts available
**HS** May–Sep
**MS** Oct–Apr
Supplements: Single room £10

## Seaton

**HAWKESHYDE MOTEL & LEISURE CENTRE**
Harepath Hill, Seaton,
Devon, EX12 2TF
Tel: 0297 20932

26 Bedrooms (All with private bathroom/shower).

M T

In five acre grounds, ideally situated within 1½ miles of the sea and the mouth of the River Axe. Enjoy squash, badminton, table-tennis, pool table, sauna, solarium, skittle alley, seven station multi-gym in our leisure centre. Quiet, comfortable bedrooms, all with private bathroom, colour TV, telephone, tea/coffee-making facilities. Ample car parking. Restaurant with beautiful views over the Axe Valley to the sea, serves excellent food. Fully licensed lounge bar.

| | B & B £ | Half Board £ |
|---|---|---|
| High Season | 21.75 | 25.75 |
| Mid Season | 20.10 | 24.75 |
| Low Season | 19.05 | 23.60 |

Children's discounts available
**HS** 20 Jun–5 Sep
**MS** 6 Sep–13 Dec
**LS** 6 Jan–19 Jun
Closed 14 Dec–5 Jan
Supplements: Single room £6.80

**THREE HORSESHOES**
Branscombe, Nr. Seaton,
Devon, EX12 3BR
Tel: 029780 251

12 Bedrooms (5 with private bathroom/shower).

M LF LP AL HT

A family-run old world inn with log fire, beams and brasses. A warm, friendly atmosphere. A large range of traditional and real ales, keg beers and ciders. Listed in Camra Good Beer Guide. Bar snacks, lunches and evening meals. Close to several seaside and fishing towns and villages, rivers and Axe Estuary. Ample parking. Special rates can be arranged for party bookings. Self-catering facilities available.

| | B & B £ |
|---|---|
| High Season | 10.50 |

Children's discounts available
Supplements: Room with bath/shower & WC £4. Single room £1. En-suite room rates vary from £14.50–£16.50

## Tiverton

**THE TIVERTON HOTEL**
Blundells Road, Tiverton,
Devon, EX16 4DB
Tel: 0884 256120

29 Bedrooms (All with private bathroom/shower).

M T LP AL

Modern purpose-built hotel situated on edge of the historic market town of Tiverton in the heart of the beautiful Exe valley. All bedrooms are spacious and have private bath, shower, WC, colour TV, air conditioning, hairdryer and free tea/coffee-making facilities. The hotel has a car park for 100 cars and is fully licensed. A superb candlelit a la carte dinner is included in half board terms.

| | B & B £ | Half Board £ |
|---|---|---|
| High Season | 22.00 | 27.00 |
| Mid Season | 20.00 | 25.00 |
| Low Season | 18.00 | 23.00 |

Children's discounts available
**HS** Jun, Jul, Aug **MS** Apr, May, Sep, Oct
**LS** Jan, Feb, Mar, Nov, Dec
Supplements: Single room £5

**WEST PITT FARM**
Uplowman, Tiverton, Devon
EX16 7DU
Tel: 0884 820296

5 Bedrooms (1 with private bathroom/shower).

M

West Pitt Farm is ideally situated for both the north and south coast, Exmoor and Dartmoor, only two miles from Junction 27 of M5. Excellent fishing facilities available including own, well-stocked coarse pool, and nearby canal, pond and fresh water fishing. Comfortable accommodation in farmhouse. Guests' lounge with oak beam, inglenook fireplace and bread oven. Bedrooms with H & C. Delicious home cooking. Games room and grass tennis courts.

| | B & B £ |
|---|---|
| High Season | 8.50 |

Children's discounts available

## Torquay

**OVERMEAD HOTEL**
Daddyhole Road, Torquay,
Devon, TQ1 2EF
Tel: 0803 27633

60 Bedrooms (55 with private bathroom/shower).

M T LF LP AL HT

A comfortable three-star family hotel situated on Daddyhole Plain, just half-a-mile from the town and harbour. Most bedrooms enjoy superb sea views and are comfortably equipped with TV, telephone and tea-making facilities. Tor Bay and Lyme Bay offer good sea fishing and the Rivers Teign and Exe are half-an-hour by car. There is also trout fishing from close by lakes. Send for our brochure 'Fabulous Fishing on the English Riviera'.

| | B & B £ | Half Board £ |
|---|---|---|
| High Season | 25.00 | 30.00 |
| Mid Season | 22.00 | 27.00 |
| Low Season | 20.00 | 25.00 |

Children's discounts available
**HS** 20 Jun–4 Sep
**MS** 23 May–19 Jun, Sep
**LS** Mar–22 May, Oct–Nov
Open all year
Supplements: Single room £2. Sea view subject to availability £1.50

## Torrington

**HUNTERS INN**
Well Street, Torrington,
Devon, EX38 8EP
Tel: 0805 23832
Classification not yet known
4 Bedrooms

M LP AL

An old world pub situated in the picturesque Torridge Valley. Ample car parking. Walking distance from fly and coarse fishing. A friendly inn serving home cooked meals in the bar at lunchtimes and evenings. Darts, skittles, pool etc. Idea spot for Exmoor coast and moors of North Devon and Cornwall. Phone or send for details.

| | B & B £ | Half Board £ |
|---|---|---|
| High Season | 12.00 | 15.00 |

*Prices in England for Fishing are per person, sharing a double room, per night, including VAT (at the current rate of 15 per cent). Check prices when you book and mention England for Fishing.*

See page 4 for details of symbols

## Woolacombe

**HOLMESDALE HOTEL**
Bay View Road,
Woolacombe, Devon,
EX34 7DQ
Tel: 0271 870335

15 Bedrooms (7 with private bathroom/shower).

M T LF LP AL HT

Holmesdale Hotel is situated 2 minutes from and overlooking Woolacombe beach — ideal for sea fishing, 3 miles drive from Ilfracombe with its regular boat fishing trips. Barnstaple is 8 miles with the Taw and Exe — river fishing and Blackwell Fisheries for trout closeby. We have a delightful restaurant with superb English and continental cuisine prepared by Carlos, a Cordon Bleu chef. Children most welcome and all fishing arrangements can be made prior to holiday.

| | B & B £ | Half Board £ |
|---|---|---|
| High Season | | 125.00* |
| Mid Season | 14.00 | 105.00* |
| Low Season | 12.00 | 90.00* |

Children's discounts available

**HS** 18 Jul–28 Aug
**MS** 16 May–17 Jul, 29 Aug–31 Oct
**LS** Feb–15 May, Nov–23 Dec
Closed Jan
Supplements: Room with bath/shower & WC £10 per week. Sea view £11 per week. *Half Board prices quoted above are per week. Special Christmas prices

## Yelverton

**PRINCE HALL HOTEL**
Two Bridges, Yelverton,
Devon, PL20 6SW
Tel: 082289 442
9 Bedrooms (6 with private bathroom/shower).

M T LF LP AL HT

An elegant, country house hotel in the heart of Dartmoor with panoramic views over 8 miles of open moorland. Ideally placed for fly fishing in the River Dart, only a few hundred yards from hotel, or in the many rivers and reservoirs within easy distance. Fishing courses available. Open log fires, a high standard of food and a well stocked bar add to your enjoyment of Prince Hall. Pets welcome.

| B & B £ | Half Board £ |
|---|---|
| 18.50 | 28.50 |

**Children's discounts available**

**TWO BRIDGES HOTEL**
Princeton, Yelverton,
Dartmoor, Devon, PL20 6SW
Tel: 082289 206

22 Bedrooms (10 with private bathroom/shower).

M T LF LP AL

An 18th-century coaching inn set in the heart of Dartmoor. Ideal centre for leisure pursuits with its own stables, with local golf courses and trout and salmon fishing on the River Dart. Recently upgraded bedrooms all have direct-dial telephone and many are en-suite with colour TV. Excellent reputation for good food and wine with a Carvery and Steak Bar. Full size snooker table for evening relaxation.

| | B & B £ | Half Board £ |
|---|---|---|
| High Season | 12.50 | 19.00 |

Children's discounts available
Supplements: Room with bath/shower & WC £5.50. Single room supplement by arrangement. Dogs £1 per day. 5% reduction for 4 days or more

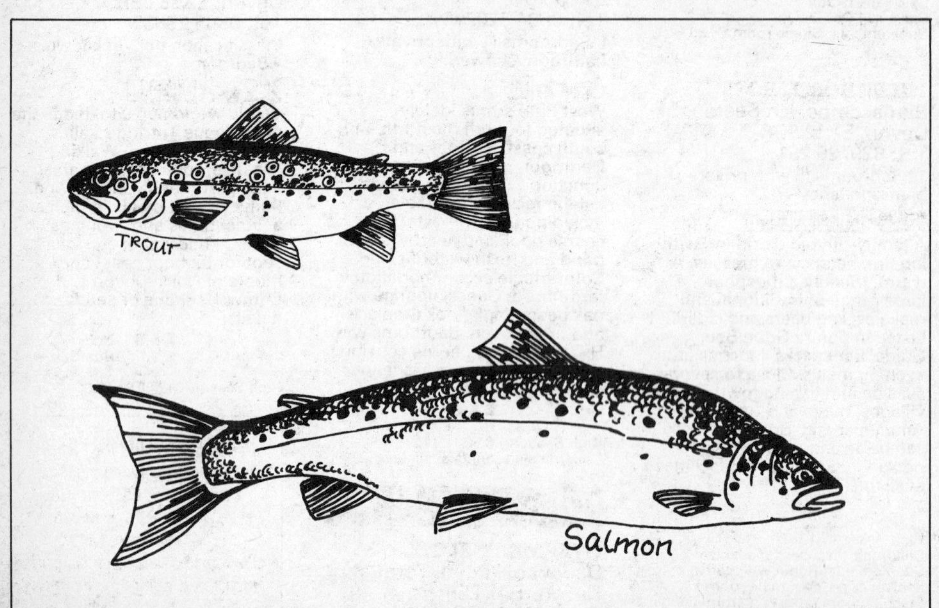

NICHOLSON
Holiday Map of DEVON
NICHOLSON
Holiday Guide to DEVON
English Tourist Board
£1.95
£3.95

English Tourist Board

# SEVERN-TRENT

*Tourist Information Centres ■ open all year round.*
*Not to scale.*

# SEVERN-TRENT

This region sits astride England from the Atlantic to the North Sea.

The crystal streams of the Derbyshire Pennines, which provided trout and grayling for Isaac Walton, drain into the mighty Trent, arguably England's most prolific coarse fishery.

Water has even been tapped from across the Welsh marches to supply industrial England and Severn-Trent's interests take it westward into the game-fishing headwaters of the Severn, which drains the great Shropshire Plain. Salmon come up past Gloucester, Worcester and Shrewsbury and the Severn and its tributaries, like the Warwickshire Avon, are first-class coarse fisheries.

The famed salmon and coarse fisheries of the River Wye are administered by Welsh Water, but remain very firmly English and the hub of England's stillwater trout fishing is still to be found in the reservoirs of Northamptonshire.

**Water Authority**

Severn-Trent Water,
2297 Coventry Road, Sheldon, Birmingham
B26 3PU
Tel: 021 743 422

**Avon Division**
Avon House, De Montford Way,
Cannon Park, Coventry CV4 7EJ

**Derwent Division**
Raynesway, Derby DE3 7JA

**Lower Severn Division**
Southwick Park, Gloucester Road,
Tewkesbury, Glos GL20 7DG

**Lower Trent Division**
Mapperley Hall, Lucknow Avenue,
Nottingham NG3 5BN

**Soar Division**
Leicester Water Centre, Gorse Hill, Anstey,
Leicester LE7 7GU

**Tame Division**
Tame House, 156–170 Newhall Street,
Birmingham B3 1SE

**Upper Severn Division**
Shelton, Shrewsbury SY3 8BJ

**Upper Trent Division**
Trinity Square, Horninglow Street, Burton-on-Trent DE14 1BL

**Welsh Water**
Cambrian Way, Brecon, Powys LD3 7HP
Tel: (0874) 3181

**Fishing Seasons**

Salmon — 2 Feb–30 Sept
Wye — 26 Jan– 17 Oct (Welsh Water)

Trout — 1 Apr–15 Oct

Rainbow Trout (in enclosed waters) —
No close season

Coarse Fish — 16 Jun–14 Mar

**Regional Tourist Boards**
Heart of England Tourist Board,
PO Box 15, Worcester WR1 2JT
Tel: (0905) 613132

East Midlands Tourist Board,
Exchequergate, Lincoln LN2 1PZ
Tel: (0522) 31521

Yorkshire and Humberside Tourist Board,
312 Tadcaster Road, York,
North Yorkshire YO2 2HF
Tel: (0904) 707961

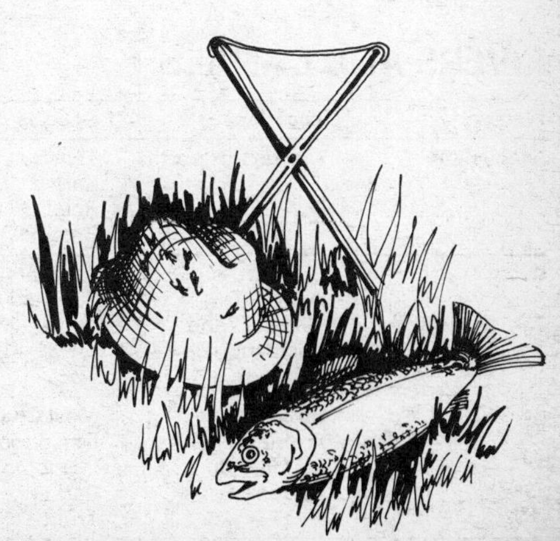

# SEVERN-TRENT ANGLING CLUBS

**Hazeldine Anglers Association**
J.W. Hazeldine, Secretary, 8 Dudley Road, Sedgley, Dudley DY3 1SX
**Ibstock & District Angling Association**
D. Parker, Secretary, 37 Thorndale, Ibstock, Leics
**Kinver Freeliner's Angling Club**
M.E. Barnett, Secretary, 2 Glenwood Close, Brierley Hill, W. Midlands DY5 2NW
**Long Eaton & District Angling Federation**
W. Parker, Secretary, 75 College Street, Long Eaton, Notts
**Montgomery Anglers Association**
T.J. Evans, Secretary, 48 Gungrog Road, Welshpool
**Moreton Angling Club**
F.D. Wilson, Secretary, 6 Lamberts Field, Bourton-on-the-Water, Glos
**The New Dovey Fishery Association (1929) Ltd**
D. Morgan Jones, Secretary, Plas, Machynlleth, Powys
**Nottingham & District Federation of Angling Societies**
William Belshaw, Secretary, 17 Spring Green, Clifton Estate, Nottingham
**Phoenix Angling Club**
J.A. Mobley, Secretary, 155 Greenhill Road, Halesowen, W. Midlands
**Red Beck Lake Fisheries Club**
Secretary, Heywood House, Pill, Bristol BS20 0AE
**Royal Leamington Spa Angling Association**
E.G. Archer, Secretary, 9 Southway, Leamington Spa CV31 2PG
**Shackerston & District Angling Association**
Mrs B.M. Andrews, Secretary, 6 Church Road, Shackerstone, Nuneaton
**Sheffield Amalgamated Anglers Society**
Secretary, 39 Sparken Hill, Worksop, Notts S80 1AL
**Stratford-on-Avon Angling Association**
D. Evason, Secretary, School House, Ullenhall, Solihull, W. Midlands B95 5PA
**Warwick & District Angling Association**
L.C. Sargeant, Secretary, 218 Warwick Road, Kenilworth, Warwicks CV8 1FD
**Whitchurch Angling Association**
B.W. Young, Secretary, 33 Smallbrook Road, Whitchurch, Shropshire
**Whitmore Reans Constitutional Angling Association**
R.H. Hughes, Hon. Secretary, c/o 6 Tettenhall Road, Wolverhampton WV1 4SA

## RIVERS AND CANALS

| Water | Location | Species | Permits |
|---|---|---|---|
| **Ashby Canal** | Market Bosworth | Tench<br>Carp<br>Roach<br>Bream | Shackerstone and District Angling Association<br>Mrs Andrews, 6 Church Road, Shackerstone, Nuneaton |
| **Avon** | Stratford-on-Avon (Old Lido and Recreation Ground) | All Coarse Fish Species | Stratford-on-Avon District Council<br>Senior Bailiff, 8 Coppice Close, Stratford-on-Avon<br>Tel: (0789) 298535<br>Bailiff on the bank |
| | Stratford-on-Avon<br>Luddington<br>Barton | Most Coarse Fish Species including Barbel<br>Trout | Stratford-on-Avon Angling Association<br>Mr D. Oldham, 32 Banbury Road, Stratford-on-Avon |

| Water | Location | Species | Permits |
|---|---|---|---|
| **Avon cont.** | Warwick<br>Leamington | Most Coarse Fish Species | Warwick and District Angling Association<br>Secretary, L.C. Sargeant, 218 Warwick Road, Kenilworth, Warwickshire<br>Local Sports Shops in Coventry, Leamington Spa, Warwick, Stratford and Rugby |
| | Offenham<br>Chaceley<br>Stratford<br>Defford<br>Evesham | Most Coarse Fish Species | Hazeldine Anglers Association<br>Secretary, J.W. Hazeldine, 8 Dudley Road, Sedgeley, Nr Dudley<br>Tel: Sedgeley 4629 |
| | Wickgrange<br>Wyke Manor | Most Coarse Fish Species | Kinver Freeliner's Angling Club<br>Secretary, M.E. Barnett, 2 Glenwood Close, Brierley Hill, West Midlands DY5 2NW (By Post) |
| **Bradford** | Bakewell (Derbyshire) | Brown Trout | Haddon Estate<br>Estate Office, Bakewell, Derbyshire<br>(Dry Fly Only) |
| **Chelt** | Gloucester | Coarse Fish | The Red Lion<br>Wainlodes Hill, Norton, Gloucester<br>Tel: Gloucester 730251<br>(Camping/Caravan Site Available) |
| **Derwent (Chatsworth Estate Waters)** | Baslow (Derbyshire) | Brown Trout<br>Wild Rainbow Trout<br>Grayling | Cavendish Hotel<br>Baslow, Bakewell, Derbyshire DE4 1SP<br>Tel: (024688) 2311 |
| **Erewash Canal** | Long Eaton | All Coarse Fish Species | Long Eaton and District Angling Federation<br>Tackle Shops in Long Eaton |
| **Grand Union Canal** | Warwick<br>Leamington | All Coarse Fish Species | Warwick and District Angling Association<br>Royal Leamington Spa Angling Association<br>Local Sports Shops |
| **Leam** | Leamington | Most Coarse Fish | Warwick and District Angling Association<br>W. Norris, Leamington Spa<br>Cooper's, Leamington Spa<br>Other Tackle Shops in Area |
| **Lugg (7 miles)** | Hereford | Grayling<br>Chub<br>Roach<br>Pike | Hereford and District AA<br>Castle Pool Hotel<br>Castle Street, Hereford<br>Tel: 0432 56321 |
| | Leamington Spa | Most Coarse Fish | Royal Leamington Spa Angling Association<br>Local Tackle Dealers |
| **Lugg** | Hereford | Chub<br>Dace<br>Grayling<br>Pike<br>Roach | Phoenix Angling Club<br>Secretary, J.A. Mobley, 155 Greenhill Road, Halesowen, West Midlands |
| **Mease** | Clifton Campville<br>Waters Upton<br>Tibberton | Most Coarse Fish Species | The Hazeldine Angling Association<br>J.W. Hazeldine, 8 Dudley Road, Sedgeley, Dudley DY3 1SX Tel: Sedgley 4629 |
| **Montgomery Canal** | Welshpool<br>Newtown | Roach<br>Tench<br>Bream<br>Carp | Montgomery Angling Association<br>Bonds, Hall Street, Welshpool<br>Turton's Tackle Shop, Llanymynech<br>Griffith's Tackle Shop, Lion Works, Newtown |

| Water | Location | Species | Permits |
|---|---|---|---|
| **Penk and Penkridge Canal** | Penkridge | Coarse Fish | Whitmore Reans Constitutional Angling Association<br>Secretary, R.H. Hughes, c/o 6 Tettenhall Road, Wolverhampton WV1 4SA<br>(S.A.E.) |
| **Roden** | Roddington Hall Farm | Coarse Fish | Whitmore Reans Constitutional Angling Association<br>Secretary, R.H. Hughes, c/o 6 Tettenhall Road, Wolverhampton WV1 4SA<br>(S.A.E.) |
| **Severn** | Bridgenorth<br>Montford Bridge<br>Stourport-on-Severn<br>Alberbury | Most Coarse Fish Species | Whitmore Reans Constitutional Angling Association<br>Secretary, R.H. Hughes, c/o 6 Tettenhall Road, Wolverhampton WV1 4SA<br>(S.A.E.) |
| | Bridgenorth (Ship Inn Waters) | Barbel<br>Chub<br>Most Coarse Fish Species | Severn Leisure<br>Ship Inn, Severnside, Highley, Nr Bridgenorth<br>Tel: Highley 861219<br>(Self Catering Flats Available) |
| | Gloucester | Barbel<br>Chub<br>Most Coarse Fish Species | Red Lion Inn<br>Wainlodes Hill, Norton, Gloucester<br>Tel: Gloucester 730251<br>(Camping/Caravan Park Available) |
| | Shrewsbury | Salmon<br>Coarse Fish | Royal Hill Caravan Park<br>Royal Hill Edgerley, Kinnerley, Oswestry, Shropshire SY10 8ES |
| | Diglis Weir | Salmon | Worcester and District United Angling Association<br>Al's Tackle Shop, 26 Malvern Road, Worcester Tel: (0905) 53780 |
| | Arley | Barbel<br>Coarse Fish | The Harbour Inn<br>Arley, Nr Bewdley, Worcs |
| | Arley<br>Bewdley | Barbel<br>Chub<br>Dace<br>Salmon | Stan Lewis<br>Tackle Specialist, 2 Severnside South, Bewdley<br>Tel: (0299) 403358<br>(The Mallards Guest House and Restaurant Tel: (0299) 404022) |
| | Welshpool<br>Newtown | Salmon<br>Trout<br>Grayling<br>Chub | Montgomery Anglers Association<br>Bond's, Hall Street, Welshpool<br>Turton's Tackle Shop, Llanymynech<br>Griffith's Tackle Shop, Lion Works, Newtown |
| | Bewdley | Barbel<br>Coarse Fish | George Hotel, Load Street, Bewdley, Worcs<br>Tel: 0299 402117 |
| | Bewdley | Barbel<br>Roach<br>Dace<br>Chub<br>Pike | Severn Valley Guest House<br>240 West Bourne St, Bewdley, Worcs DY12 1AG Tel: (0299) 402192 |
| | Alveley<br>Hampton Lodge<br>Unicorn | Barbel<br>Coarse Fish | Kinver Freeliner's Angling Club<br>By post from Secretary, M.E. Barnett, 2 Glenwood Close, Brierley Hill, West Midlands |

| Water | Location | Species | Permits |
|---|---|---|---|
| **Severn contd.** | Worcester<br>Montford Bridge<br>Welshpool<br>Bicton | Most Coarse<br>Species<br>Salmon | Hazeldine Anglers Association<br>Secretary, J.W. Hazeldine, 8 Dudley Road, Sedgeley, Nr Dudley<br>Tel: Sedgeley 4629 |
| **Soar** | Kegworth | Barbel<br>Chub<br>Roach<br>Bream<br>Other Species | Long Eaton and District Angling Federation<br>Tackle Shops in Long Eaton |
| | Loughborough | | "Proctors" Pleasure Park<br>Barrow Upon Soar, Leics<br>Tel: (0509) 412434 |
| | Loughborough (Cast Metal Section) | | Borough of Charnwood<br>Charnwood Leisure, Brown's Lane, Loughborough<br>Local Tackle Shops |
| **Stour** | Warwick | Most Coarse<br>Fish | Warwick and District Angling Association<br>Local Tackle Shops |
| | Clifford Chambers | | Stratford-on-Avon Angling Association<br>D. Oldham, 32 Banbury Road, Stratford-on-Avon |
| **Teme** | Ludlow | Trout<br>Coarse Fish | Cliffe Hotel, Dinham, Ludlow, Shrophire<br>Tel: 0584 2063 |
| **Tern** | Market Drayton | Brown Trout<br>Rainbow Trout | Tern Valley Fishery<br>Broomhall Grange, Peatswood,<br>Market Drayton, Shropshire TF9 2PA |
| **Trent** | Castle Donington | Trout<br>Chub<br>Roach<br>Bream | Priest House Hotel<br>Kings Mills, Castle Donington, Nr Derby<br>Tel: 0332 810649 |
| | Besthorpe<br>Girton<br>South Clifton | Most Coarse<br>Fish Species | Sheffield Amalgamated Anglers Society<br>Bailiff on river bank |
| | Nottingham<br>Radcliffe<br>Burton Joyce | Barbel<br>Carp<br>Chub<br>Roach<br>Dace<br>Pike | Nottingham and District Federation of Angling Societies<br>Bailiff on bank |
| | Willington | Mixed Coarse<br>Fish | Derby Anglers Association<br>Rising Sun Public House<br>Cross Roads, Willington |
| | Long Eaton | Mixed Coarse<br>Fish | Long Eaton Victoria AS<br>Permits on Bank |
| | Trent Bridge | Mixed Coarse<br>Fish | Earl Manners AC<br>Permits on Bank |
| | Nottingham (Victoria Embankment) | Roach<br>Chub<br>Carp | Free Fishing |
| | Colwick Park | Mixed coarse<br>Fish | Nottingham City Council<br>Permits from lodge<br>Tel: 0602 870785 |

| Water | Location | Species | Permits |
|---|---|---|---|
| **Trent contd.** | Holme Pierrepoint | Mixed coarse Fish | National Water Sports Centre<br>Ranger on Bank<br>Tel: 0602 821212 |
| | Hoveringham | Mixed coarse Fish | Midland AS<br>Bailiffs on bank |
| | Fiskerton Rolleston | Chub<br>Dace<br>Roach | Nottingham Piscatorial Society<br>Tackle Shops in Nottingham<br>Post Office, Rolleston |
| | Laugherton North Clifton | Bream<br>Roach<br>Eels | Lincoln and District AA<br>Bailiff on Bank |
| **Wye (Derbyshire)** | Bakewell | Brown Trout<br>Wild Rainbow Trout | Haddon Estate Water<br>Peacock Hotel, Rowsley, Nr Matlock, Derbyshire<br>Tel: (0629) 733518<br>(Dry Fly Fishing) |
| | Baslow | Brown Trout<br>Wild Rainbow Trout | Chatsworth and Monsal Dale<br>Cavendish Hotel, Baslow, Derbyshire DE4 1SP<br>Tel: (024 688) 2311 |
| **Wye (Herefordshire)** | Hereford (9½ miles) | Mixed Coarse Fish | Hereford and District AA<br>Castle Pool Hotel, Hereford |
| | Ross-on-Wye | Mixed Coarse Fish | Ross-on-Wye AA<br>GB Sports, 10 Broad Street<br>Ross-on-Wye |
| | Ross-on-Wye | Salmon | Royal Hotel<br>Palace Pound<br>Ross-on-Wye<br>Hereford<br>Tel: 0989 65105 |
| | | Salmon<br>Trout | Pengethley Manor<br>Nr Ross-on-Wye<br>Tel: 0989 87211 |

# LAKES AND RESERVOIRS

| Water | Location | Species | Permits |
|---|---|---|---|
| **Arrow Valley Park Lake** | Redditch | Carp<br>Tench<br>Roach<br>Rudd<br>Bream | Redditch Borough Council<br>Warden at Lake |
| **Belvoir Lakes** | Grantham | Bream<br>Roach<br>Pike<br>Tench<br>Rudd<br>Perch | Estate Office<br>Belvoir Castle, Grantham |
| **Bull Pool and Sheaf Pool** | Whitchurch (Shropshire) | Carp<br>Rudd<br>Crucian Carp<br>Roach<br>Bream | Whitchurch Angling Association<br>Local Tackle Shops |

| Water | Location | Species | Permits |
|---|---|---|---|
| **Charnwood Water** | Loughborough | Carp<br>Tench<br>Crucian Carp<br>Roach<br>Perch | Borough of Charnwood<br>Charnwood Leisure Centre, Brown's Lane, Loughborough<br>Local Tackle Shops |
| **Clumber Lake** | Worksop | Trout<br>Carp<br>Bream<br>Roach | The National Trust<br>Clumber Park, Worksop<br>Bailiff on bank |
| **Coombe Abbey Lake** | Coventry | Bream<br>Roach<br>Tench<br>Pike<br>Perch | Coombe Abbey Country Park<br>Bailiff at waterside |
| **Docklow Pools** | Leominster | Carp<br>Tench<br>Crucian Carp<br>Bream<br>Rudd<br>Roach<br>Trout | West End Farm<br>Docklow, Nr Leominster, Herefordshire<br>Tel: (056 882) 256<br>(Cottage accommodation available) |
| **Draycote Water** | Rugby | Rainbow Trout<br>Brown Trout | Severn-Trent Water<br>Fishing Lodge at Reservoir |
| **Dunham Lakes** | Newark | Coarse Fish | Sheffield and District Angling Association<br>Bridge Garage, Dunham |
| **Foremark Reservoir** | Burton-on-Trent | Brown Trout<br>Rainbow Trout | Severn-Trent Water<br>Brookdale Farm, Milton<br>Leicester Water Centre, Gorse Hill, Anstey, Leicester<br>Tel: (0533) 352011 |
| **Gailey Lower Reservoir** | Wolverhampton | Pike<br>Perch<br>Tench | British Waterways Board<br>Mr T.G. Leatherland, Fisheries Officer, Willow Grange, Church Road, Watford, Herts (S.A.E.) |
| **Haddon Estate Dams** | Bakewell | Brown Trout | Haddon Estate Office<br>Bakewell, Derbyshire |
| **Knipton Reservoir** | Grantham | Bream<br>Roach<br>Rudd<br>Tench | Estate Office<br>Belvoir Castle, Grantham |
| **Kyre Pool (Wellfield Pool) (Snuffmill Pool) (Haye Farm Pool)** | Bewdley | Carp<br>Tench<br>Roach<br>Bream<br>Rudd<br>Perch | Stan Lewis<br>Tackle Specialist, 2 Severnside South, Bewdley Tel: (0299) 403358<br>(The Mallards Guest House and Restaurant Tel: (0299) 404022) |
| **Ladybower Reservoir** | North Derbyshire | Brown Trout<br>Rainbow Trout | Severn Trent Water<br>Fishery Office at Reservoir<br>Derwent Hotel, Bamford<br>Fisherman's Supplies, 131 Sheffield Road, Chesterfield |

| Water | Location | Species | Permits |
|---|---|---|---|
| **Linacre Reservoir** | Chesterfield | Trout | Linacre Fly Fishing Assocition<br>Secretary, J.G. Nixon, 4 Netherthorpe, Staveley<br>Fisherman's Supplies, 131 Sheffield Road, Chesterfield |
| **Mill Farm Fishery** | Lutterworth | Carp<br>Tench<br>Roach<br>Bream | Mill Farm Fishery<br>Farmhouse at top of lane |
| **Nanpantan** | Loughborough | Coarse Fish | Severn-Trent Water<br>W.H. Wortley & Son, 45 Baxter Gate, Loughborough |
| **Naseby Reservoir** | Northampton | Carp<br>Tench<br>Rudd | British Waterways Board<br>T.G. Leatherland, Fisheries Officer, Willow Grange, Church Road, Watford<br>S.A.E. for Permits<br>Reopening after stocking on 16/6/87 |
| **Nuddock Wood Trout Fishery** | Scunthorpe | Brown Trout<br>Rainbow Trout<br>Brook Trout | Nuddock Wood Trout Fishery<br>Permits on site |
| **Ogston Reservoir** | Chesterfield | Trout | Severn-Trent Water<br>S.T.W., Dimple Road, Matlock<br>New Napoleon Inn, Woolley Moor, Near Ogston Reservoir |
| **Patshull Park Great Lake** | Wolverhampton | Trout | Patshull Park Fisheries Ltd<br>Burnhill Green, Wolverhampton<br>Fishing Lodge at Lake |
| **Proctor's Lake** | Loughborough | Carp<br>Tench<br>Bream<br>Roach<br>Pike<br>Perch | Proctor's Pleasure Park<br>Barrow-upon-Soar, Leics<br>Tel: 0509 412434<br>Permits at entrance |
| **Red Beck Lake** | Evesham | Carp | Red Beck Lake Fisheries Club<br>Peter Mohan, Heywood House, Pill, Bristol<br>Tel: 027581 2129 |
| **Ross Salmon Fisheries** | Ross-on-Wye | Stillwater<br>Salmon<br>Trout | Ross Salmon Fisheries<br>The Fishery Lodge<br>Upton Bishop, Ross-on-Wye<br>Tel: 098 985 455 |
| **Rudyard Lake** | Stoke-on-Trent | Roach<br>Bream | British Waterways Board<br>Bailiff on site<br>Match Bookings — Information and Booking Assistant, British Waterways Board, Hire Cruiser Base,<br>Chester Road, Hewhull, Nantwich, Cheshire Tel: 0270 625122 |
| **Shustoke Reservoir** | Coleshill | Trout | Shustoke Fly Fishers<br>Permits on site after 12th April<br>Tel: 0675 81702 |
| **Staunton Harold Reservoir** | Melbourne | Coarse Fish | Severn-Trent Water<br>Melbourne Tackle and Gun, 52/54 High St, Melbourne, Derbyshire<br>Tel: 0332 2091 |

| Water | Location | Species | Permits |
|---|---|---|---|
| **Sulby Reservoir** | Leicester | Carp<br>Tench<br>Bream<br>Pike | British Waterways Board<br>T.G. Leatherland, Fisheries Officer, Willow Grange, Church Road, Watford<br>S.A.E. for Permits |
| **Thornton Reservoir** | Leicester | Trout | Cambrian Fisheries<br>On site from 1st March<br>Tel: 053 021 7107 |
| **Tittesworth Reservoir** | Leek | Trout | Tittesworth Fly Fishers Ltd<br>Fishing Lodge at Reservoir<br>Tel: 053 834 389 |
| **Trimpley Reservoir** | Kidderminster | Trout<br>Coarse Fish | Trimpley Angling Association<br>Secretary, D.E. Nobes, 10 College Road, Kidderminster<br>Tel: 0562 68568 |
| **Welford Reservoir** | Leicester | Bream<br>Tench<br>Roach<br>Pike | British Waterways Board<br>T.G. Leatherland, Fisheries Officer, Willow Grange, Church Road, Watford<br>S.A.E. for Permits |
| **Winthorpe Lake** | Newark | Coarse Fish | Sheffield and District A.A.<br>The Level Crossing, Winthorpe |

# ACCOMMODATION

## DERBYSHIRE
### Baslow

**CAVENDISH HOTEL**
Baslow, Bakewell,
Derbyshire, DE4 1SP
Tel: 024688 2311

23 Bedrooms (All with private bathroom/shower).

M T LP AL HT

Built as the famous Peacock Inn in the 1780s, the Cavendish was restored in 1975 and extended in 1984. It has 23 bedrooms, a recommended dining room and drawing rooms with roaring log fires. The hotel is managed by its owner Eric Marsh and run by professional and friendly staff. The Cavendish is set on the Duke of Devonshire's Chatsworth Estate of which every room enjoys a magnificent view, and whose exclusive fishing is available to guests.

| | Bed Only £ |
|---|---|
| High Season | 57.50 |

Supplements: Extra bed £5. Inn room £65. Breakfast from about £3.50. Lunch and dinner from about £15

### Buxton

**THE LEE WOOD HOTEL**
Manchester Road, Buxton,
Derbyshire, SK17 6TQ
Tel: 0298 70421

42 Bedrooms (All with private bathroom/shower).

M T LF HT

Situated in its own grounds, facing south, the three-star Lee Wood Hotel has been fully modernised to meet present day requirements. All bedrooms have private bathroom, TV, in-house movies, telephone, hairdryer, trouser press and tea/coffee-making facilities. Bar snacks available daily and the restaurant offers both table d'hote and a la carte menus. Fishing on Ladybower Reservoir 14 miles from the hotel.

| | B & B £ | Half Board £ |
|---|---|---|
| High Season | 24.50 | 34.00 |
| Mid Season | 22.50 | 31.50 |
| Low Season | 20.50 | 29.50 |

Children's discounts available
**HS** 22 May–10 Nov
**MS** 27 Mar–21 May
**LS** 11 Nov–26 Mar
Closed 24–28 Dec
Supplement: Single room £6 Monday–Thursday

## GLOUCESTERSHIRE
### Bourton-on-the-Water

**OLDE FOSSEWAY HOTEL**
Cirencester Road, Bourton-on-the-Water, Cheltenham,
Gloucestershire, GL54 2LE
Tel: 0451 20387

6 Bedrooms (2 with private bathroom/shower).

M AL

A privately-run, licensed hotel with a homely atmosphere. Traditional English hospitality and food always available. Fishing rights at 3 local lakes and a stretch of the Severn.

| | B & B £ | Half Board £ |
|---|---|---|
| High Season | 12.50 | 17.50 |
| Low Season | 10.50 | 15.50 |

Children's discounts available
**HS** Apr–Sep
**LS** Oct–Mar
Supplements: Room with bath/shower & WC £2.50 per room. Single room £5

*Check prices when you book and mention England for Fishing.*

See page 4 for details of symbols

## Cheltenham

**HOME FARM**
Seven Springs, Cheltenham, Gloucestershire, GL53 9NG
Tel: 0242 87 219
Classification not yet known
6 Bedrooms (1 with private bathroom/shower).
M LF LP AL
A 6 bedroomed guesthouse, 1 double room with en-suite bath and WC. Situated close to the source of the River Thames with a small, well-stocked trout lake. We are within a 10-mile drive of Cotswold Water Park, South Cerney, 3 miles from Whitcombe Reservoir and 7 miles from the River Severn.

| | B & B £ |
|---|---|
| High Season | 10.00 |

Children's discounts available
Closed 20 Dec–20 Jan
Supplements: Room with bath/shower & WC from £5

## Fairford

**THE HYPERION HOUSE HOTEL**
London Street, Fairford, Gloucestershire, GL7 4AH
Tel: 0285 712349
23 Bedrooms (20 with private bathroom/shower).
M T LF HT
The Hyperion House Hotel is situated in the southern Cotswold town of Fairford. Dry fishing is available on the scenic River Coln which runs through the town. Coarse fishing is available on the nearby River Thames, between Lechlade and Cricklade and on several artificial lakes close to the hotel, where carp, tench and roach provide excellent sport. Day tickets for all the above venues are available locally. Tight lines.

| | B & B £ | Half Board £ |
|---|---|---|
| High Season | 20.00 | 29.00 |
| Low Season | 19.00 | 27.50 |

**HS** 2 Apr–1 Nov
**LS** 2 Nov–1 Apr
Supplements: Single room £10.
Fishing permit

*Check prices when you book and mention England for Fishing.*

## Kelmscott

**MANOR FARM**
Kelmscott, Nr. Lechlade, Gloucestershire, GL7 3HJ
Tel: 0367 52620
2 Bedrooms
M LF LP AL
Manor Farm has a friendly, relaxed atmosphere and is ideally situated for touring, fishing, golfing and walking. It is a 315-acre working dairy farm and has a large garden. Kelmscott is a quiet village famous for William Morris Manor. All rooms with central heating, tea/coffee-making facilities. Full English breakfast, packed lunches by arrangement. Lounge with colour TV.

| | B & B £ |
|---|---|
| High Season | 11.00 |
| Mid Season | 10.00 |
| Low Season | 9.50 |

Children's discounts available
**HS** Jun–Sep
**MS** Apr, May
**LS** Oct–Mar
Supplements: Single room £5

## Lower Slaughter

**MANOR HOTEL AND RESTAURANT**
Lower Slaughter, Cheltenham, Gloucestershire, GL54 2HP
Tel: 0451 20456
21 Bedrooms (All with private bathroom/shower).
M T LF LP HT
The Manor — a magnificent honey-coloured building, ideally situated in one of the most beautiful Cotswold villages, is surrounded by wooded grounds and a trout stream. Owned by Eric and Narney Roby who create a relaxing atmosphere offering fine wines and fresh daily menus. Facilities: heated indoor swimming pool, sauna, solarium, tennis and croquet. The hotel is ideal for country walking and within easy distance of superb game fishing for anglers.

| | Bed Only £ | B & B £ | Half Board £ |
|---|---|---|---|
| High Season | 30.00 | 35.00 | 50.00 |
| Mid Season | 27.50 | 32.50 | 47.50 |
| Low Season | 25.00 | 27.50 | 40.00 |

**HS** 1 Apr–5 Nov
**MS** 1 Feb–Mar
**LS** 6 Nov–Jan
Supplements: Single room £8

## Minsterworth

**SEVERN BANK**
Minsterworth, Nr. Gloucester, Gloucestershire, GL2 8JH
Tel: 045275 357
Classification not yet known
7 Bedrooms
M LF LP AL
Severn Bank is a small, exclusive country hotel situated in the beautiful Gloucestershire countryside in its own 6-acre grounds alongside the River Severn, 4 miles west of Gloucester. We offer a warm welcome in spacious comfort. The non-smoking bedrooms have superb views over the river and countryside, wash basins, tea/coffee-making facilities and colour TV. There are several excellent restaurants and pubs nearby. Licensed. Free brochure on request.

| | B & B £ |
|---|---|
| High Season | 12.00 |

Children's discounts available
Supplements: Single room £12. £16 for single occupancy in double room.
Closed Christmas Eve, Christmas Day

## Stroud

**THE AMBERLEY INN**
Amberley, Stroud, Gloucestershire, GL5 5AF
Tel: 045387 2565
14 Bedrooms (All with private bathroom/shower).
M T AL
A friendly, Cotswold inn set high on Minchinhampton Common with magnificent views of the lovely Woodchester valley. Two bars with real ale, an attractive small restaurant serving good English food, and comfortable bedrooms with modern bathrooms. Holiday includes one day of trout fishing at Rainbow Lake (15 miles) with a 5-fish limit and your water authority licence. A free bottle of wine provided if you do not catch anything.

| | Half Board |
|---|---|
| | £ |
| High Season | 36.00 |
| Mid Season | 35.00 |
| Low Season | 31.50 |

**HS** 22 May–2 Nov **MS** 27 Mar–21 May
**LS** 1 Jan–26 Mar
Supplements: Single room supplement on request. *Rates from 3 November 87 on application

## Upper Slaughter

### LORDS OF THE MANOR HOTEL

Upper Slaughter, Bourton-on-the-Water, Cheltenham, Gloucester, GL54 2JD
Tel: 0451 20243
15 Bedrooms (All with private bathroom/shower).
M T HT
Lords of the Manor Hotel is a 17th-century Cotswold rectory lovingly restored as a country house hotel, where the emphasis is on high standards of food, wine, service and comfort. The hotel stands in seven acres of grounds with its own trout lake and stream available for the exclusive use of residents.
**HS** Apr–Oct
**LS** Nov–Mar
Closed 4 Jan–19 Jan
Prices for HS B & B £25.45.
LS £75–£85 for 2 nights.

## HEREFORDSHIRE Hereford

### CASTLE POOL HOTEL

Castle Street, Hereford, Herefordshire, HR1 2NR
Tel: 0432 56321
27 Bedrooms (All with private bathroom/shower).
M T LF LP AL HT
A quiet, secluded hotel in Georgian Hereford, yet only minutes from the Wye, the cathedral and the town centre. All bedrooms en-suite with colour TV, tea/coffee-making facilities. Real ales, excellent food and summer barbecues. Extensive game and coarse fishing, including salmon, on Rivers Wye and Lugg at modest rates. Purpose built platform on the Wye for disabled anglers. Special Break rates. Trout/fly fishing weekend courses for novices on selected dates.

| | B & B | Half Board |
|---|---|---|
| | £ | £ |
| High Season | 21.00 | 31.75 |
| Low Season | 19.00 | 28.75 |

Children's discounts available
**HS** 1 Apr 87–31 Mar 88
**LS** To 31 Mar 87
Supplements: Single room £8 & £9

### THE RED LION HOTEL

Bredwardine, Nr. Hereford, Herefordshire, HR3 6BU
Tel: 09817 303
10 Bedrooms (7 with private bathroom/shower).
M LF LP AL HT
The 17th-century hotel is situated in the hamlet of Bredwardine that nestles on the banks of the River Wye, just 12 miles out of Hereford. The Wye is probably the premier salmon river in England and is renowned for its famous 'springers' as well as offering year around sport. We are one of the very few hotels that can offer fishing on their own waters, with some 8 miles under our direct control. We specialise in sporting holidays offering comfortable accommodation.

| | B & B | Half Board |
|---|---|---|
| | £ | £ |
| High Season | 45.00 | 60.00 |
| Mid Season | 30.00 | 48.00 |

Children's discounts available
**HS** Mar–Jun **MS** Jul–Oct
Closed Nov–Feb
Supplements: Single room in HS £30, MS £20.

## Ross-on-Wye

### PENGETHLEY MANOR

Nr. Ross-on-Wye, Herefordshire, HR9 6IL
Tel: 098987 211
20 Bedrooms (All with private bathroom/shower).
M T LP AL HT
Come and enjoy our luxurious Georgian country manor, our gourmet restaurant and superb wine cellar. Appreciate the peace and tranquillity of our gardens and grounds. Relax by our heated outdoor pool in summer and roaring log fires in winter. We have our own trout lake and there is salmon fishing nearby. Special rates available including English breakfast and dinner for a stay of 2 or more nights. Small parties catered for.

| | B & B | Half Board |
|---|---|---|
| | £ | £ |
| High Season | 47.00 | 67.00 |
| Mid Season | 45.00 | 64.50 |
| Low Season | 40.00 | 58.50 |

Children's discounts available
**HS** Jul–Dec, Feb
**MS** Mar–Jun
**LS** Jan
Supplements: Single room £15

### ROYAL HOTEL

Palace Pound, Ross-on-Wye, Herefordshire, HR9 5HZ
Tel: 0989 65105
31 Bedrooms (All with private bathroom/shower).
M T LF LP AL HT
The hotel has a fishing licence for the River Wye. We have fishing permits for Friday, Saturday, Sunday and Monday for salmon, and day permits may be purchased in the town. We hold special interest fishing breaks at the hotel from £90.75 for 2 days per person including dinner, bed, breakfast, packed lunch and tuition.

| | Half Board |
|---|---|
| | £ |
| High Season | 36.00 |
| Mid Season | 34.00 |
| Low Season | 32.00 |

Children's discounts available
**HS** Sep
**MS** May–Jul, Oct
**LS** Nov–Apr
Supplements: Single room £8. £5 per person De Luxe Room. £3 per person Superior Room

### SARACENS HEAD HOTEL

Symonds Yat East, Ross-on-Wye, Herefordshire, HR9 6JL
Tel: 0600 890435
11 Bedrooms (4 with private bathroom/shower).
M T LF
The Saracens Head Hotel nestles in the beautiful Wye Valley and the Forest of Dean. It is situated on the River Wye which is famous for its salmon and trout fishing. The Saracens Head Riverside Restaurant boasts the finest food.

| | B & B | Half Board |
|---|---|---|
| | £ | £ |
| High Season | 16.50 | 25.00 |

Children's discounts available
Supplements: Single room B & B £15.50, HB £24. Winter 2 Day Break (15 Oct–13 Apr) £38–£45 per person

## LEICESTERSHIRE
## Castle Donington

**PRIEST HOUSE HOTEL**
Kings Mills, Castle Donington, Nr Derby, Leicestershire, DE7 2RR
Tel: 0332 810649

15 Bedrooms (All with private bathroom/shower).

M T LF

Historic watermill on the banks of the River Trent. Coarse fishing, including the occasional trout, on hotel's own water. Log fires, real ales and friendly service from this three-star family hotel. Small matches welcome by arrangement, private dinners for fishermen a speciality.

| | B & B £ | Half Board £ |
|---|---|---|
| High Season | 22.50 | 30.50 |

Children's discounts available
Supplements: Single room £10

## Empingham

**WHITE HORSE**
Main Street, Empingham, Oakham, Leicestershire, LE15 8PR
Tel: 078086 221

11 Bedrooms (8 with private bathroom/shower).

M T LF AL HT

Situated next to the Dam on Rutland Water, the largest manmade and finest still-water trout fisheries in Europe. Stocked with brown and rainbow trout. Fishing Lodge at Whitwell (2 miles) offers weighing and gutting room. There are 15 miles of bank fishing with boats that may be reserved, available for hire. The White Horse is renowned for good quality, freshly cooked food. Both Rutland Water and inn open all year. We offer special bargain breaks. Egon Ronay recommended.

| | B & B £ |
|---|---|
| High Season | 19.50 |

Children's discounts available
Supplements: Room with bath & WC £4. Full packed lunch £4, lunches from £2.25 to £6.45. Afternoon teas £1.45

## NOTTINGHAMSHIRE
## Newark

**THE MANOR HOTEL AND RESTAURANT**
Main Road, Long Bennington, Newark, Nottinghamshire, NG23 5DJ
Tel: 0400 81374

Classification not yet known
13 Bedrooms (All with private bathroom/shower).

M T LF LP AL

In a quiet village location on the Nottinghamshire/Lincolnshire border, close to the River Trent and the historic town of Newark-on-Trent, this charming, country Manor Hotel and Restaurant makes an ideal base for people wishing to take advantage of the excellent fishing in the area. The Manor is set in 4 acres of grounds. The splendid restaurant offers both a varied menu and excellent cuisine. All rooms are en-suite.

| | B & B £ | Half Board £ |
|---|---|---|
| High Season | 17.00 | 25.00 |

Supplements: Single room £2.50.
Children free if sharing room with parents.

**ROBIN HOOD HOTEL**
Lombard Street, Newark, Nottinghamshire, NG24 1XB
Tel: 0636 703858

21 Bedrooms (All with private bathroom/shower).

M T LF HT

The Robin Hood Hotel is a two-star hotel situated in the centre of Newark, a quarter of a mile from the Trent. All bedrooms have private bathroom, TV and tea/coffee-making facilities. Night porter. Early breakfast and packed lunches available on request. Car parking for 50 cars.

| | B & B £ |
|---|---|
| High Season | 47.50 |

Children's discounts available.
Supplements: Single room £5.

## Nottingham

**POST HOUSE HOTEL**
Bostocks Lane, Sandiacre, Nottingham, Nottinghamshire, NG10 5NJ
Tel: 0602 397800

107 Bedrooms (All with private bathroom/shower).

M T LP AL HT

A modern Trusthouse Forte hotel, all rooms having private bath, situated in peaceful, rural surroundings with many attractive waters easily accessible.

| | Bed Only £ | B & B £ | Half Board £ |
|---|---|---|---|
| High Season | 27.00 | 32.00 | 40.00 |
| Low Season | 18.00 | 21.00 | 30.00 |

Children's discounts available
**HS** Monday to Thursday
**LS** Friday to Sunday
Supplements: Single room £5.
Executive rooms £7 per room per night

## SHROPSHIRE
## Clun

**BIRCHES MILL**
Clun, Nr. Craven Arms, Salop, Shropshire, SY7 8NL
Tel: 05884 409

3 Bedrooms

M LF LP AL

Birches Mill is situated beside a trout stream (The River Usk). There is good fishing in The River Clun and the Teme Valley (brown trout). There is also a private lake locally (brown & rainbow trout). Birches Mill is a recently converted 17th-century riverside farmhouse with oak beams and inglenook fire places, central heating, electric blankets in all rooms. Super food, own produce organically grown, vegetarians welcome. Riverside gardens for residents use.

| | B & B £ | Half Board £ |
|---|---|---|
| High Season | 12.00 | 19.50 |
| Mid Season | 11.00 | 18.50 |
| Low Season | 9.75 | 17.25 |

Children's discounts available
**HS** Jun–Sep
**MS** Oct, Apr–May, ex Bank Holidays
**LS** Nov–Mar, ex Christmas & New Year

## Ludlow

**CLIFFE HOTEL**
Dinham, Ludlow, Shropshire, SY8 2JE
Tel: 0584 2063

Classification not yet known
10 Bedrooms (5 with private bathroom/shower).

M LG LP AL

We are a small, family-run hotel,

situated within 2 minutes of the River Teme. We are fully licensed with a large garden and patio, serving traditional ales. Day tickets for game and coarse fishing are available on the Teme, and numerous stillwaters, all within 30 minutes drive of the hotel. Fresh bait may be ordered and local information is usually on hand. Special out-of-season rates.

| | B & B £ |
|---|---|
| High Season | 12.00 |

Children's discounts available
Supplements: Room with bath/shower and WC £2.50. Single room supplement £1 and £5. Weekly rates available

## Shrewsbury

**PRINCE RUPERT HOTEL**
Butcher Row, Shrewsbury, Shropshire, SY1 1UQ
Tel: 0743 52461

63 Bedrooms (All with private bathroom/shower).

M T LF LP AL

Shrewsbury is an excellent centre for fishermen. The River Severn virtually encloses the town and there are many good coarse fishing stretches. Good catches of salmon are taken during the season. Game fishing is available at Clywedog, Llanidloes and Lake Vernwy. The Prince Rupert Hotel combines the character of the 15th century with the best modern hotel accommodation. It is renowned for its hospitality, service and fine cuisine.

| | B & B £ | Half Board £ |
|---|---|---|
| High Season | 27.50 | 37.00 |

Children's discounts available
Supplements: Single room £5. Children sharing parents room £15 up to age 14

## WARWICKSHIRE
## Rugby

**AVONDALE GUEST HOUSE**
16 Elsee Road, Rugby, Warwickshire, CV21 3BA
Tel: 0788 78639

6 Bedrooms

M LF

A family-run Victorian guest house quietly situated within The Rugby School conservation area. A short walk to town centre and all amenities. Non fishing wives can relax in our comfortable lounge or visit Stratford-upon-Avon, Warwick Castle, Leamington Spa, Coventry and Birmingham. Excellent fishing 3 miles. Personal attention, early breakfasts, flasks, packed lunches available. Fridge/freezer/drying facilities provided.

| | B & B £ | Half Board £ |
|---|---|---|
| High Season | 12.00 | 16.50 |
| Low Season | 10.00 | 14.50 |

Children's discounts available
**HS** 20 May–30 Sep **LS** 1 Oct–19 May

**MARTON FIELDS FARM**
Marton, Nr. Rugby, Warkwickshire, CU23 9RS
Tel: 0926 632410

4 Bedrooms

M LF LP HT

A warm welcome awaits you at our 240-acre working farm. Spacious Victorian farmhouse, central heating, washbasins in bedrooms (2 twin, 1 double, and 1 single) plus tea/coffee-making facilities. Visitors sitting and dining rooms. Full English breakfast including home made bread and marmalade. Lovely countryside with River Itchen on farm. Less than 10 miles to Draycote Water Bishops Bole Nr. Rugby & Chesterton Mill Nr. Leamington Spa.

| | B & B £ |
|---|---|
| High Season | 12.00 |

Supplements: Single room £12, 2nd night onwards cost reduces to £10 per guest

## Stratford-upon-Avon

**CLIFFORD MANOR HOTEL**
Clifford Chambers, Stratford-upon-Avon, Warwickshire, CV37 8HU
Tel: 0789 292616

8 Bedrooms (6 with private bathroom/shower).

M T LF

Queen Anne manor house, set in 10 acres of garden and woodland. Coarse fishing in moat within the grounds, also fishing in nearby river. Fishing facilities also in Stratford-upon-Avon, a distance of two miles.

| | B & B £ |
|---|---|
| High Season | 35.00* |
| Mid Season | 35.00* |
| Low Season | 35.00* |

**HS** May–Sep
**MS** Mar–Apr, Oct
**LS** Nov, Jan, Feb
Supplements: *Prices quoted for different seasons vary from £35–£65

**MOAT HOUSE INTERNATIONAL**
Bridgefoot, Stratford-upon-Avon, Warwickshire, CV37 6YR Tel: 0789 67511

249 Bedrooms (All with private bathroom/shower).

M T

Luxury 4-star hotel situated in own grounds on banks of River Avon, within few minutes walk of town centre. All bedrooms have private bathroom, air-conditioning, colour TV, mini bars, 24 hour room service and laundry facilities. Excellent coarse fishing on River Avon with own Fishing Rights, local information available to guests. Game fishing within easy reach on the famous Trout waters.

| | Half Board £ |
|---|---|
| High Season | 35.00 |

Children's discounts available

## WORCESTERSHIRE
## Bewdley

**GEORGE HOTEL**
Load Street, Bewdley, Worcestershire, DY12 2QB
Tel: 0299 402117

13 Bedrooms (5 with private bathroom/shower).

M T LF LP AL HT

A 16th-century, family-run coaching inn. We pride ourselves on our home cooking and well kept ales. Late bar available to residents. Private stretch of fishing on the Severn which provides some of the best barbel fishing possible. Fishing bait and tackle shop within walking distance of the hotel and the river is only 150 yards away.

| | B & B £ | Half Board £ |
|---|---|---|
| High Season | 12.50 | 18.75 |

Children's discounts available
Supplements: Room with shower £2

# NORTH-WEST

*Tourist Information Centres ■ open all year round.*
*Not to scale.*

# NORTH WEST

This is "highland" England at its best. The North West encompasses the famed Lake District of Cumbria and the western slopes of the Pennine backbone of England. High rainfall and steep slopes send rushing rivers to the Solway and to the Irish Sea and bring up salmon and sea trout in to the Eden, Lune and Ribble and countless lesser streams. The 'Lakes' themselves are home to trout, char and pike while numerous reservoirs throughout the region provide trout and coarse fisheries.

Not all of the north west is mountainous. The southern half is made up of the great Cheshire Plain, a land of salt mines and reed-fringed meres, famed for bream but also rich in carp, tench, roach and pike. The River Dee is administered by Welsh Water even although the Chester part is English.

**Water Authorities**

North West Water, Dawson House, Great Sankey, Warrington WA5 3LW
Tel: (0925) 724321

**Regional Fisheries Office**
New Town House, Buttermarket Street, Warrington WA1 2OG
Tel: (0925) 53999

**Northern District**
North Cumbria Area Office, Chertsey Hill, London Road, Carlisle
Tel: (0228) 25151

**Central District**
Beathwaite, Levens, Kendal, Cumbria
Tel: (0448) 60567

**Southern District**
New Town House, Buttermarket Street, Warrington WA1 2OG
Tel: (0925) 53999

**Welsh Water**
Cambrian Way, Brecon, Powys LD3 7HP
Tel: (0874) 3181

**Northern Division**
Shire Hall, Mold
Tel: (0352) 58551

**Fishing Seasons**

Salmon — 1 Feb–31 Oct
  Eden catchment — 15 Jan–14 Oct
  Dee (Cheshire) — 1 Mar–15 Oct

Sea Trout — 1 May–15 Oct
  Rivers: Annas, Bleng, Esk, Mite, Irt, Calder, Ehen — 1 May–30 Oct
  River Dee (Cheshire) — 1 Mar–30 Sept

Trout (including Rainbow Trout) — 15 Mar–30 Sept

Rainbow Trout (Lakes, Reservoirs and enclosed waters) — No close season

Char — 15 Mar–30 Sept
  Coniston Water 1 May–31 Oct
  Windermere (moving boat and artificial lures) — 15 Mar–30 Sept

Coarse Fish — 16 Jun–14 Mar

**Regional Tourist Boards**
North West Tourist Board, The Last Drop Village, Bromley Cross, Bolton, Greater Manchester, BL7 9PZ
Tel: (0204) 591511

Cumbria Tourist Board, Ashleigh, Holly Road, Windermere, Cumbria LA23 2AQ
Tel: (096 62) 4444

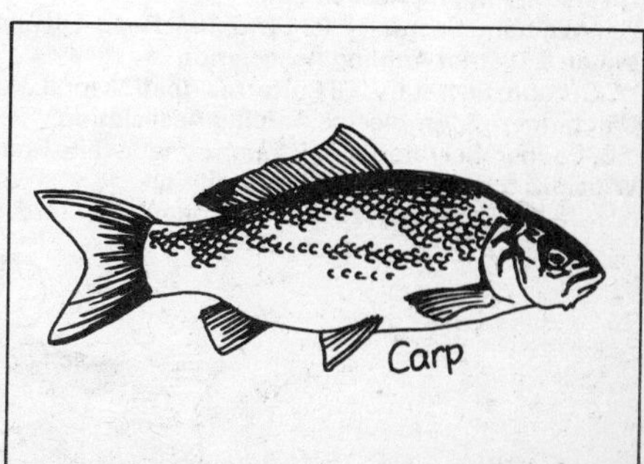

# NORTH WEST ANGLING CLUBS

**Accrington & District Fishing Club**
A. Balderstone, Secretary, 42 Towneley Avenue, Huncoat, Accrington, Lancs
**Bentham Angling Association**
A.R. Green, Secretary, The Post Office, Main Street, Bentham, Lancs LA2 7HL
**Bolton Anglers Club**
T. McKee, Secretary, 1 Lever Edge Lane, Bolton
**Congleton Anglers Society**
N.J. Bours, Secretary, 8 Norfolk Road, Congleton, Cheshire CW12 1NY
**Darwen Anglers Association**
Mr J. Priestley, Secretary, 24 Knowlesly Road, Darwen, Lancs BB3 2NE
**Egremont & District Anglers Association**
Clive Fisher, Secretary, 69 North Road, Egremont, Cumbria
**Errwood Fly Fishing Club**
Alan Hudson, Secretary, 12 Glenwood Grove, Woodsmoor, Stockport
**Ingleton Angling Association**
N.W. Capstick, Secretary, Bower Cottage, Uppergate, Ingleton, Carnforth LA6 3BG
**Kent (Westmorland) Angling Association**
Secretary, The Hyena, 9 Fountain Brow, Kendal, Cumbria
**Liverpool & District Anglers Association**
J. Johnson, Secretary, 97 Liverpool Road (North), Maghull, Merseyside L31 2HG
**Lonsdale Angling Club**
W.L. Dagger, Secretary, 71 Cleveleys Avenue, Lancaster, Lancs
**Lymm Angling Club**
J.S. Graham, Secretary, 15 Boswell Avenue, Warrington, Cheshire WA4 6DQ
**Macclesfield Waltonian Angling Society**
Secretary, 4 The Green, Cookshill, Caverswall, Stoke-on-Trent ST11 9EQ
**Northern Anglers Association**
Brendan Dawes, Secretary, 51 Brennand Street, Burnley, Lancs BB10 1SU
**Oldham & District Amalgamated Anglers Association**
H. Garside, Secretary, 60 Queensway, Greenfield, Nr Oldham OL3 7AH
**Penrith Angling Association**
R.F. Allinson, Secretary, 7 Scaws Drive, Penrith, Cumbria
**Rowland Game-Fishing Association**
B. Hoggarth, Secretary, 1 Moorfield Road, Leyland, Preston, Lancs PR5 3AR
**Sedbergh Anglers**
G. Bainbridge, Secretary, El Kantara, Garsdale Foot, Sedbergh, Cumbria
**South Manchester Angling Club**
David Crookall, Secretary, 12 Wincombe Street, Rusholme, Manchester M14 7PJ
**Southport Angling Association**
Malcolm Bannister, Secretary, 7 Sunny Road, Southport, Lancs
**Stanley Park Angling Society**
Ian Heyworth, Secretary, 212 West Park Drive, Blackpool, Lancs
**Staveley Angling Association**
A. Mawson, Secretary, "Blakebank", Staveley, Nr Kendal, Cumbria
**Ulverston Angling Association**
H.B. Whittam, Secretary, 29 Lyndhurst Road, Ulverston, Cumbria
**Wigan & District Angling Association**
W. Gratton, Secretary, 66 Balcarres Road, Aspull, Wigan
**Windermere & Ambleside Angling Association**
J.B. Cooper, Secretary, 'Rylstone', Limethwaite Road, Windermere, Cumbria
**Winsford & District Anglers Association**
J.S. Bailey, Secretary, 22 Plover Avenue, Winsford, Cheshire

# RIVERS AND CANALS

| Water | Location | Species | Permits |
|---|---|---|---|
| **Brathay** | Ambleside | Salmon<br>Sea Trout | Windermere and Ambleside Angling Association<br>Local Shops, Hotels and Tourist Information Centres |
| **Bridgewater Canal** | Timperley to Leightown Bridge | Mixed Coarse Fish | Northern Anglers Association<br>Local Tackle Shops |
| **Calder** | Mitton | Mixed Coarse Fish | North West Water<br>Mrs Haynes, Mitton Hall Farm, Mitton, Near Whalley |
| | Whalley | Mixed Coarse Fish | Marsden Star Angling Society<br>Local Tackle Shops |
| **Crossens** | Southport | Mixed Coarse Fish | Southport Angling Association<br>Crossens Tackle Shop, 186A Rufford Road, Southport<br>J.E. Robinson, 71 Sussex Road, Southport |
| **Dane** | Middlewich | Roach<br>Bream<br>Chub | Winsford and District Anglers Association<br>Harrisons Pet Store, Delamere Street, Winsford |
| **Dee (Cheshire)** | Chester | Grayling<br>Chub<br>Roach<br>Bream<br>Dace | Chester Association of Anglers<br>Martins Tackle,<br>Bridge Street, Chester |
| | Chester (Part) | | Free Fishing with Welsh Water Licence |
| | Farndon Bridge | Salmon<br>Trout<br>Sea Trout<br>Coarse Fish | Dee AA<br>Secretary, 2 Snowdon Crescent<br>Lache Lane, Chester |
| **Derwent** | Keswick | Salmon<br>Trout<br>Pike<br>Perch | Kelso Anglers Association<br>Tackle Shops in Keswick |
| | Keswick | Trout<br>Grayling<br>Pike<br>Perch | Derwentwater Hotel<br>Portinscale, Keswick |
| **Doe** | Ingleton | Trout<br>Sea Trout<br>Salmon | Ingleton Angling Association<br>P. Berry, Newsagents, Main Street, Ingleton |
| **Eden** | Ravenstonedale | Brown Trout | Black Swan Hotel<br>Ravenstonedale, Kirkby Stephen |
| | Kirkoswald | Salmon<br>Trout | Midland Hotel, Lazonby<br>Tel: Lazonby (076 883) 331<br>By arrangement through:<br>Prospect Hill Hotel, Kirkoswald, Penrith<br>Tel: Lazonby (076 883) 500 |
| | Lazonby | Salmon<br>Trout | Bracken Bank Lodge Limited<br>Lazonby, Penrith Tel: Lazonby (076 883) |
| | Appleby | Game Fish | Eden Bank Hotel, Bolton<br>Appleby in Cumbria Tel: 093 14 219 |

| Water | Location | Species | Permits |
|---|---|---|---|
| **Eden contd.** | Penrith | Salmon<br>Trout | The Mill Inn, Mungrisdale, Penrith<br>Tel: 059 683 632 |
| **Ehen** | Egremont | Salmon<br>Sea Trout<br>Trout | Egremont and District Anglers Association<br>W.N. Holmes, Main Street, Egremont |
| **Greta** | Ingleton | Trout<br>Sea Trout<br>Salmon | Ingleton Angling Association<br>P. Berry, Newsagents, Main Street, Ingleton |
| **Hodder** | Clitheroe | Salmon<br>Sea Trout<br>Trout<br>Grayling | The Inn at Whitewell<br>Forest of Bowland, Nr Clitheroe, Lancashire<br>Tel: 02008 222 |
| | Hurst Green | Game Fish | Shireburn Arms Hotel, 1 Whalley Road<br>Hurst Green, Nr Blackburn, Lancs<br>Tel: 0254 86 518 |
| **Huddersfield Narrow Canal** | Lock 24 to Bridge 85 | Trout<br>Coarse Fish | Oldham and District Amalgamated Anglers Association<br>Local Tackle Shops<br>Bailiffs on water |
| **Kent** | Kendal | Salmon<br>Sea Trout<br>Trout | Kent (Westmoreland) Angling Association<br>Kendal Sports, 30 Stramongate, Kendal<br>Tel: Kendal (0539) 21554<br>Carlson's Fishing Tackle, Kirkland, Kendal<br>Tel: Kendal (0539) 24867 |
| | Kendal | Trout | Staveley Angling Association<br>Chemist Shop, Staveley, Nr Kendal |
| **Lancaster Canal** | Preston to Tewitsfield and Glasson Arm | Coarse Fish | Northern Anglers Association |
| **Leeds and Liverpool Canal** | Chorley to Long Inge Bridge<br>Bank Newton Top Lock to Leeds | Coarse Fish | Northern Anglers Association |
| | Halsall to Liverpool | Coarse | Liverpool and District Anglers Association<br>All Tackle Shops on Merseyside |
| **Liddle** | Longtown Nr Carlisle | Salmon<br>Sea Trout<br>Trout | March Bank Country House Hotel<br>Scotsdyke, Via Longtown, Carlisle<br>Tel: (0228) 791325 |
| **Lune** | Lancaster (Halton) | Salmon<br>Sea Trout<br>Trout<br>Coarse Fish | Lansil Angling Club<br>Secretary, J.E.N. Barnes, 88 West End Road, Morecambe, Lancs<br>Tel: (0524) 416006 |
| | Halton | | North West Water<br>R.A. Maxfield, 5 Moor Lane, Lancaster |
| | Skerton | | North West Water<br>R.A. Maxfield, 5 Moor Lane, Lancaster |
| | Tebay | | Tebay Fishing Club<br>Black Swan Hotel, Ravenstonedale, Kirkby Stephen, Cumbria<br>Tel: 05873 204 |
| | Caton (Hermitage) | | Northern Anglers Association<br>J.H. Tucker, 6 Nelson Street, Preston<br>Tel: Preston 702672<br>(Special Day Permit — in advance) |

| Water | Location | Species | Permits |
|---|---|---|---|
| **Lune contd.** | Sedbergh | Salmon<br>Sea Trout<br>Trout | Sedbergh Anglers<br>Sports Shop, Main St, Sedbergh |
| **Macclesfield Canal** | Macclesfield Bridge 37 to Marple Top Locks High Poynton | Coarse Fish | Northern Anglers Association |
| **Ribble** | Preston (Parts) | Coarse Fish | Northern Anglers Association |
| | Clitheroe | Game and Coarse Fish | Ribble Valley Borough Council<br>Church Walk, Clitheroe (Mon–Fri 9am–4.45pm)<br>The Warden, Edisford Caravan Site, Edisford Bridge (Apr–Oct) |
| | Preston<br>Longridge | | Bolton and District Anglers Association<br>All Local Tackle Shops |
| | Mitton Bridge to Calderfoot | Game and Coarse Fish | North West Water<br>Mrs Haynes, Mitton Hall Farm, Mitton, Near Whalley |
| | Hurst Green | Game Fish | Shireburn Arms Hotel, 1 Whalley Road<br>Hurst Green, Nr Blackburn, Lancs<br>Tel: 0254 86 518 |
| **Rothay** | Ambleside | Salmon<br>Sea Trout<br>Trout | Windermere and Ambleside Angling Association<br>Local Shops, Hotels and Tourist Information Centres |
| **Rufford Canal** | Tarlton to Rufford | Coarse Fish | Liverpool and District Anglers Association<br>All Tackle Shops on Merseyside |
| **Sankey — St Helens Canal** | Bewsey Old Hall to Ferry Inn | Coarse Fish including Carp | Lymm Angling Club<br>Bailiff on bank |
| **Shropshire Union Canal** | Ellesmere Port to Chester | Coarse Fish | Liverpool and District Anglers Association<br>All Tackle Shops on Merseyside |
| | Ellesmere Port to Bridge 45, Knighton and Other Stretches | Coarse Fish | Northern Anglers Association |
| **South Tyne** | Alston | Salmon<br>Sea Trout<br>Trout | Alston and District Angling Association |
| **Twiss** | Ingleton | Trout<br>Sea Trout<br>Salmon | Ingleton Angling Association<br>P. Berry, Newsagents, Main Street, Ingleton |
| **Weaver** | Winsford | Carp<br>Tench<br>Roach<br>Bream | Winsford and District Anglers Association<br>Harrisons Pet Store, Delamere Street, Winsford |
| **Wenning** | Bentham | Salmon<br>Sea Trout<br>Trout | Bentham Angling Association<br>Churchill's, Station Road, Bentham |
| **Wyre** | Garstang | Salmon<br>Trout<br>Chub<br>Roach | Lonsdale Angling Club<br>Tackle Shops in Lancaster and Morecambe<br>Bolton and District Anglers Association<br>All Local Tackle Shops |

# LAKES AND RESERVOIRS

| Water | Location | Species | Permits |
|---|---|---|---|
| **Alexandra Park Lake** | Moss Side<br>Manchester | Perch<br>Roach<br>Tench<br>Carp | City of Manchester Recreational Services<br>Moss Side Centre, Moss Lane East, Manchester<br>Tel: 061 226 0131 ext 240<br>Permits sold on bank |
| **Bailrigg Lake** | Lancaster | Carp<br>Tench<br>Catfish<br>Rudd<br>Perch<br>Bream | Lonsdale Angling Club<br>Membership Secretary, Mr M. Moore, 135 Willow Lane, Lancaster<br>(No day tickets) |
| **Barrowford Reservoir** | Burnley | Trout<br>Bream<br>Roach<br>Perch | Marsden Star Angling Society<br>Tackle Shops in Nelson, Burnley |
| **Bassenthwaite** | Keswick | Trout<br>Pike<br>Perch | Lake District Special Planning Board<br>Temple's Sports Shop, Station Street, Keswick |
| **Bigland Hall Fishery** | Newby Bridge | Pike<br>Perch<br>Roach<br>Rudd<br>Tench | Bigland Hall Estate Office<br>Blackbarrow, Newby Bridge<br>Tel: 0448 31361 |
| **Bigland Hall Trout Fishery** | Newby Bridge | Rainbow Trout | Bigland Hall Estate Office, Blackbarrow, Newby Bridge Tel: 0448 31361 |
| **Blackley New Road Upper Lake** | Manchester | Trout<br>Mixed Coarse Fish | City of Manchester Recreational Services<br>Reece Tackle Shop, Blackley New Road, Nr Blackley |
| **Boggart Hole Clough Lake** | Blackley<br>Manchester | Roach<br>Perch<br>Carp | City of Manchester Recreational Services<br>Permits from attendant |
| **Boretree Tarn** | Newby Bridge | Pike<br>Perch | Lonsdale Angling Club<br>Tackle Shops in Lancaster and Morecambe |
| **Brookside Trout Fishery** | Crewe | Brown Trout<br>Rainbow Trout<br>Brook Trout | Brookside Trout Fishery<br>Church Lane, Betley, Nr Crewe, Cheshire<br>Tel: Crewe (0270) 820528<br>(Barbless hooks only) |
| **Lake Burwain** | Foulridge<br>Nr Colne | Trout<br>Carp<br>Tench<br>Bream<br>Roach<br>Pike | Lake Burwain Fishing<br>(Foulridge Reservoir)<br>Day tickets at Lake<br>Match permits from:<br>Mr J.C. Peate, c/o The Anchorage, Foulridge, Colne, Lancashire<br>Tel: 0282 863933 |
| **Buttermere** | Keswick | Trout<br>Char<br>Pike<br>Perch | Rannerdale Farm,<br>Buttermere |
| **Calderstones Park Lake** | Liverpool | Mixed Coarse Fish | City of Liverpool<br>Recreation and Open Spaces Department, The Mansion House, Calderstones Park, Liverpool<br>Tel: 051 724 2371 |

| Water | Location | Species | Permits |
|---|---|---|---|
| **Chorlton Water Park** | Manchester | Mixed Coarse including Carp Crucian Carp | City of Manchester Recreational Services Permit on bank or Head Office |
| **Clayton Hall Sand Quarry** | Leyland | Roach Tench Bream | Leyland and Farington Centre N.A.A. A.C. Angling, Towngate, Leyland, Lancs |
| **Cleabarrow Tarn** | Bowness | Carp | Windermere, Ambleside and District Angling Association (Local permit only) |
| **Coniston Water** | Coniston | Trout Char Pike Perch | Free Fishing |
| **Crummock Water** | Keswick | Trout Char Pike Perch | Rannerdale Farm Buttermere Tel: 059685 232 |
| **Debdale Lower Reservoir** | Manchester | Trout Coarse Fish | City of Manchester Recreational Services Permits at Reservoir (Disabled Facilities) |
| **Debdale Upper Reservoir** | Manchester | Mixed Coarse | City of Manchester Recreational Services Permits at Reservoir |
| **Derwentwater** | Keswick | Trout Pike Perch | Derwentwater Hotel Portinscale, Keswick Tel: 07687 72538 |
| | Keswick | Salmon Trout Pike Perch | Keswick Anglers Association Tackle Shops, Keswick |
| **Earnsdale Reservoir** | Darwen | Brown Trout Rainbow Trout | Darwen Anglers Association County Sports Shop, 181 Duckworth Street, Darwen, Lancs Tel: 0254 72187 |
| **Errwood Reservoir** | Whalley Bridge Buxton | Brown Trout Rainbow Trout | Errwood Fly Fishing Club Shadyoak Hotel, Long Hill, Whalley Bridge |
| **Esthwaite Water** | Hawkshead | Trout Pike | Red Lion Inn, Hawkshead, Nr Ambleside, Cumbria Tel: 09666 213 |
| **Haweswater** | Shap | Trout | North West Water Free Fishing |
| **Heaton Park Boating Lake** | Manchester | Pike Perch Roach Carp | City of Manchester Recreational Services Permit from Tackle Office or Attendant (Restricted Fishing during Public Boating Season) |
| **High Arnside Tarn** | Ambleside | Trout | Windermere, Ambleside and District Angling Association Local Shops, Hotels and Tourist Information Centres |
| **Hurleston Hall Fishery** | Ormskirk | Rainbow Trout | Hurleston Hall Fishery per 81 Yew Tree Road, Ormskirk, Lancashire Tel: Ormskirk (0695) 75901 (Booking essential) |
| **Jumbles Reservoir** | Bradshaw | Mixed Coarse Fish | North West Water Free Fishing |

| Water | Location | Species | Permits |
|---|---|---|---|
| **Kentmere Tarn** | Kendal | Brown Trout | Staveley Angling Association<br>Chemist Shop, Staveley |
| **Lough Trout Fishery** | Carlisle | Brown Trout<br>Rainbow Trout | Lough Trout Fishery<br>Thurstonfield, Carlisle Tel: 0228 76552 |
| **Lymm Dam** | Warrington | Carp<br>Tench<br>Pike<br>Bream | Lymm A.C.<br>Bailiff on bank |
| **Meadow Fishery** | Chester | Brown Trout<br>Rainbow Trout<br>Brook Trout | Meadow Farm<br>Mickle Trafford, Chester<br>Tel: 0244 300236 |
| **Mitchell House Reservoirs** | Accrington | Rainbow Trout | Accrington and District Fishing Club<br>Tackle Shops in Accrington |
| **Moss Eccles Tarn** | Hawkshead | Brown Trout | Windermere, Ambleside and District Angling Association<br>Local Shops, Hotels and Tourist Information Centres |
| **Parsonage Reservoir** | Blackburn | Brown Trout<br>Rainbow Trout | Bowland Game Fishing Association<br>Roe Lee Tackle Box, Whalley New Road, Blackburn |
| **Pinfold Tarn** | Ravenstonedale | Rainbow Trout | Black Swan Hotel<br>Ravenstonedale, Kirkby Stephen, Cumbria<br>Tel: 05873 204 |
| **Platt Fields Park Lake** | Rusholme | Coarse Fish | City of Manchester Recreational Services<br>Permits on bank |
| **Princes Park Lake** | Liverpool | Coarse Fish | City of Liverpool<br>Free Fishing — No Permit Required |
| **Rivington Reservoirs (Upper/Lower and Anglezark)** | Adlington | Trout<br>Coarse Fish | North West Water<br>Anderton Yard, Horwich, Bolton<br>Tel: Horwich 696118<br>(Under Review) |
| **Roddlesworth Reservoirs (Upper/Lower)** | Preston | Trout<br>Coarse Fish | North West Water<br>Anderton Yard, Horwich, Bolton<br>Tel: Horwich 696118 |
| **Rydal Water** | Ambleside | Salmon<br>Sea Trout<br>Trout<br>Pike<br>Perch | Windermere, Ambleside and District Angling Association<br>Local Shops, Hotels and Tourist Information Centres |
| **School Knott Tarn** | Windermere | Trout | Windermere, Ambleside and District Angling Association<br>Local Shops, Hotels and Tourist Information Centres |
| **Sefton Park Lake** | Liverpool | Mixed Coarse Fish | City of Liverpool<br>Free Fishing — No Permit Required |
| **Shakerley Mere** | Holmes Chaple | Mixed Coarse Fish | Congleton Anglers Society<br>Bailiff on duty on site |
| **Stanley Park Lake** | Blackpool | Mixed Coarse Fish | Stanley Park Angling Society<br>Permit on bankside |
| **Stanley Park Lake** | Liverpool | Mixed Coarse Fish | City of Liverpool<br>Free Fishing — No Permit Required |

| Water | Location | Species | Permits |
|---|---|---|---|
| **Statham Pool** | Warrington | Mixed Coarse Fish | Lymm Angling Club<br>From Bailiff on bank |
| **Stocks Reservoir** | Clitheroe | Brown Trout<br>Rainbow Trout<br>Brook Trout | Bentham Trout Farm<br>Low Mill, Bentham, Lancs<br>Tel: 0468 61305 |
| **Swantley Lake** | Lancaster | Mixed Coarse Fish including Orfe | Lonsdale Angling Club<br>Tackle Shops in Lancaster and Morecambe |
| **Tatton Mere** | Knutsford | Mixed Coarse including<br>Roach<br>Bream<br>Hybrids<br>Rudd<br>Carp | Cheshire County Council<br>Tatton Park, Knutsford, Cheshire<br>Knutsford entrance Pay Kiosk<br>Ranger staff for early anglers |
| **Teggsnose Reservoir** | Macclesfield | Carp<br>Bream<br>Roach<br>Tench | Macclesfield Waltonian Angling Society<br>Macclesfield Tile Centre, Windmill Street, Macclesford |
| **Thirlmere** | Keswick | Trout | North West Water<br>Mintsfleet Road South, Kendal<br>Tel: Kendal 21505<br>Free Fishing<br>Post Office, Thirlspot<br>Kings Head Hotel, Thirlmere |
| **Twin Lakes Trout Fishery** | Chorley | Brown Trout<br>Rainbow Trout<br>Brook Trout | Twin Lakes Trout Fishery<br>Brickcroft Lane, Croston, Nr Preston, Lancs<br>Permits at Fishery Shop |
| **Ullswater** | Penrith | Trout<br>Schelly<br>Perch | No Permit Required |
| **Upper Langendale Valley and Reservoirs** | Nr Glossop | | North West Water<br>Mintsfleet Road South, Kendal<br>Tel: Kendal 21505 |
| **Walton Hall Park** | Liverpool | Mixed Coarse Fish | City of Liverpool<br>Free Fishing |
| **Wastwater** | Seascale | Trout<br>Pike<br>Perch | National Trust Campsite<br>Wasdale Head |
| **Westlow Mere Trout Fishery** | Congleton | Brown Trout<br>Rainbow Trout | Congleton Anglers<br>Local Tackle Shop<br>Hut at Mere |
| **Whalley Abbey Trout Fishery** | Blackburn | Rainbow | Whalley Abbey Trout Fishery<br>Clitheroe by-Pass, Whalley, Nr Blackburn<br>Tel: 0254 822211 |
| **Windermere** | Windermere | Trout<br>Char<br>Perch<br>Pike | Low Wood Hotel<br>Windermere<br>Tel: 0966 33338 |

# SEA ANGLING

### The Wirral
New Brighton, West Kirby and Thurstaston all provide fishing possibilities. However, the whole of the area is rather dangerous and most local anglers prefer to travel away to more convenient and productive venues.

### Southport
Flounder, dab and small plaice make up the bulk of the summer catches. During the winter, whiting and the occasional cod can be expected. Offshore marks produce skate, tope, dogfish, mackerel, cod, and whiting. Shore fishing marks in the Southport area include the beach at Formby, Southport Beach and the Pinfold Channel. Pier anglers can pay Southport Corporation a modest sum for a ticket to fish Southport Pier.

### Blackpool
Summertime beach fishing on any of the beaches in the Blackpool area is out of the question. For summertime sport the estuaries of the River Ribble and River Wyre provide the best chance of escaping the holiday crowds. In winter, things are different and then it is worth fishing the local beaches. The same applies to pier and promenade fishing. Lytham St Anne's promenade and the sea wall at Blackpool are then worth trying. The North Pier at Blackpool can also be fairly good to fish from. This pier costs a few five-pence pieces per day but gives the angler the chance of a good sized winter cod or some whiting. Blackpool cod seldom reach a weight of more than 15 lb but the fish that are caught are all decent sizes, averaging 6 lb to 10 lb.

### Cleveleys
Situated midway between Blackpool and Fleetwood, Cleveleys offers fair sport with flatfish, whiting and cod. Cleveleys breakwater and the promenade at Anchorsholme are the most productive spots to fish.

### Fleetwood
Noted mainly as a commercial fishing port, Fleetwood has quite a lot to offer the angler as well. Charter boats can be hired and it is possible to launch small boats as well. Boat marks produce cod, skate, dogfish, whiting, silver eels and flatfish. The occasional tope and conger eel may also be encountered. Shore fishermen can fish from Easton Beach, Marine Beach and from various points in the estuary of the River Wyre. Fleetwood Town Pier is also worth a try, as too is the Jubilee Quay in the area between the ferry and the fish dock.
The docks and the estuary are good for flatfish, particularly flounders and silver eels. Local beaches and the pier produce more of a mixed bag — cod, whiting, flatfish, eels, dogfish and the very occasional bass. Lugworm is a favourite local bait and can be dug from Marine Beach. Soft-back and peeler crabs make a good all-round bait in this area. These can be found round the wall of the Jubilee Quay.

### Morecambe and Heysham
During the past few seasons Morecambe Bay has been much in the angling newspapers, with catch after catch of very big thornback ray. Local charter and private boats fishing various marks within the bay continually make contact with packs of heavyweight thornbacks, most of which fall to mackerel bait. Individual boat catches of up to twenty big ray in a single day's fishing are commonplace and a number of fish in excess of 20 lb have been taken. Shore anglers have always enjoyed fair beach and pier fishing in this area and this, coupled with the good boat fishing, has made the Morecambe area most popular.
All the local beaches are worth trying, as too are the outfall-pipe area, the sea wall, the battery slipway and the Central Pier. Lugworm can be dug in the area. Flatfish, mostly dabs, flounders and small plaice, make up the bulk of the beach catches, but there is always the chance of making contact with the odd bass and, in the winter, whiting.

### Barrow-in-Furness
Between Morecambe and Barrow there are many places where fishing is possible and anglers keen on flatfish will do well to explore this very tidal stretch of coastline. Barrow itself offers reasonably good fishing for flatfish, silver eels, pouting, cod, mackerel, bass and mullet. Some of the best fishing in the area is round the Roa Island Hotel and the Causeway at Foulney Island. The stone jetty directly opposite the Roa Island Hotel fishes well for good-sized cod and whiting. The occasional tope and bass can also be expected, but both are far from common. Between

Barrow and Whitehaven miles of flat sand offer plenty of scope for exploration, particularly for flatfish.

**Whitehaven**
In my opinion Whitehaven is the start of true cod country. Along this stretch of coastline, with mixed rock and beach fishing available, anglers have plenty of scope for good mixed fishing. The West Pier and North Pier, local names for the harbour walls at Whitehaven, provide fair fishing for flatfish, silver eels, pouting and the occasional mackerel. Wellington Beach is a fair flatfish and silver eel mark and the rocks at St Bees Head are likely to produce all kinds of fish including cod and whiting. The cliff paths down to these rocks tend to be dangerous in wet weather and at night, so great care should be exercised when fishing this area.

At Parton there is also some fair rock fishing but on flood tides these rocks can become very dangerous so keep a weather eye on the tide and move inshore before it rises and cuts you off from safety. It is sometimes possible to gather crabs for bait at Parton Rocks. Lugworm, however, is scarce and has to be bought locally or dug farther up the coast at Workington.

**Workington**
Harrington Beach, to the south of the town and Siddick Beach to the north are well worth visiting. These beaches fish best for flounder, dab and small plaice. Boat fishing along this coast can be very good, and boats can be launched at Harrington. The best fishing seems to be one to three miles offshore. Catches include skate, cod, whiting, dogfish and mackerel. Baited feathers are good for most species, although the skate are best fished with a plain running leger.

**Maryport to Gretna Green**
From Maryport to Gretna the fishing is mainly over flat sand and mud. At Maryport itself the promenade beach, Grasslot Beach and the south and north pier are worth trying. Pollack, codling and flatfish are the common species. Boats can be launched at Maryport and the offshore fishing is good. Ragworm can be dug in many places. To the north of Maryport the coastline faces bleakly out on to the wastes of the Solway Firth. Various points along this coastline are fishable and creeks which wind inshore often produce good catches of prime flounders.

# ACCOMMODATION

## CHESHIRE
### Chester

**CURZON HOTEL**
54 Hough Green, Chester, Cheshire, CH4 8JQ
Tel: 0244 678581
[4 crowns]
16 Bedrooms (All with private bathroom/shower).
[symbols] M T LG LP AL HT
An exclusive, small hotel, one mile from Chester city centre. Family-owned and managed Victorian house, recently converted into 16 bedrooms, all en-suite. TV, telephone, tea/coffee-making facilities in all rooms. Licensed bar and dining room. Single, double and twin rooms. Large private car park.

| | Bed Only £ | B & B £ | Half Board £ |
|---|---|---|---|
| High Season | 20.00 | 24.00 | 30.00 |
| Mid Season | 17.00 | 21.00 | 27.00 |
| Low Season | 15.00 | 18.00 | 22.00 |

Children's discounts available
**HS** Jun–Aug
**MS** Sep–Oct
**LS** Nov–May
Supplements: Single room supplement £3

## CUMBRIA
### Alston

**LOWBYER MANOR HOTEL**
Hexham Road, Alston, Cumbria, CA9 3JX
Tel: 0498 81230
Classification not yet known
12 Bedrooms (All with private bathroom/shower).
[symbols] M LG LP AL
Charming 17th-century Manor House, fully modernised and converted for guests' comfort. All rooms en-suite and centrally heated. Courtyard restaurant with a la carte menu, under personal supervision of owners. Comfortable lounge with TV, library for peace and quiet, cosy bar with inglenook. Coarse and fly fishing. Drying facilities; refrigeration facilities; packed lunches on request. Ample private parking.

| | Bed Only £ | B & B £ | Half Board £ |
|---|---|---|---|
| High Season | 13.25 | 18.75 | 28.25 |

Children's discounts available
Supplements: Single room supplement £6.25

See page 4 for details of symbols

## Ambleside

**QUEEN'S HOTEL**
Market Place, Ambleside, Cumbria, LA22 9BU
Tel: 05394 32206

30 Bedrooms (22 with private bathroom/shower).

M T LF LP AL HT

The Lake District offers a wide range of game and coarse fishing; fly fishing for brown and rainbow trout in the Tarns; perch and brown trout in the lakes and rivers; also sea trout and salmon. A warm, Cumbrian welcome awaits you at the Queen's Hotel, well-situated in the centre of Ambleside, where you can be sure of quiet relaxation, comfort and first-class service in the friendly atmosphere of a family-run hotel.

| | B & B £ | Half Board £ |
|---|---|---|
| High Season | 18.00 | 25.50 |
| Mid Season | 15.00 | 20.50 |

Children's discounts available
**HS** Bank holiday weekends
**MS** All others
Supplements: Room with bath/shower & WC £2.50. Single room £2

## Appleby-in-Westmorland

**EDENBANK FARM**
Bolton, Appleby-in-Westmorland, Cumbria, CA16 6AN
Tel: 093 14 219
4 Bedrooms

M T LF LP AL HT

This peaceful, secluded working farm, set on the edge of The Lake District and within easy reach of Yorkshire Dales makes it the ideal base for both anglers and non-anglers. It has its own stretch of private fishing on the River Eden. Amenities include packed lunches, drying facilities, freezer storage. There is tea/coffee-making facilities and central heating in all rooms. Tuition available.

| | B & B £ |
|---|---|
| High Season | 10.00 |
| Mid Season | 9.00 |
| Low Season | 8.00 |

Children's discounts available
**HS** Jun–Sep, Bank Holidays
**MS** Oct, Mar–May **LS** Nov–Feb
Supplements: Fishing rights on application

## Cockermouth

**KIRKSTILE INN**
Loweswater, Cockermouth, Cumbria, CA13 0RU
Tel: 090085 219

10 Bedrooms (8 with private bathroom/shower).

M LP AL

The 16th-century inn is ideally situated between the lakes of Loweswater and Crummock Water which offer excellent game and coarse fishing. For sea anglers the Solway coast is only approx. 12 miles away. After a long day's fishing relax with a pint of real ale and a bar supper, or enjoy dinner in the traditional oak beamed restaurant.

| B & B £ | Half Board £ |
|---|---|
| 13.00 | 21.75 |

Children's discounts available
Supplements: Room with bath/shower & WC £6. Single room £6.50

**SCALE HILL HOTEL**
Loweswater, Nr. Cockermouth, Cumbria, CA13 9UX
Tel: 090085 232
14 Bedrooms (13 with private bathroom/shower).

M LF LP AL

The valley boasts 3 lakes, all containing trout, pike and perch, whilst Crummock Water, half-a-mile away, is also wellknown for its char! Loweswater is stocked with trout by the National Trust who own the lake, and also the rowing boats which are available together with permits from Scale Hill. There are 2 small lakes within 10 miles which are regularly stocked with rainbow trout.

| | B & B £ | Half Board £ |
|---|---|---|
| High Season | 20.00 | 30.00 |
| Low Season | 16.00 | 24.00 |

Children's discounts available
**HS** Easter–October
**LS** November–Easter
Closed January & February
Supplements: Room with bath/shower & WC £2. Single room £4

## Coniston

**SUNNY BANK MILL**
Torver, Coniston, Cumbria, LA21 8BL
Tel: 0966 41300
Classification not yet known
6 Bedrooms (All with private bathroom/shower).

M LF AL

An old mill beside Torver Beck offering top quality en-suite accommodation with TV and tea/coffee-making facilities. Large lounge. Access at all times. Laundry and drying facilities. Private trout and salmon stream, and lake frontage onto Coniston water with boat for hire. Sea estuary and canal within 10 miles. Packed lunches – evening meals by arrangement. License applied for. Short break and weekly terms on application.

| | B & B £ |
|---|---|
| High Season | 36.40 |
| Low Season | 32.36 |

**HS** May–Sep **LS** Oct–Apr
Supplements: Single room £2.

## Grasmere

**WHITE MOSS HOUSE**
Rydal Water, Grasmere, Cumbria, LA22 9SE
Tel: 096665 295
7 Bedrooms (All with private bathroom/shower).

M T LF LP

A small luxury hotel, situated in the heart of the English Lakes. White Moss House, once owned by Wordsworth, now has an outstanding reputation for food and wine. Described as 'the best English food in the country', the five-course dinner and the excellent cooked breakfast use only the finest fresh local produce. The River Rothay, Rydal Water and Grasmere Lake are only a few minutes walk from the hotel and free fishing is available for guests on all local water.

| | B & B £ | Half Board £ |
|---|---|---|
| High Season | 27.50 | 45.50 |

**HS** Mid Mar–Mid Nov
Closed Mid Nov–Mid Mar
Supplements: Single room £10.

## Hawkshead

**FIELD HEAD HOUSE HOTEL**
Outgate, Hawkshead, Cumbria, LA22 0PY
Tel: 09666 240

8 Bedrooms (7 with private bathroom/shower).

M T LF LP AL HT

Quietly situated midst beautiful scenery, Field Head House Hotel is an elegant, warm and historic country house with modern facilities and run by owners Bob and Eeke van Gulik. Nearby trout fishing on lakes and rivers, Windermere (10 minutes) for char and pike. Sea fishing trips, permits, boats, tackle, tuition and expert local advice arranged. Excellent food (fresh vegetables from own gardens) at times to suit you and a warm toddy on your return.

| | B & B £ | Half Board £ |
|---|---|---|
| High Season | 17.00 | 30.00 |

Children's discounts available
Supplements: Room with bath/shower & WC £3

**RED LION INN**
Hawkshead, Nr. Ambleside, Cumbria, LA22 0NS
Tel: 09666 213
8 Bedrooms (All with private bathroom/shower).

M T

Esthwaite Water. Set in the Vale of Esthwaite, some two miles from Hawkshead village. Superb fishing for brown trout, rainbow trout, pike — a water for all seasons.

| | B & B £ | Half Board £ |
|---|---|---|
| High Season | 16.50 | 25.00 |

Children's discounts available
Supplements: Single room £2

*Prices in England for Fishing are per person, sharing a double room, per night, including VAT (at the current rate of 15 per cent). Check prices when you book and mention England for Fishing.*

## Kendal

**HILL FOLD FARM**
Burneside, Kendal, Cumbria, LA8 9AU Tel: 0539 22574
3 Bedrooms

M LP

Hill Fold is a 400-acre dairy/sheep farm situated 3 miles north of Kendal, close to the rolling hills of Potter Fell, within easy reach of lakes and sea. You will find colour TV, log fires in lounge, H & C heaters, shaver points, exposed beams in bedrooms. Bathroom with separate WC. Fishing river: trout, sea trout, salmon, private tarn, trout/fly. Lakes fishing: char etc. Sea fishing: Morecambe Bay. Fishing fee by arrangement. Wholesome meals, genuine hospitality.

| | B & B £ | Half Board £ |
|---|---|---|
| High Season | 8.00 | 12.00 |

Children's discounts available

## Keswick

**DERWENTWATER HOTEL**
Portinscale, Keswick, Cumbria, CA12 5RE
Tel: 07687 72538

46 Bedrooms (All with private bathroom/shower).

M T LP AL HT

Like a jewel set in the heart of the lakelands, Derwentwater reflects a timeless beauty that enchants all who visit her. Perched on the shores is Derwentwater Hotel, in 16 acres of prime lakeland grounds with lots of lake and river to fish without paying for permits. Boat hire a short stroll away, but above all your hotel is a home away from home dedicated to answer your every need and staffed by people who really care.

| | Half Board £ |
|---|---|
| High Season | 30.50 |
| Mid Season | 27.00 |
| Low Season | 25.00 |

Children's discounts available
**HS** 1 Apr–30 Sep
**MS** 1 Oct–31 Dec
**LS** 1 Jan–31 Mar
Supplements: Single room £7

## Kirkby Stephen

**THE BLACK SWAN HOTEL**
Ravenstonedale, Kirkby Stephen, Cumbria, CA17 4NG
Tel: 05873 204

9 Bedrooms (7 with private bathroom/shower).

M T LF LP AL HT

A delightful family-run hotel set amidst magnificent Cumbrian fells, in a picturesque and secluded village. Five miles of wild brown trout fishing on the River Eden, a well stocked tarn for rainbows and association water on the River Lune for sea trout and salmon. Renowned for good food, hospitality and comfort. Special 3, 5 and 7 night inclusive rates.

| | B & B £ | Half Board £ |
|---|---|---|
| High Season | 17.00 | 29.00 |

Children's discounts available
Closed Jan–Feb
Supplements: Room with bath/shower & WC £3.00. Single room £5

## Newby Bridge

**THE SWAN HOTEL**
Newby Bridge, Ulverston Cumbria, LA12 8NB
Tel: 05395 31681

36 Bedrooms (All with private bathroom/shower).

M T LP AL

This privately-owned hotel, overlooking the fine stone bridge at the southern end of Lake Windermere, offers peaceful nights and relaxing days. The Swan, which has provided shelter and refreshment since the 17th century, now provides all the facilities appreciated by the keen angler. Hotel's private fishing, exclusive rod on nearby White Moss. Tarn, Bouth and the WA and DA waters. Choice of restaurant and wine bar. 20 mins from the M6 (Junction 36).

| | B & B £ | Half Board £ |
|---|---|---|
| High Season | 27.00 | 35.00 |

Children's discounts available

See page 4 for details of symbols

## Penrith

**THE MILL INN**
Mungrisdale, Penrith,
Cumbria, CA11 0XR
Tel: 059683 632

8 Bedrooms (2 with private bathroom/shower).

M LF LP AL

A friendly welcome is assured at this cosy 16th-century lakeland inn, peacefully located at the foot of the Skiddaw range. AA, RAC and Les Routiers listed. Tea/coffee-making facilities and electric blankets in all bedrooms. Central heating. Log fires in bar and residents' lounge. Free-house with real ale. Resident proprietor (keen salmon fishers) arrange day permits on a two-mile private stretch of River Eden. Trout fishing also available.

| | B & B |
|---|---|
| | £ |
| Mid Season | 12.00 |
| Low Season | 12.00 |

Children's discounts available
**HS** 22 May–31 Oct
**MS** 17 Apr–21 May
**LS** 1 Nov–16 Apr
Supplements: Room with bath/shower & WC £2.00. Room with shower only £1.50

## Penton

**CRAIGBURN FARM**
Catlowdy, Penton, Carlisle,
Cumbria, CA6 5QP
Tel: 022877 214

7 Bedrooms (All with private bathroom/shower).

M T LP AL

A friendly atmosphere with personal attention awaits you at this spacious 18th century farmhouse, in a quiet rural setting. Game fishing in the Rivers Liddle, Esk and Lyne, all within 10 miles. Coarse fishing also 10 miles. A family-run beef/sheep farm of 250 acres. We serve delicious home cooking with fresh produce. Excellent for touring, fishing, shooting, walking, bird watching, pony riding, swimming. Pool table, darts board.

| | B & B | Half Board |
|---|---|---|
| | £ | £ |
| High Season | 9.00 | 15.00 |

Children's discounts available

## Rothay Bridge

**ROTHAY MANOR HOTEL**
Rothay Bridge, Ambleside,
Cumbria, LA22 0EH
Tel: 0966 33605

18 Bedrooms (All with private bathroom/shower).

M T LF LP

Set in its own grounds a quarter of a mile from the head of Lake Windermere, the Manor was built in 1830 as a private residence, and the drawing rooms and candlelit dining rooms are those of an elegant Regency house. Run by the Nixon family for the last 20 years, the hotel has gained a reputation as one of the country's leading Country House hotel, the excellence of service, cuisine and relaxed atmosphere. Free local permit for residents.

| | B & B | Half Board |
|---|---|---|
| | £ | £ |
| High Season | 35.00 | 52.00 |
| Low Season | 30.00 | 40.00 |

Children's discounts available
**HS** 17 Apr–31 Oct **LS** 2 Nov–12 Feb
Closed 1 Nov–12 Feb
Supplements: Single room £16 per night High Season. Balcony room £4 per night. Suite £13.

## Ulverston

**HIGHFIELD COUNTRY HOTEL**
Blawith, Ulverston, Cumbria,
LA12 8EG
Tel: 0229 85238

12 Bedrooms (All with private bathroom/shower).

M LF LP AL

Highfield is a lovely period house set in two and a half acres overlooking the Crake Valley, one mile from Coniston Water. Fishing waters are only a few minutes away. The relaxed country house atmosphere is enhanced by log fires, a well-stocked bar and games room. Our restaurant menu is varied and seasonal, prepared by our resident chef.

| | Bed Only | B & B | Half Board |
|---|---|---|---|
| | £ | £ | £ |
| High Season | 18.50 | 21.50 | 31.50 |
| Low Season | 16.50 | 19.50 | 28.50 |

Children's discounts available
**HS** Apr–Sep **LS** Oct–Mar
Closed 1–14 Jan
Supplements: Single room £2.

## Windermere

**LOW WOOD HOTEL**
Windermere, Cumbria,
LA23 1LP
Tel: 05394 33338

82 Bedrooms (All with private bathroom/shower).

M T LP AL

Low Wood Hotel has ¾ mile of lake frontage. Both coarse and game fish are caught. In addition licences are held for visitors' use to fish the private waters in the nearby rivers. Try char fishing, a new experience? Friendly, helpful staff under the management of John Swift will ensure your angling tales are almost believed. Open fires, central heating, 3 bars, traditional beers, all make an enjoyable happy holiday.

| | B & B | Half Board |
|---|---|---|
| | £ | £ |
| High Season | 29.50 | 38.50 |
| Mid Season | 27.50 | 35.00 |
| Low Season | 23.50 | 34.00 |

Children's discounts available
**HS** 30 May–1 Nov
**MS** 1 Apr–29 May
**LS** 1 Jan–31 May, 2 Nov–31 Dec

## LANCASHIRE
## Blackburn

**SHIREBURN ARMS HOTEL**
1 Walley Road, Hurst Green,
Nr. Blackburn, Lancashire,
BB6 9QJ
Tel: 0254 86 518

12 Bedrooms (7 with private bathroom/shower).

M LF LP AL

The 17th-century Shireburn Arms Hotel is set in the heart of the beautiful Ribble valley. It offers superb fishing on limited stretches of the Rivers Hodder and Ribble. The hotel is ideal for the fisherman to relax and enjoy a meal with a good bottle of wine in the cosy, beamed restaurant. Most rooms are en-suite, all with colour TV, trouser press and tea/coffee-making facilities.

| | B & B |
|---|---|
| | £ |
| High Season | 15.00 |

Supplements: Room with bath/shower and WC £5.00. Single room £4.50

## Blackpool

**SINGLETON LODGE**
Lodge Lane, Singleton,
Nr. Blackpool, Lancashire,
FY6 8LT
Tel: 0253 883854

4 Bedrooms (All with private bathroom/shower).

M LF LP AL HT

Here is a chance to visit and enjoy all types of fishing that are available on the Fylde coast — trout, seat trout, salmon or private water — sea fishing from Fleetwood where chartered boat and tackle are available. Coarse fishing in our own grounds. The choice is yours. A very warm, friendly atmosphere and superb country fare at our elegant Georgian country house are always on hand to welcome you.

| | B & B | Half Board |
|---|---|---|
| | £ | £ |
| High Season | 15.00 | 22.00 |

Children's discounts available
Supplements: Single room £4.50

## Carnforth

**ROYAL STATION HOTEL**
Market Street, Carnforth,
Lancashire, LA5 9BT
Tel: 0524 733636

12 Bedrooms (9 with private bathroom/shower).

M T LP AL

A refurbished, comfortable hotel with friendly atmosphere. All rooms have direct-dial telephone, tea/coffee-making facilities, radio, colour TV and trouser press. We offer English, French and Italian cuisine. Full central heating. Carnforth is surrounded by beautiful countryside of Lonsdale and is 20 minutes from the English Lakes. RAC two-star, AA three-star.

| | B & B |
|---|---|
| | £ |
| High Season | 13.75 |

Children's discounts available
Supplements: Room with bath & shower £3.00. Single room £2.25

## Clitheroe

**THE INN AT WHITEWELL**
Forest of Bowland,
Whitewell, Nr. Clitheroe,
Lancashire, BB7 3AT
Tel: 02008 222
Classification not yet known
11 Bedrooms (6 with private bathroom/shower).

M T LF LP AL HT

Period inn in a dramatically beautiful riverside setting. Antique furniture and log fires. Economical bar lunches and suppers available for residents as an alternative to the restaurant. Seven miles of trout, sea trout and salmon fishing on the River Hodder which flows past the lawn. Tap room with pool table and darts.

| | B & B |
|---|---|
| | £ |
| High Season | 21.50 |

Children's discounts available

*Prices in England for Fishing are per person, sharing a double room, per night, including VAT (at the current rate of 15 per cent). Check prices when you book and mention England for Fishing.*

**THORNEYHOLME COUNTRY HOUSE**
Dunsop Bridge, Clitheroe,
Lancashire, BB7 3BB
Tel: 02008 271
Classification not yet known
7 Bedrooms (5 with private bathroom/shower).

M

A fine 17th-century shooting lodge, tastefully refurbished in two-and-a-half acres of elegant gardens. Ideally situated in the Trough of Bowland for walkers, fishermen and tourists alike. 30 minutes from the M6. Restaurant offers varied a la carte menu changing every Friday, providing both traditional and exotic cuisine. Relax in our lounge and bar. Ample parking available. 'Discretion' is our motto!

| | Bed Only | B & B | Half Board |
|---|---|---|---|
| | £ | £ | £ |
| High Season | 27.00 | 32.00 | 50.00 |
| Mid Season | 25.00 | 30.00 | 48.00 |
| Low Season | 21.00 | 26.00 | 44.00 |

Children's discounts available
**HS** Jun–Sep
**MS** Oct–Nov, Apr–May
**LS** Dec–Mar
Supplements: Room with bath/shower & WC £2.50. Single room £6. Suite £5

## Lancaster

**SLYNE LODGE HOTEL**
Slyne, Lancaster,
Lancashire, LA2 6AZ
Tel: 0524 823389

13 Bedrooms (All with private bathroom/shower).

LF LP AL HT

With sea, river, canal and lake fishing, all between half and five miles away, seaside Morecambe and historic Lancaster both 3 miles away, and the Lakes and the Yorkshire Dales less than an hour's drive away, this varied area has appeal for fishermen and non-fishermen. On the A6 north of Lancaster, our rooms are quiet, self-contained and separate from the bars, and the restaurant which is open all day.

| | B & B |
|---|---|
| | £ |
| High Season | 17.00 |
| Low Season | 15.00 |

Children's discounts available

## Preston

**BROUGHTON PARK HOTEL**
418 Garstang Road,
Broughton, Preston,
Lancashire, PR3 5JB
Tel: 0772 864087

98 Bedrooms (All with private bathroom/shower).

M T LP AL HT

A country house hotel set in its own grounds of woods and lawns in the heart of Lancashire countryside. Coarse fishing available in Preston-Lancashire Canal and the River Ribble, sea angling at Morecambe. Blackpool and Fleetwood for plaice, codling, bass and mackerel. Boat trips for parties can be arranged. Many day ticket waters for fly fishing (rainbow and brown trout). All bedrooms with bathroom, tea/coffee-making facilities, TV, telephone, radio. Health club.

| | B & B<br>£ | Half Board<br>£ |
|---|---|---|
| High Season | 24.50 | 35.00 |
| Low Season | 18.50 | 27.50 |

Children's discounts available
**HS** Sep–Jun (excl weekends)
**LS** Weekends, Jul–Aug
Supplements: Room with bath/shower and WC £15 in HS

## MERSEYSIDE
## Moreton

**LEASOWE CASTLE HOTEL**
Leasowe Road, Moreton,
Merseyside, L46 3RF
Tel: 051 606 9191

45 Bedrooms (All with private bathroom/shower).

M T

The hotel is on the Wirral peninsula and is of historical interest being built in 1593 as a castle. It was converted to a three-star hotel 4 years ago. All bedrooms have private bathroom, colour TV, direct dial-telephone, hairdryer, trouser press, tea/coffee-making facilties. There is a health club with gym, sauna and sunbeds. Fishing is available along 2 miles of promenade with possibly some of the most ideal conditions for beach fishing in the country.

| | B & B<br>£ | Half Board<br>£ |
|---|---|---|
| High Season | 24.15 | 31.10 |

Children's discounts available.

*Wrasse*

# English Tourist Board
# Book Choice

**Planning a holiday can be almost as exciting as the holiday itself! Here's a selection of some of the best travel and leisure books, all produced or endorsed by the English Tourist Board and available from your local bookseller.**

### WHERE TO STAY

*1987 series*

Official annual English Tourist Board guides to all types of accommodation, from the grandest hotels through to the simplest hostels. All establishments are registered with the ETB and are clearly described so you know what you are getting for your money! There are three *Where to Stay – England* guides:

| | |
|---|---|
| Hotels, Motels, Guesthouses & Universities | £4.95 |
| Farmhouses, Bed & Breakfast, Inns & Hostels | £3.95 |
| Holiday Homes & Holiday Centres | £3.95 |
| Also in the *Where to Stay* series: | |
| Britain – Camping & Caravan Parks | £3.95 |

### ACTIVITY & HOBBY HOLIDAYS

*1987 edition*

Annual ETB guide to hundreds of really different holidays with accommodation and most equipment included: action and sports, arts and crafts, study courses, holidays for unaccompanied children . . . in fact, something for everyone!

Price £2.25

### LONDON'S CHURCHES: A Visitor's Companion

*Published in association with Grafton Books*

A beautifully illustrated guide to one hundred of London's most interesting churches. The authors, Elizabeth and Wayland Young, combine a wealth of detail and anecdote on each church with a fascinating history of church architecture from Romanesque to Lutyens.

Paperback edition £7.95
Hardback edition £12.95

### ENGLAND'S SEASIDE

*1987 edition. Published in association with Pastime Publications*

Guide to hundreds of seaside hotels and guest houses which promise a special welcome to families. Just choose the area or resort that's right for your family, then book with confidence.

Price £1.95

### ENGLAND FOR GOLF and ENGLAND FOR FISHING

*1987 editions. Published in association with Pastime Publications*

Two new guides containing indispensable information for anyone wishing to play golf or go fishing whilst away from home. Golf clubs and fishing grounds which welcome visitors and nearby hotels that can cater for them, plus features and tips from celebrities in the golf and fishing fields.

Price £1.10 each

### NICHOLSON'S HOLIDAY GUIDES AND MAPS

*Published in association with Robert Nicholson Publications*

New series of guides and maps designed for the tourist with details of local heritage, attractions, entertainment, transport, restaurants, pubs . . all you need to plan your trip. Devon and the Lake District are the first two areas to be covered in the series.

| | |
|---|---|
| Holiday Guide to Devon | £3.9 |
| Holiday Map of Devon | £1.9 |
| Holiday Guide to the Lake District & Cumbria | £3.9 |
| Holiday Map of the Lake District & Cumbria | £2.5 |

## DISCOVER ENGLAND

*Published in association with Weidenfeld & Nicolson*

Five beautifully illustrated titles on fascinating aspects of England's history and heritage, each written by an expert in his field: English Castles, Prehistoric England, Great English Houses, Roman England and English Cathedrals.

Hardback, price £8.50 each

## THE ART OF HOLIDAY PHOTOGRAPHY

*Published in association with Fotobank Books and Chameleon Publications*

No more need to be ashamed of your holiday snaps! Written by photo-journalist Roger Hicks, this lavishly illustrated book explains how to achieve successful results in all kinds of holiday situations and features articles by six leading holiday photographers.

Hardback, price £9.95

## NICHOLSON'S GUIDE TO ENGLISH CHURCHES

*Published in association with Robert Nicholson Publications*

Informative and lively, this is a practical guide to over 850 English parish churches of outstanding interest and beauty. An ideal touring companion.

Price £5.95

## BRITISH RAILWAY JOURNEYS

*Published in association with Fourth Estate Publications*

Four fascinating books to liven up your train journeys with facts, figures and anecdotes about places passed along the way and the railways themselves. The books cover major routes out of London: Paddington to the West, King's Cross to the North, Euston to the Midlands and North West and Victoria and Waterloo to the South.

Price £2.95 each

## THE DOMESDAY BOOK – England's Heritage Then and Now

*Published in association with Hutchinson*

This best-selling book is a highly informative, gloriously illustrated history of the Domesday Book which looks at the 12,500 settlements originally listed and examines what they are today.

Hardback, price £16.95

## THE CHILDREN'S BOOK OF DOMESDAY ENGLAND

*Published in association with Kingfisher Books*

A colourful book designed for younger readers which looks at what life was really like in Domesday England and how the Domesday Book was compiled.

Hardback, price £4.95

**For the best choice in books on England, look for the English Tourist Board logo at your local bookshop.**

# INDEX OF RIVERS AND CANALS

# INDEX OF LAKES AND RESERVOIRS

# INDEX OF SEA FISHING

# INDEX OF ADVERTISERS

ENGLAND FOR FISHING 1987

Published by Pastime Publications in association with the English Tourist Board

This coupon should be cut out and mailed direct to the establishment in which you are interested (please **do not** send it to the English Tourist Board).

Remember to enclose a stamped addressed envelope for your reply.

Tick box required

☐ Please send me a brochure or further information, and details of prices charged.

☐ Please advise me, as soon as possible, if accommodation is available as detailed overleaf.

To:
(name & address of establishment)

My name is:
(Block letters)

Address:

Telephone number:

Please complete the reverse side if you are interested in making a booking P.T.O.

# ENQUIRY COUPON

ENGLAND FOR FISHING 1987

Published by Pastime Publications in association with the English Tourist Board

This coupon should be cut out and mailed direct to the establishment in which you are interested (please **do not** send it to the English Tourist Board).

Remember to enclose a stamped addressed envelope for your reply.

Tick box required

☐ Please send me a brochure or further information, and details of prices charged.

☐ Please advise me, as soon as possible, if accommodation is available as detailed overleaf.

To:
(name & address of establishment)

My name is:
(Block letters)

Address:

Telephone number:

Please complete the reverse side if you are interested in making a booking P.T.O.

# ENQUIRY COUPON

**Complete this side if you are interested in making a booking, but please read the advice on page 5 first.**

I am interested in accommodation for adults and children (ages: )
(Please give the number of persons and the ages of the children if applicable)

From (date of arrival): To (date of departure):

or alternatively from: to:

Accommodation required:

Meals required:

Other/special requirements:

I enclose a stamped addressed envelope (or international reply coupon) for your reply:

Signed: Date:

**Complete this side if you are interested in making a booking, but please read the advice on page 5 first.**

I am interested in accommodation for adults and children (ages: )
(Please give the number of persons and the ages of the children if applicable)

From (date of arrival): To (date of departure):

or alternatively from: to:

Accommodation required:

Meals required:

Other/special requirements:

I enclose a stamped addressed envelope (or international reply coupon) for your reply:

Signed: Date:

ENGLAND FOR FISHING 1987

Published by Pastime Publications in association with the English Tourist Board

ENQUIRY COUPON

This coupon should be cut out and mailed direct to the establishment in which you are interested (please **do not** send it to the English Tourist Board).

Remember to enclose a stamped addressed envelope for your reply.

Tick box required

☐ Please send me a brochure or further information, and details of prices charged.

☐ Please advise me, as soon as possible, if accommodation is available as detailed overleaf.

To:
(name & address of establishment)

My name is:
(Block letters)

Address:

Telephone number:

Please complete the reverse side if you are interested in making a booking P.T.O.

ENGLAND FOR FISHING 1987

Published by Pastime Publications in association with the English Tourist Board

ENQUIRY COUPON

This coupon should be cut out and mailed direct to the establishment in which you are interested (please **do not** send it to the English Tourist Board).

Remember to enclose a stamped addressed envelope for your reply.

Tick box required

☐ Please send me a brochure or further information, and details of prices charged.

☐ Please advise me, as soon as possible, if accommodation is available as detailed overleaf.

To:
(name & address of establishment)

My name is:
(Block letters)

Address:

Telephone number:

Please complete the reverse side if you are interested in making a booking P.T.O.

**Complete this side if you are interested in making a booking, but please read the advice on page 5 first.**

I am interested in accommodation for adults and children (ages: )
(Please give the number of persons and the ages of the children if applicable)

From (date of arrival): To (date of departure):

or alternatively from: to:

Accommodation required:

Meals required:

Other/special requirements:

I enclose a stamped addressed envelope (or international reply coupon) for your reply:

Signed: Date:

**Complete this side if you are interested in making a booking, but please read the advice on page 5 first.**

I am interested in accommodation for adults and children (ages: )
(Please give the number of persons and the ages of the children if applicable)

From (date of arrival): To (date of departure):

or alternatively from: to:

Accommodation required:

Meals required:

Other/special requirements:

I enclose a stamped addressed envelope (or international reply coupon) for your reply:

Signed: Date:

# *Fishing Notes*